SOLOMON IN ALL HIS GLORY

WALTER WAGNER

AUTHOR:
The Chaplain of Bourbon Street

SOLOMON IN ALL HIS GLORY

WALTER WAGNER

VISION HOUSE PUBLISHERS
SANTA ANA, CALIFORNIA 92705

"Go forth . . . and behold King Solomon."
—Song of Solomon 3:11

PART I

Ecclesiastes 1:4

> *"One generation passeth away, and another generation cometh: but the earth abideth for ever."*

Chapter One		3
Two		29
Three		33
Four		43
Five		55
Six		63
Seven		73
Eight		83

PART II

Psalms 127:1

> *"Except the Lord build the house, they labour in vain that build it: except the Lord keep the city, the watchman waketh but in vain."*

Chapter Nine		91
Ten		107
Eleven		119
Twelve		131
Thirteen		139
Fourteen		145
Fifteen		153
Sixteen		159
Seventeen		171
Eighteen		175

PART III

Ecclesiastes 2:19

"And who knoweth whether he shall be a wise man or a fool? yet shall he have rule over all my labour wherein I have laboured, and wherein I have shewed myself wise under the sun. This is also vanity."

Chapter Nineteen 185

Twenty 199

Twenty-One 209

Twenty-Two 217

Twenty-Three................................. 227

Twenty-Four 233

Twenty-Five 245

Twenty-Six 255

Twenty-Seven 265

PART I

*"One generation passeth away,
and another generation cometh:
but the earth abideth for ever."*
—Ecclesiastes 1:4

1

Chapter One

The prize was the Promised Land ... and beyond.

The prize was an empire.

Astride a royal mule, the twenty-year-old son of David and Bathsheba expertly held the reins in his long, thin fingers. At his back, the white, fortified walls of Jerusalem hurried to the heavens, alabaster proud and impregnable since the city had been captured by his father and consecrated to God. Ahead lay the spring of Gihon and a sacred ceremony so epic in its ramifications that men to the latter days would recall it with awe and wonder.

The sure-footed animal strained against the golden bit between its jaws, but young Solomon, tall and taut in his jeweled leather saddle, held him firm. He hardly heard the thousands of hosanna-shouting Israelites as he looked across to a familiar grove of mulberry trees standing on a heavy-shouldered, rock-webbed hill—a circle of spikes under a black pavilion of leaves.

At a moment like this, a lesser man would exclude all thoughts except the pageantry of the moment, because only once in the crescent of a lifetime would such a supreme prize be offered, a prize won at so fearful a cost. Yet Solomon could not divert his attention from the grove. He reflected that an excess of the blood-red juice of the mulberry could drive a reluctant warrior, a bashful virgin, a toothless wolf, to the brink of sudden, unexplainable courage—or madness. From his firm lips, a faint smile flickered, revealing a flash of even teeth hued goat's milk white. He recalled that only a few days before he and the prophet Nathan had journeyed by foot to the grove and made a succulent noon meal of the ripe fruit. Then while grizzled, loyal Nathan composed himself in a tranquil nap, Solomon examined the veins

3

of the leaves and texture of the bark, and marveled that trees so brilliantly arrayed could flourish in the harsh, boulder-strewn hillside.

A hot east wind from the Dead Sea had gusted through the headdress of foliage, shimmering the leaves of the grove which was fed to blazing beauty by ripples of underground water. Solomon had noted, not for the first or last time, that the unseen is more powerful and miraculous than the seen.

When Nathan awoke, they had talked of the things of God and of men until night shaded the sky.

"Long live King Solomon!"

The insistent, full-throated cries from the multitude momentarily smothered his reverie.

Solomon was not yet a king—and after the holy anointing he would not be merely a king.

An empire demanded an emperor!

Generations of once-anonymous, persecuted sheep herders, nomads, and slaves had bred a soon-to-be-crowned emperor of a unique people with unrivaled power across the face of the earth. But how had the Hebrew nation and he come to this climactic moment of pending coronation?

Realization of the enormous accomplishments of Israel and hope for what was yet to be accomplished suffused the tanned, angular face with alternating expressions of dedication and doubt, resolve and remorse. His eyes, blue as the fringe of flame that once leaped from thousands of campfires of his father's outlaw army, danced with courage and apprehension.

Solomon knew his ascension to the throne was more than a personal triumph. It was the triumph of a special, remorseless, inevitable history; the reward for faith and obedience to the Most High. Except for Yahweh, the one true God, this time of glory and grandeur would have been impossible. He was the end product of a destiny decreed long ago—a destiny chiseled into reality from the dreams of inspired, stalwart ancestors. But now Solomon did not consider himself a worthy successor to the giants who preceded him in guiding the complex affairs of the land of Israel.

Though well guarded by trusted soldiers of his father's personal bodyguard, Solomon scanned the crowd. His eyes searched for the gleam of a fatal dagger or unfriendly face. A single assassin recruited by any of his multifarious enemies, could quickly emerge from the surrounding mass of bodies and murder him before he was proclaimed ruler. But all he saw was the frenzy of adoration and continuing cheers from faces flushed with approval and love.

The affectionate demonstration helped Solomon cast off, at least temporarily, the dread of assassination. Besides, he was certain Yahweh would protect him.

Soon he no longer heard the shouts of the crowd. Even as he made his way at a slow gallop in the splendidly chaotic parade of priests, warriors, and court officials, he had at this unlikeliest time and place a deep need to probe the why of this breathtaking leap from sheep herder to emperor. Why had a straggling band of wanderers achieved identity, nationhood, and become an empire which would shortly be his to preserve and protect? His need to look backward before he could look forward had never before been necessary. He had contented himself until now with an easy, superficial acceptance of the Hebrew past. But that was no longer enough, not nearly enough as he approached the threshold of power over Israel and its dominions. And so he riveted his attention to the fountainhead of his heritage.

The first promise of a homeland that would billow into a horizon-hurdling empire was sworn in the highlands of Ur to revered Abraham, the spiritual father of all families of Earth. God had chosen Abraham to seed a realm, declaring to him, "Get out of your country, to a land that I will show you; and I will make of you a great nation."

It was an oath that fed the yeast of youth into the aging bones of Abraham, survivor of seventy-five coarse winters and scalding summers.

Driving his flocks before him, Abraham departed for busy Canaan, west of the Jordan, where the aquatic reeds of the papyrus grew. He pitched a tent on the plain of Moreh under a graceful, purplish-gray, resinous terebinth, its winged branches coiled for flight. He built a stone altar to God, and then the Lord came to Abraham with the soaring pledge:

"Unto your seed will I give this land."

But the gift was not to be a waiting paradise. It would have to be earned through prayer, intelligence, daring—and battle.

When famine scarred and pocked the land of Canaan, Abraham was reluctantly forced into Egypt with his wife Sarah. Never had Pharaoh seen so comely a woman as Sarah, and he coveted the princess God had destined to be honored as mother of the Hebrews. The monarch's lust, however, was thwarted by a stratagem of Abraham, who convinced Sarah to disguise herself as his sister rather than admit she was his wife, for it was prudent to assume Pharaoh would kill him in order to possess her. It was thwarted, too, by the anger of God, who showed His vast displeasure with the king's passion by sending great plagues to the people of the Nile.

In stormy puzzlement, the ruler of the Egyptians summoned Abraham to the throne room and snapped an accusing finger at him. The seal ring on Pharaoh's right hand, symbol of his supreme authority, glittered menacingly. So awesome was his power, that Pharaoh's subjects believed his sovereignty would remain after his death. When he was mummified, placed inside two sealed coffins, and interred in a huge triangular pyramid, it was thought he would become the god Osiris, ruler of the dead.

But standing now before Pharaoh, a short, unprepossessing figure in a surprisingly ill-fitting, scarlet cloak, Abraham no longer feared him. He stood resolutely, aware that the God who had come to him in Ur and Moreh was far more powerful than Pharaoh, powerful enough to punish the Egyptian monarch for interfering with Yahweh's plan for Sarah.

"What is this you have done to me?" thundered the sheik of all lands from the fertile delta to ancient Pathros. "Why did you not tell me that Sarah was your wife?"

"My beloved is a fair woman to look on," answered Abraham. "The fault is mine. I entreated my wife to present herself as my sister so that Pharaoh's men would not kill me, Sarah would be saved, and my soul should live."

An eloquent and wise reply, thought Pharaoh. Perhaps too eloquent, too wise. Perhaps it was not eloquence or wisdom, but guile. Pharaoh struggled with a mounting rage which threatened to overcome his reason. There had not been the slightest hint of insult in Abraham's answer, but was there not disrespect? Why hadn't this puny vizier of flocks and she asses showed the same dread which mottled the faces of all others who confronted the royal brother of the sun? Why weren't Abraham's eyes filled with terror; why didn't he quake or beg for mercy? Didn't this nettlesome sheep herder know a single command would have him butchered like an ox?

Abraham sensed Pharaoh's dilemma, yet he had no choice but to be firm and forthright. If he were executed, the nation of Hebrews would be throttled before its birth. If Pharaoh would not free Sarah, there would be no seed from which the nation could flower.

The Egyptian king balanced his pride and ardor against the afflictions Abraham's God had visited on his subjects.

"Now therefore behold your wife," conceded Pharaoh, with the feeling that he was losing far more than a caravan laden with priceless treasure. "Take her, and go your way."

Abraham smiled with relief. His head reeled with the wonder of what had occurred: the Lord had entered this gold-encrusted room, the apotheosis of all the might of Egypt, and vanquished Pharaoh.

Sarah embraced her freedom joyfully. Aside from her personal distaste for Pharaoh, her foremost incentive for emancipation was the knowledge that she was to be Abraham's partner in the creation of a people especially selected by God.

But Sarah proved to be as barren as she was beautiful, and with each passing year her travail increased when Abraham's essence failed to produce a child. Her womb was empty as the Sinai. Apprehension that she would never cradle an infant to her breast was seldom out of mind. Untiring in her faith in God, Sarah yet despaired when her years for child-bearing had irrevocably fled.

Early one morning, while camped on the Plain of Mamre, Abraham quietly entered his wife's tent. Sarah did not hear or see her husband. She was transfixed by her reflection in her polished bronze mirror. Disconsolately, she counted the deep wrinkles that traveled from her neck to the sockets of her still luminous eyes.

Abraham's despair was as great as Sarah's as he watched her measure the loss of youth and middle age. Sarah was in the winter of life and it would be impossible for her to become a mother. Had God sworn falsely to him?

Stealing from her tent, Abraham ambled down a winding path to a curtain of limbs under a live oak to seek protection from the burning sun.

His life and Sarah's would soon be over, he thought, and they would leave no progeny behind. Of what use had it been for Sarah to be freed from Pharaoh?

With his faith plummeted to its nadir, Abraham suddenly

heard a voice: "I am the Almighty God. Walk before Me, and be perfect."

Abraham looked up, shielding his stare with a bony hand.

"I will bless Sarah," said God to Abraham, "and give you a son by her. Yes, I will bless her, and she shall be a mother of nations; kings of peoples shall come from her."

Startled and incredulous, Abraham fell on his face. "How," he asked in his heart, "shall a child be born to me when I am an hundred years old? And how shall Sarah, who is ninety, bear a child?"

God heard Abraham's thoughts and answered, "Sarah shall bear you a son indeed."

Fleet-footed as a doe, Abraham scampered back to Sarah's tent and told her of the Lord's assurance of a miracle. " 'At this set time in the next year,' He said to me, 'you shall be with child.' "

Tracing the wrinkles across the geography of her face with a trembling hand, Sarah found it difficult to accept Abraham's enthusiasm and certitude. She could not believe her aged body would function in the intricate rhythm demanded by mother-hood. Sarah glanced at her newest maidservant, a perfectly pro-portioned beauty from Canaan. The girl's hair was plaited and she wore a yellow cloak, her trim feet encased in brown sandals. For such a full-hipped and nubile woman, the midwife and stone birthstool for the period of labor would probably not be needed. *Her* child would spark to life unassisted. But Sarah was not a nineteen-year-old maidservant.

Despite her doubt, Sarah allowed herself the luxury and com-fort of belief, warming herself with the assurances of God and her husband.

She turned once more to her mirror. To her astonishment, her eyes were more luminous than ever and she seemed younger than before.

At the appointed time, the Lord visited Sarah as He had said, and did unto her as He had spoken.

The midwife and the birthstool were not needed.

Soon Sarah's laughter skittered through the tent. She trilled to her maidservants, "God has made me laugh, so that all that hear will laugh with me, for I have born Abraham a son in his old age." The encampment was quickly engulfed in a wave of mirth. The high, happy cadence echoed down the path to the live oak, and the wind carried the music of the women's laughter to the far corners of Mamre.

In compliance to the wish of the Lord, Abraham named his son Isaac—child of promise.

Abraham rejoiced in the knowledge that his people, the elect of God, would now survive and multiply because of His direct intervention. Word for word, Abraham remembered the renewed covenant with God, who had told him before the birth of Isaac, "I will give to you and to your seed after you the land in which you are a stranger, all the land of Canaan, for an everlasting possession."

The recipient of the covenant was pleased with the way Isaac sprinted toward manhood. His son was quiet, gentle, dutiful, hard-working, and took no advantage of his position as the heir of Abraham, who by now had become exceedingly wealthy and the unchallenged, respected chieftain of a few thousand nomads blessed by God. No task was too difficult or menial for Isaac. He fed the wolfish dogs that guarded Abraham's flocks, drifted into prickly brambles to round up strays, gathered firewood from the forested mountains, and hunted game with great zeal and success. A sage father, Abraham was not overly protective. He fought off the temptation of surrounding Isaac with always-watching guards. But whenever Isaac was out of sight or late returning to the encampment, Abraham's brow furrowed with concern and his stomach rumbled with anxiety. God would not visit Sarah with child again and thus Isaac was of more value than a mountain of shekels. He was irreplaceable; *he was the Hebrew future.* Abraham never failed to thank God when Isaac reappeared safely.

Soon Abraham felt that Isaac was nearly self-sufficient, and he looked forward to the day of his son's marriage. Abraham did not expect to live to see his grandchildren, but he was tranquil nevertheless, his heart at peace, knowing that Isaac would carry forth the founding of a nation. Abraham spent his time worshipping the Lord, enjoying the companionship of Sarah, and preparing Isaac for leadership of his people. Abraham was sure he would die without further incident. His life had already been, if anything, too eventful and adventurous.

Then, without warning, Abraham received a command from God that darkened his spirit and sundered and perplexed his soul. In a moment all that had been pure white in Abraham was transformed to onyx. He suddenly felt abandoned and useless. The totality of what had been sworn to him was now vanishing like a vapor.

The command, Abraham thought impulsively, was wildly unreasonable, more brutal than the lash of a slave trader. If Abraham obeyed—how could he not obey—the cost would be the destruction and despoilation of everything he valued most.

He drowned himself in contemplation of the full consequences of this new decree from the Most High.

"Take now your son, your only son Isaac, whom you love, and get into the land of Moriah," God declared, "and offer him there for a burnt offering."

Abraham thought he was about to plunge into the pit of madness. But, according to tradition, madness was punishment meted out only to those who had disobeyed the laws of God. And Abraham was certain he had not disobeyed God.

Why then must Isaac, rather than a ram or a fatted calf, be slain? Abraham and his people had long since put aside the barbarism of human sacrifice, though the rite was still practiced among those who groveled before idols. There were still tribes of Canaanites who put children to the torch, and in northern Mesopotamia, among those who gave their allegiance to the storm god Baal, male children were also set afire. Was the savagery of human immolation to be restored by a God that Abraham considered the quintessence of mercy and justice? Was his God no better than Baal?

Isaac was the child of promise, bred of a miracle. If his stripling body were to corrode the clear air of Moriah with the acrid stench of burning flesh, how then would God multiply Abraham's seed? Why would God send a miracle and then withdraw it? To what purpose was Isaac born?

And what of the promise of a Hebrew nation? Did it again face extinction as it had when Pharaoh coveted Sarah? Did God conjure covenants only to make them disappear like the doves of Noah in the wily hands of a marketplace magician?

Abraham would have traded all his wealth for the life of Isaac. He would have gone in Isaac's stead to Moriah and given himself to the fire.

Would God consider such a bargain?

Abraham searched the sky and waited for an answer.

But the silence *was* his answer. After his first panic spent itself,

Abraham realized the truth—God could bargain with men; men could not bargain with God.

Early the next morning, the progenitor of a seemingly doomed people rose from his couch, reluctant to face the day. But he cut the wood for the offering and bade good-bye to Sarah, who was equally uncomprehending as to the reason for the imminent death of her son.

Abraham climbed heavily onto his mule. Two of his young servants went with him, one riding ahead, the other to the rear. Abreast of Abraham, sitting his mount in princely fashion, rode Isaac, blissfully unaware of the pyre awaiting him forty-two miles ahead on the rocky hilltop of Mount Moriah.

The small group of travelers began their northward journey from the oasis-sanctuary of Beersheba. They were careful not to stray from the well-traveled main road, a precaution against lurking Hittite marauders.

Isaac's alert hunter's eyes missed nothing. He witnessed new sights on the unexpected trek with an ever-present sense of excitement: a rare white camel bred to race rather than carry burdens; an armored band of Philistine soldiers with glittering, double-edged swords as terrifying as the tight scowls above their black beards; the corrugated lime terrain as they passed Hebron, the royal city of Canaan. They also passed a village called Bethlehem, unimpressive to Isaac with its clutch of domed houses pressed closely together. A short distance outside Bethlehem, Isaac's interest soared when he spotted a nimble, fast-moving roe, its forked antlers, a cluster of elegant danger, standing as high as the boy's shoulders. Had there been time to track the deer for fresh meat, it would have been an even match.

At the end of three days, Moriah loomed implacably. Soon Abraham signaled a halt and slid awkwardly off his beast. He noted sourly that his mules, which often displayed stubbornness and had to be coaxed or whipped into movement, had not hesitated for a moment during this journey toward the accursed foothills.

"Remain with the animals!" Abraham growled the order to his servants with uncharacteristic harshness. "Isaac and I will go on foot to worship." His next command was to Isaac, uttered with all the tenderness he could summon, "My son, you will carry the wood."

From a pouch on the hind of his too-eager mule, Abraham

removed an irregularly shaped bundle. He unrolled the linen wrapping and with his flint ignited the goblet filled with pitch and oil-drenched rags. Now he dug into his cloak. Abruptly, a stone knife glinted in his hand.

Oblivious to the blade, Isaac asked innocently, "My father, we have the fire and the wood, but where is the lamb for the offering?"

In a voice choked with torment, Abraham replied, "God will provide a lamb".

They clambered up the mountain until Abraham was led by the Lord to the place of sacrifice. Here he laid aside the torch and knife, then with considerable effort, stooped and assembled rocks until there were enough for a makeshift altar. As calmly as he could, Abraham than directed Isaac to place the wood on the altar.

Abraham could feel the perspiration flood his hands, and with each fleeting second, unbearable tension was building inside him. Faith pushed him toward what must be done, but fatherhood still made him doubt if slitting the throat of his son was truly the will of a merciful God.

Removing the hand-worked belt of twisted vines that circled his cloak, Abraham bound the wrists of the unprotesting Isaac, whose keen vision spotted another animal a short distance away —a ram tangled in a clump of bushes.

"Isaac," said Abraham wearily as he moved him onto the altar, "thou art the lamb which God has provided." Before he could read his son's expression, Abraham bent and kissed Isaac's forehead, a final kiss of farewell.

His eyes clouded by tears, Abraham retrieved the knife. The cut would be from right to left. One swift stroke and Isaac's blood would stain the mountain.

Unexpectedly, the sun ripened the sky with a harvest yellow, wiping away the mist as Abraham brought the knife to within an inch of Isaac's throat.

"Abraham!" The voice was unmistakable.

"Here am I," he said, looking up.

"Lay not your hand upon the lad ..."

A surge of joy poured through Abraham.

"Neither do anything to him ..."

A new command and a sudden, last-minute reprieve for Isaac! But why?

"For now I know that you fear God, seeing you have not withheld your son, your only son, from Me."

How could he have questioned God? How could he have failed to understand that Yahweh had acted to test his faith?

Now Abraham felt a deep friendship between God and himself.

He smiled down at Isaac, and briskly slit his fetters.

But the Lord must yet be acknowledged with thankfulness for the deliverance of Isaac.

Abraham caught sight of the snared ram. He swiftly freed it, brought the bleating sheep to the altar, used his blade, and put the torch to the wood.

God had His burnt offering, and as Abraham watched the fire devour the skin of the animal, the stench did not assault his nostrils; the odor was sweeter than all the perfumes of Egypt.

Again God called to Abraham:

"By myself have I sworn, for because you have done this thing, and have not withheld your son, your only son; that in blessing I will bless you, and in multiplying I will multiply your seed as the stars of the heaven, and as the sand which is upon the seashore; and your seed shall possess the gate of his enemies; and in your seed shall all the nations of the earth be blessed; because you have obeyed My voice."

The thought occurred to Abraham that he had not been idly named—for the name of Abraham meant Father of a Multitude.

The trip back to Beersheba was as happy as the pilgrimage to Moriah had been sad. Sarah hugged Isaac to her breast, shouting praise to the Lord.

Content beyond measure, Sarah died at age one hundred and twenty-seven. Abraham wept and mourned for the wife with whom he had shared so much. During the seven days of his lamentation, he resolved that Sarah must be buried with special dignity, in a manner befitting the high esteem in which she was held by the Lord. It would be ignominious and dishonorable to Sarah's cherished memory for her to rest in earth belonging to someone who did not believe in the one true God. Abraham's need was to *purchase* ground for her tomb, although he was aware it would be almost impossible. Buying so much as a foot of land had never been accomplished by any of his people. Hebrews had no right to own Canaanite land, even for a sepulchre.

Yet it would be more dishonorable to Sarah if the attempt to give her this final tribute was not made.

And so Abraham went to restless Hebron. Two tribes—the clever Hittites and giant Amorites—had long contended for absolute supremacy over the city with neither totally victorious. They lived in an uneasy state of half-war, half-peace.

When Abraham learned that Ephron was the owner of the land he sought, he approached the Hittite chieftain with optimism since he had heard that Ephron's taste for treasure was insatiable.

Just inside the Hebron gate, the Hittite elders sat each day in a semi-circle, administering justice and conducting business. Abraham, wearing his finest embroidered wool cloak, observed closely how the Hittites traded among themselves for fields, herds, and spices. The Hittites were shrewd, but when an agreement was struck, it was binding. Each exchange was sworn to and duly witnessed.

Patiently and politely, Abraham waited his turn. When at last he presented himself before the powerful Hittite elite, he bowed in respect. "I am a stranger and a sojourner among you," he said. "Give me possession of a burying place with you so that I may put my wife to rest."

"My lord," answered one of the elders with a touch of sarcasm, "you are a mighty prince among us. In the choice of our sepulchres bury your dead. None of us shall withhold from you his sepulchre."

Abraham knew he was being taunted, but said, "If it be your mind that I should bury my dead, present me to Ephron that he may give me the Cave of Machpelah for as much money as it is worth."

From the audience of elders came a honeyed cry. "Nay, my lord, hear me. The field I give you, and the cave that is therein. In the presence of the sons of my people I give it; bury your dead."

It could only be Ephron who spoke with such authority and prerogative of position and ownership. Abraham measured the squat, round-chested Hittite leader, sensing he also spoke with the honey found inside a lion—sweet but difficult and dangerous to obtain.

The affair was extremely complicated. If Abraham accepted Ephron's offer, it would be binding since it had been made in the presence of witnesses. But Ephron could later reverse himself and reclaim his land, claiming no money had been paid to him, which was perfectly acceptable under the Hittite code. Also, if Abraham accepted the land as a gift, he would be yoked to Ephron, and he could not permit himself to remain beholden to an unbeliever. Besides, Abraham understood his acceptance would violate the code of the bazaar: only an opening gesture had been proffered; he was not expected to take Ephron at his word. Abraham decided to press payment on the Hittite lion. In the end, of course, Ephron would refuse.

"I will give you money for the field. Take it of me and I will bury my dead there," said Abraham. Even as he spoke Abraham knew Ephron and the snickering Hittites would consider his offer either insolence or idiocy.

Ephron dropped all pretense, anxious to abruptly end the laughable episode. He had tarried long enough with this arrogant alien hiding behind a mask of politeness. This prince without a country could be dispensed with easily by insisting on a sum so high that to pay it would mean a humiliating loss of face.

"The land is worth four hundred shekels of silver," the chief of the Hittites announced without a hint of compromise.

Abraham had not come to riches through stupidity. Four hundred shekels was an insult. In all the land of Canaan, none but a fool would pay so much for so little.

But before Abraham could reply, Ephron added with a cunning smile, "What is that between me and you?"

To Abraham it was everything. He had once stood steadfast against Pharaoh and he would stand sure against this lesser ruler, even if throughout Canaan he would be thought a simpleton. It was the acquisition of land, however small the parcel and however large the overpayment, that was of transcendent importance. Abraham knew it would not be wise to haggle. Before Ephron could withdraw his offer, Abraham struck the bargain.

Astonished, Ephron let loose a bellowing, gleeful roar. The story of his canny trading would amuse his concubines, and with Abraham's silver he could purchase several new women for his harem. As Ephron lumbered away, his mind focused particularly on the pepper-skinned, full-breasted daughter of a drunken, impoverished potter who had offered his virgin seventeen-year-old for a few shekels and a skin of wine.

Abraham returned for Sarah's body, thinking that even in

death she had triumphantly served God and her people. For now, east of memorable Mamre, the field and trees surrounding the Cave of Machpelah—this hugely significant, jot of land—was the legitimately acquired property of the Hebrews.

And there Sarah was buried. A long procession of mourners following, she was the first Hebrew put to rest in Hebrew-owned earth.

Now Abraham no longer felt himself a stranger and a sojourner among the Canaanites. He too, was content. However modest the beginning, the Hebrew dynasty—which would last forever—had begun.

* * *

Solomon, nearing the site of anointment, considered the ways of God and how often they defied the understanding of man; how frequently He, who had scooped out the mountains and hurled the stars into heaven, mysteriously worked His will. Just as Abraham's purchase of Machpelah was God's will, so his coronation, near to realization, was also God's will. He had not sought the throne, yet it was to be his as the result of an enigmatic, unpredictable confluence of events that only Yahweh could perceive.

Solomon knew there were those who were already scorning him as little more than a boy-king lacking the needed experience to guide the fortunes of Israel and her conquered lands. They considered him a callow usurper who had cynically plotted for power; the pawn of Bathsheba and Nathan who would reign over but not rule the world's most strategic kingdom. Solomon could not forget those, still to be contended with, who considered him their hated enemy solely because he had been selected to replace David.

Nathan had taught him how the hallowed covenant between God and Abraham—a homeland pledged in exchange for faith—had come to fruition as the result of a few moments of bargaining in a bazaar. The seemingly unimportant transfer of the Cave of Machpelah was the initial, lawful thrust of Abraham and his fellow wanderers into the sacred soil of the Promised Land.

Nathan never tired of recounting the story of the patriarch. Once when Solomon was fifteen years old and Nathan began reading of Abraham from the cracked papyrus scrolls, Solomon had lost his temper. "Enough! I, too, have read the scrolls and listened endlessly to your unblemished praise of Abraham. I know more of him than has been taught me of the deeds of my own father. Abraham was not the only lily in the Hebrew field."

Nathan's reply was as a tongue of fire. In an unquavering tone that did not bend before the royal offspring, the prophet boomed, "Remember always, my young lord, that those who carried Sarah's funeral litter into the recess of the Cave transported far more than a lifeless body. Into that Cave they carried dreams and visions. On that litter rested the hope of the Lord! Into Machpelah was carried the covenant!"

The wick of the lamp in Solomon's palace chamber shivered under the ferocity of Nathan's reply. The anvil of Solomon's outburst crumbled under the hammer of Nathan's indignation.

As Solomon sat in galvanized silence, Nathan added—the timbre of his speech softer now—"Remember, too, that the acorn of Machpelah has grown into the oak of an empire. And one day you shall be the protector of that oak."

Throughout his life, Solomon had heard much talk of his becoming king, none of which he took seriously. He ran neither toward the throne, nor did he run from it. Above all, he comported himself with politeness and respect whenever he was in the presence of his father. He sought love from David, not his crown. Solomon would have dismissed the thought of the throne entirely except for Nathan and Bathsheba. The prophet repeatedly reminded him of his kingly destiny, and of Bathsheba's constant affirmation that at his birth David had sworn, "Assuredly Solomon your son shall reign after me."

Sensitive to the nuances of language, Solomon pointed out on one occasion, when perhaps for the thousandth time his mother repeated David's words, "The king declared me *your* son, not his."

"It is one and the same, as Yahweh and the Most High are one and the same," Bathsheba replied impatiently, dismissing his subtle observation with a wave of her pungently-perfumed handkerchief.

Solomon did not at all share his mother's disdain for the refinements of phraseology or her certainty that he would one day sit in David's royal wooden chair. There were ample reasons for him to doubt his accession. His mother might well have been a mere concubine and he an illegitimate son if David had not ordered his ruthless army commander, Joab, to arrange for Bathsheba's luckless Hittite husband to die in battle. David had hardheartedly disposed of Uriah so he could marry Bathsheba. If David in truth had promised Bathsheba that Solomon would reign, could not his motive have been ardor for the dazzling beauty of Uriah's widow and the impulsive pride of a new father? And even if it had been given honestly, who could insist that David make good his promise? Solomon realized he was the issue of love. And he was also the issue of lust, adultery, and murder, even though the Lord had forgiven David when he repented of his sins.

As he was growing up, Solomon was never entirely certain of his father's innermost feelings toward his mother or himself. Certainly Bathsheba did not dominate David's affections. He had seven other wives and a score of concubines. And Solomon was but one of nineteen sons fathered by the king in Hebron and Jerusalem. Bathsheba had remained the apparent favorite among David's wives, but he was not the favorite son. That important honor once belonged to Absalom, who might have been crowned had he not prematurely attempted to usurp the throne and rebelled against David. This later resulted in his death by the hand of Joab. Absalom's mother was the smoke-eyed Maacah, daughter of King Talmai of Geshur, a buffer state between Israel and Aram. David had not loved Absalom's mother. She was simply a trophy of war, captured in battle. David married her in the name of diplomacy—her dowry was a treaty with the Geshurites, who could be troublesome if not pacified and joined in common cause through a royal wedding.

Next in line for the throne was the ambitious Adonijah, son of the equally ambitious Haggith. Adonijah felt—with some justification—that he should be king since he was the eldest living son. But Adonijah had also made a premature attempt to usurp the crown, which angered David. In the end, it had been David's personal decree, not usurpation or inheritance by virtue of age that had been the decisive factor in choosing his successor.

David now was seventy years old, and many said he was suffering from senility, that in all probability he had given the identical vow of his throne to each of his wives and possibly to many or all of his numerous sons.

In his youth, Solomon had often wondered if his father considered him a living, unwelcome reminder of a romantic alliance that he profoundly regretted. Yet Solomon found no hint of such an attitude on the rare occasions when he was summoned to sit at the feet of his father in the drafty, cedar-columned throne room to observe him conduct affairs of state. And no such attitude was manifest on those even more rare occasions when David would visit his chamber to mark the progress of his lessons with Nathan. His father displayed an avid interest in his education, and rather than speak of himself, his problems, or the gossip of the palace, each meeting would begin with a question that David had evidently devised to challenge him.

"My son, what is everything and what is nothing?"

"The world is nothing and God is everything."

"What is life's greatest certainty?"

"Death."

"What does a king fear most?"

"That there will not be peace for his people."

David seemed well pleased with Solomon's answers, but such uncomplicated thrust and parry did not mean his father was preparing him to rule. Possibly David asked all his sons the same questions and received similar answers.

Solomon hungered for his father to tell him in detail all the incredible events of his long life. Only after constant urging, and then usually with tantalizing briefness, would David speak of his anointing by Samuel while he was yet a shepherd. Sometimes David talked about playing his harp for Saul to soothe the king's nerves, his slaying of Goliath, his days in exile as a hunted fugitive, his defeat of the Philistines, and the capture of the Jebusite stronghold which he had renamed Jerusalem and established as the religious and political capital of Israel. But all too soon his father, eyes glazed with the mists of memory, would absentmindedly excuse himself and pad slowly from his quarters.

Nathan's visits, on the other hand, were seldom brief or uneventful. The most momentous visit of all had come early today when he had been awakened by the vigorous prodding of the prophet.

Solomon had worked at his cluttered table until morning composing a poem. Tired at last, he went to sleep, planning to rise at noon and continue his writing

He had slumbered only a short while when Nathan insistently roused him from his couch and handed him a bowl engraved with a scarab of four beatle wings and filled with grapes, figs, and pomegranates.

"Prepare at once, King Solomon. The throne is yours!" Nathan announced, curving his body before him in a deep bow.

Drowsiness fled from Solomon like a herdsman from the royal tax collector. Nathan's sense of humor was bizarre. *King* Solomon! The idea was outlandish.

"Your language is as careless as Bathsheba's," Solomon said with a head-shaking grin as he ate a pomegranate. "Unless my father is dead, he is yet king."

"David lingers on, and while he lives he has done that which is now closest to his heart. He has given you his throne. The scepter has passed."

"If it has passed, and I find it impossible to believe, then the staff of power has come to rest in the eager hands of the three who plot for it—my brother Adonijah, his champion Joab, and Abiathar the priest, who is as close to my father as Nathan."

As soon as the reference to Abiathar had been made, Solomon regretted it. He had no wish to add to Nathan's pain, knowing the prophet had long been unhappy at Abiathar's growing influence with David.

Nathan answered without rancor. "Abiathar is the prisoner of human jealousy, which I have often taught the noble Solomon is the same as spiritual death. Only the Lord may show jealousy since He shows it for a rightful purpose. In his envy of Zadok, who is his equal as a high priest, Abiathar has violated his vows. He gives David no faithful service."

Only Nathan's serious mien and the aura of urgency surrounding him prevented Solomon from insisting that the prophet be gone. The young prince of Israel desired to end the bizarre conversation. Palace politics bored him, and he still considered the notion of his becoming king absurd.

"Adonijah has slain oxen and fat cattle and sheep in abundance," Nathan continued with growing impatience. "He already pretends to rule, but he has not been given the authority to take the throne."

"Then my father sits firm in the royal place of honor, as he has for forty years."

"Your father is filled with age. Abishag, the comely Shunammite, nurses him with her young body so that he may have warmth. But he continues to quiver with chills for which the physicians have no remedy."

"For the sake of Israel, may the Lord grant my father another forty years of life. Nathan, are you readying your prayers for the king before the tomb claims him?"

"David is aware the tomb is near. Therefore, he proclaimed you king early this morning. I would have come to you sooner, but your father asked me to oversee the arrangements for your coronation."

"If there is a coronation, I will attend as an on-looker and not as the anointed one," said Solomon, putting aside his barely eaten breakfast.

"Apparently I have not made myself clear," continued Nathan. "I have failed to impress my new king with the honor that awaits him, or the gravity of the moment. Within my hearing and that of Bathsheba, Zadok, and Benaiah, who still serves devotedly as the captain of the royal bodyguard, David said, 'Take with you the servants of your Lord, and cause Solomon my son to ride upon my own mule, and bring him down to Gihon. And let Zadok the priest and Nathan the prophet anoint him their king over Israel. And blow with the trumpet, and say, 'God save King Solomon.' Then you shall come up after him, that he may come and sit upon my throne. For he shall be king in my stead. And I have appointed him to be ruler over Israel and over Judah.' "

"If those are my father's words, then his afflictions are greater than I suspected. His mind wanders into unreality."

"Your father is yet clear in thought. And his proclamation will be respected and obeyed by the people. It does not please David that Adonijah has moved with stealth and arrogance to take that from him which he gained with bravery and great sacrifice."

"But I am not fit to be king. Under no circumstances would I be fit," Solomon declared.

"God and your father have judged your qualifications. In the second after David declared you king, Benaiah said, 'As the Lord has been with my lord the king, even so be he with Solomon, and make his throne greater than the throne of my lord King David.' "

'A throne greater than David's! That is inconceivable, for Adonijah or myself."

"The king made no objection to Benaiah's words. He smiled with satisfaction and urged your anointing to be accomplished as soon as possible, with proper ceremony, so that he may confer with you as sovereign. There is much to be done."

Solomon's eyes drifted to the table and his unfinished poem. He retrieved the scroll and held it out for Nathan's inspection. The prophet ignored the papyrus and Solomon chose to ignore the small insult.

"I speak not from modesty or lack of ambition," said Solomon, "but I am young. For the present I have no desires except to contemplate God, to write my verses and perhaps plant an orchard of grapes."

"When you are king there will be much time—and much need—to contemplate God. And did not David, while he was king, write more than three-score psalms on which the children of Israel are weaned? It is easier for a king to be a poet than a poet to be a king. And you shall have your grape orchard, the most scarlet in the world with sun-colored flowers from which will flow the finest wines in the empire."

Until this moment Solomon had treated Nathan's news lightly, almost with scorn. But now, as he began to pace his chamber, he realized that the proffer of the crown was genuine.

"Nathan, you mean well for me," he said in complete earnest. "I know you are saintly, not the schemer and scoundrel that many will call you for pleading my cause before my father, although you have done so without my permission. I believe you are set apart for the special use of God as I am set apart for the use of God in no discernible way except as a vagabond strolling from one imperfect journey of the mind to another. I am a rich beggar, and that is the extent of my blessing for now. I am grateful to you and all who support me, particularly my father who pays me sudden homage and extends a confidence in my ability I have scarcely noted before."

"Time grows short, King Solomon."

"No, dear Nathan, I am not a king, and I will not be king."

"Why should you refuse to serve your people?"

Solomon pointed his index finger at the prophet, a dagger of accusation. "You, Nathan, have given me reason enough."

Nathan's features were a knife of surprise.

"You have been teacher and friend, Nathan, and have taught me too well."

Before continuing, Solomon stopped his pacing and withdrew the finger into the scabbard of his hand. He wanted Nathan's full attention, undistracted by movement or gesture.

"Hear me, prophet of Israel. From your lips I have heard the incredible deeds of our Hebrew heroes. Who am I to walk in their place? I have not covenanted with God as did Abraham. I have not been tested as was Isaac. Unlike Jacob, I did not renew the covenant with God and father our twelve tribes."

Solomon paused at the enormity of his words, but there was more.

"Nor have I emerged from common bondage to achieve power second only to Pharaoh, as did Joseph after his brothers sold him into slavery. It was not to the tenth son of David, but to Moses that Yahweh appeared at the burning bush and later gave the law in the wilderness. To that stammering servant of God, Israel owes much of its divine worship, not to me. I have done nothing to equal the feats of our venerated judges; Ehud, Deborah, Gideon, and Samson. The piety of the priest Eli and the prophet Samuel is not the piety of a whelp rescued from bastardy through the connivance of a father famished for the loveliness of Bathsheba. And though he was oppressed by dark spirits, King Saul was also directed by God, and he labored for Israel with a stormy skill that is not at my command."

The king-apparent was breathing hard, his cheeks flushed. "And finally, I was not the slayer of Goliath. My father was younger than this all but neglected son of his when he took stone and sling to vanquish the eleven-foot Philistine. "What giants have I vanquished?"

Nathan was composed, resolute. "My king," he replied, "you have mastered the surface of my lessons, but what lies beneath has eluded you. The time of the wilderness and the warrior is past. It is time now for the peace-giver. Therefore did your father call you Solomon, child of peace. Therefore did I call you Jedidiah, beloved of the Lord. At your birth David's wars were already at an end. Therefore were you marked from the first by the Lord and your father to bring amity and prosperity to Israel. There are giants without breastplates yet to slay, and you will find these enemies more clever and stronger than the adversaries of the battlefield."

"But, war is yet certain," objected Solomon. "My father's conquests are many, his foes beyond counting. And our own tribes intrigue and bicker among themselves. The wilderness is gone, but the need for a warrior king remains."

"Does Solomon dare risk his life to prove his judgment is correct?"

Solomon laughed, "Who would seek the head of a rich beggar?"

"When Adonijah learns you are David's choice, consider what your life will be worth. And that of your mother, Zadok, and Benaiah. My own chance for survival is the least of it, for I am nearly as old as David and do not fear an honorable grave. But as it was with Absalom, our bodies will be thrown into an unmarked pit and heaped with cold stones. No prayers will be said for us. The game we play is not a diversion for children. You, Solomon, are as the swift, resourceful leopard of Lebanon which has caught the hunter's eye and wavers between attack or retreat."

"Adonijah seeks power, not blood."

"Solomon is mistaken—"

The redolent fragrance of a familiar perfume—a nuptial of cinnamon, lotus, and frankincense—preceded Bathsheba into the chamber. Across her arms, like a bed of mandrake, lay a purple robe.

"My mother comes well prepared," Solomon said, arching a disapproving eyebrow. 'It will make a splendid coronation gift for Adonijah."

"Don the regal cloak and speak not to me of Haggith's cub who claws for that which is not his, who has disgraced David's house, asserting himself a king and after the royal manner gathers chariots and fifty soldiers to run before him."

"Your son does not have the claws of Adonijah," Nathan said with disdain. "He hesitates to leave the lair to claim his prey."

"Solomon hesitates?" Bathsheba's lightly painted eyebrows were puzzled semicircles of disbelief.

"While he pauses," the prophet added, "the lightning gathers at Adonijah's shoulder. He will hurl his bolts soon enough."

From the courtyard below they were interrupted by the sound of cheering.

"The word has spread quickly among the people, and they beg for you," said Bathsheba, forcing the cloak into Solomon's hands. "A new star shines in the sky of Jerusalem. Now garb and prepare yourself as befits a king."

"Modesty, wisdom, and experience also befit a king," Solomon replied with annoyance. "Did the dyemaker thread those riches into the royal robe?"

Nathan wheeled and pivoted for the door.

"Stay, Nathan!" Bathsheba called, pleadingly.

"For what reason?" he said, not bothering to hide his exasperation. "I thought I was a prophet and teacher to a king. It appears I have failed and instructed a dullard who cares not for the command of Yahweh, the command of his father, the deepest wish of his mother, the urging of his prophet, the approval of his people, or the responsibility for Israel and its dominions. I will tell the lord David that Solomon is a self-indulgent, disobedient son who by his refusal of the throne threatens the Hebrew future and assures the death of himself and all who love him."

Solomon stiffened. "Is our choice only between the grave and glory?"

"Only that," Nathan answered laconically.

"For myself, I wish neither," Solomon said.

"The choice must be made."

"Such is no choice."

"Choose then nevertheless."

Could Nathan be right? Could so much depend on his accepting the throne? No one in Israel was more learned or closer to God than Nathan. As a prophet, Nathan's function was not to interpret the will of God, but to utter precisely the actual words which God gave him to proclaim. There were false as well as true prophets, but Nathan had proved his worth and his fearlessness as a spokesman through whom the word of God was revealed. He had courageously opposed David's desire to build a grandiose temple to God, persuading David that because he had shed so much blood God would be displeased and that He wanted the temple erected by the son who would replace him. It had been Nathan, only Nathan, who had been valorous enough in a face-to-face confrontation to condemn his father for his adultery with his mother. Nathan's forthrightness led to David's earnest repentance and the blessings that subsequently showered upon the house of David proved that God had forgiven him and that Nathan was a true prophet.

For the first time since Nathan had jostled him awake, Solomon allowed himself to consider obeying the prophet that his father had wisely obeyed. His glance strayed from Nathan to Bathsheba. Both stood indomitable.

Solomon walked to the window. When the people caught sight of him, their cheers grew tumultuous. Instinctively he raised his arm in acknowledgement, tarrying and absorbing the acclamation for several minutes before he whirled and demanded of Nathan and Bathsheba, "How am I to be certain all this is the work of God and not the plans of well-meaning conspirators?"

"Yahweh would not ask that you put your hand with the wicked," Nathan said sternly.

Bathsheba implored: "Two shouts echo through the city: 'God save King Adonijah' and 'God save King Solomon.' The throne will host but one of David's sons, and the Lord has made clear His wish that you govern Israel."

Solomon hesitated a few seconds before he said softly, calmly: *"I will be king."*

There was a long hush in the room—Nathan and Bathsheba overcome with surprise, relief, and gratitude. Finally Nathan said, "Israel has been delivered. And Yahweh, whose unmistakable choice you are, has triumphed."

Bathsheba embraced her son, and to her perfume was added the salt of blissful tears.

Solomon slipped hurriedly into the cloak, and with Nathan and Bathsheba he sped to the courtyard. He marveled at how swiftly word of his coronation had spread. An imposing escort awaited, a throng of praise-saying well wishers—priests, merchants, farmers, peddlers, potters, a cupbearer shaking his sistrum noisemaker, carpenters, shepherds and ironworkers. One of the palace gardeners handed Bathsheba a magnificent bouquet of pink-edged yellow roses, the flower which symbolized peace among the Israelites. From the harems of Jerusalem had come Philistine eunuchs with their concubines, the women sending up a nervous, happy concatentation of giggles. Mothers held excited children who clutched animal dolls, whistles, and rattles. Also waiting were the fighting mercenaries, the Cherethites and Pelethites, who composed David's personal bodyguard, the elite of his army. A one-eyed Cherethite soldier held the reins of the royal mule which no one except the king was allowed to ride.

* * *

Now Solomon's procession had reached Gihon, the rocky site in the Valley of the Kidron beneath the City of David, so cherished a place that it had been named for the second river that flowed from Eden.

Solomon was pleased and relieved that the path from Jerusalem to Gihon had been spanned without a threatening or unpleasant incident. His father's show of military force, a visible percaution against an attack from any of Adonijah's more fanatic followers, had been unnecessary, or else had proved a deterrent. The aged battle tactician who could find no warmth for his withered body had lost none of his ability as a strategist.

The cavalcade to coronation proved his first victory—beggars to moneychangers emptying their lungs, crying out their unanticipated, rousing support every step of the way. As Solomon brought the mule to a halt and dismounted, the shophar was sounded once by a priest. Two blasts from the curved ram's horn trumpet meant danger. His father's battle host had heard the twin careening lances of alarm through each of their hard-fought campaigns. A single shrill call from the instrument announced that a formal gathering had assembled for a high purpose,

The one blast was not yet spent by the time Solomon, followed by Nathan and Bathsheba, completed the climb up the short incline to the altar. Set on high ground, the altar enabled Solomon to see the uplifted faces of thousands, now silent since the first note of the shophar winnowed through the air. Across the Valley loomed the three summits of the Mount of Olives, through which his father had passed in temporary retreat from Jerusalem in the wake of Absalom's rebellion, David later putting down the insurrection after ferocious combat in the forest of Ephraim east of the Jordan.

Zadok, long-jawed and resolute, emerged from the tent shrouding the Ark of the Covenant, which David had efficiently arranged to be at the right place at the right time. The presence of the holy Ark emphasized the importance of the ceremony. It was Israel's supreme possession, more than the cattle on a thousand hills. Solomon himself dared not touch the oblong acacia chest overlaid inside and out with pure gold. That privilege was reserved solely for the high priest, and he could view its contents only once a year. In the Ark lay the tablets of the law given to

Moses, the evidence of God's enduring pledge to the Hebrews.

Surrounding the Ark was the presence of God. If even the most devout believer put his hand to it without special, priestly permission—which was seldom given—he would be mortally punished. The well-meaning Judahite, Uzzah, had died instantly when he reflexively and innocently steadied the Ark being pulled by oxen to Jerusalem.

In Zadok's hands was a horn of oil, and from it he poured the scented liquid over the head of Solomon, saying, "You, by command of Yahweh and our lord David, are king over Israel and over all that Israel possesses. You are the king who reigns before Him who has given us Solomon from the seed of Abraham and has made of us a great nation." Nathan then took the horn of oil from Zadok and anointed Solomon. The prophet said nothing, tilting his head to heaven, his lips trembling. Solomon knew Nathan was sending forth a prayer of thanksgiving.

The short ceremony ended, and with it the silence. From the far corners of the Kidron the throng enveloped the new king in a vast outpouring of tribute.

The joyful noise to the Lord would not die. King though he was, Solomon could not order stillness. The praise and celebration continued without ceasing, though the freshly anointed ruler yearned to share his innermost thoughts with his people.

On the ride back to the palace, Solomon's way was bathed in cheers. They piped the pipes and the earth quivered with the sound of them. He passed under the south gate near the royal gardens, then leaped from the mule and crossed under the doorsill to where David and the throne waited. In a flourish of purple he disappeared into the palace.

The symphony of the shophar—which the Israelites felt carried the cries of the multitude to God and which God and His angels also played on special occasions—filled the air with acclaim and joy.

Chapter Two

The shophar's melody and the rapturous, heaven-rending sound of the celebrants was also heard at Rogel Well, eleven hundred yards down the Valley, by three ambitious men—a self-declared king, a high priest, and a warrior of Israel second only to David in reputation and deed. Even if they had bestirred themselves from the black tent long since faded by the sun, Adonijah, Abiathar, and Joab would not have witnessed Solomon's coronation. The site of anointing was hidden from their view by a bend in the Kidron.

They had come together for their own celebration, the covenant of salt. A private, solemn meal, their eating, drinking, and vows bound them irreparably in friendship and dedication to a common goal—no less than David's throne.

They had eaten well from a leather-covered table. A calf had been killed and cooked in spices. From heavy gold goblets they repeatedly toasted Adonijah's reign with tasty, fermented wine imported from Helbon in Tyre. This was particularly appropriate because it was the favorite drink of kings.

Craggy-faced Joab, his scythe of dark beard flecked with quills of gray, poured his goblet full again from the hyacinth-colored goatskin bag. Before he could raise the drink to his lips, he heard another wave of acclaim.

"Why the uproar?"

Abiathar's black, hypnotic eyes closed and his head bobbed in prayer. "Yahweh has acted," he said with conviction. "The host of Israel hastens to attend Adonijah, the new king. All praise to our lord David. All praise to God, the beneficent, the righteous, the merciful, the just."

"The words of Abiathar are certain," said Adonijah, his ivory,

29

chiseled features flushed garnet with excitement. "Abiathar and Joab, you have served me well. Your reward will be gifts that only a king can bestow."

An unnamed feeling, akin to what he once had sensed prior to an ambush, pulsed through Joab. Thus far all had gone well for Adonijah. But Joab was aware that David, until the grave claimed him, was capable of wielding a well-executed ax of surprise. And in this dangerous business of choosing a new king the unexpected could not be discounted. Joab had willingly cast his lot with Adonijah as the least objectionable son of David. The rest of them, especially Solomon, who seemed to enjoy neither the pleasures of women nor the exhilaration of war, he dismissed as royal eunuchs incapable of protecting the nation from its enemies. Though he had heard the long-standing rumor of David's promise to Bathsheba that Solomon would succeed him, he considered it nonsense. Solomon would not make a competent captain of a hundred.

Yet again came the blare from the distance, shouts riding in on the cry of the shophar.

Joab rose to his feet, weaving slightly as he maneuvered slowly toward the entrance of the tent, slashing the curtain aside with the mace of his fist. He did not see the host of people anticipated by Abiathar, but only the lone, gangling figure of Abiathar's son, Jonathan, running toward him.

Joab returned to his drink and drained the goblet. Unaccountably, the wine tasted bitter.

"The blood of Tyre's grape tastes as the poison of gall and the sorrow of wormwood," Joab said to his companions, the feeling of an ambuscade closing in on him ever stronger. "I taste the judgment of God."

"Only our enemies shall drink gall," Adonijah replied.

"And the wormwood will be the burden of those who fear, not welcome, the decision of Yahweh to give the throne to Adonijah," added Abiathar.

A burst of motion caromed into the tent. Jonathan, who had been a message carrier for David in the battle of the Ephraim wood, was out of breath. He had run only a short distance, yet he felt he had come from a far place.

"The valiant Jonathan," Adonijah said lightly. "Good news must bring you to us in such haste."

Jonathan wished he was back in the adventurous service of

David. As spy and messenger, he had helped deliver the crucial details of Absalom's secret attack plans to David and was in part responsible for the king's victory, for saving David's life, and preserving his throne."

"Speak the glad tidings, my son," Abiathar urged, "for that is why I sent you among the people, to learn their mood and when Adonijah may take the palace."

Jonathan's tongue caught in his throat and panic gave him the whipped look of defeat.

Joab, who had seen the same expression on the terror-beaded faces of soldiers cowering before a battle, shrugged. "Then it is as I feared. All is gall and wormwood."

"For the sake of Yahweh, speak!" Abiathar's demand was the impatient insistence of crumbling self-confidence. And though Joab was half-drunk, Abiathar could not entirely dismiss the sudden pessimism of David's general. Neither could Adonijah. His mood changed swiftly and he steadied his trembling hands against the table. He realized if the news was favorable Jonathan would not look crestfallen. Besides, Abiathar's son had always been quick of tongue.

"Tell us the reason for the shouting and why the shophar sounds," Adonijah insisted.

Jonathan caught his breath and prayed for an anodyne, which did not come. His gaze tied to the earthen floor, he whispered hoarsely, "Our lord David has made Solomon king."

"Solomon!" Joab declared, spitting the name out like a curse. "Solomon, who wears the purest loincloth in Jerusalem, an insignificant poem-maker and a coward who has never sped a javelin to its target. How can Solomon be king over a nation of valiant fighting men? If what you say is true, then David's gift for surprise has turned to madness."

"Solomon sits on the throne," said the dejected Jonathan. "He has been anointed by Zadok and Nathan. And the people applaud the choice. This is the noise you have heard."

Already knowing the answer, Adonijah asked with as much self-control as he could muster, "There is no mistake?"

"None," said the baleful messenger. "I was the only witness to the coronation who did not cheer."

The three ambitious men of Israel remained mute as each instantaneously projected the consequences for himself now that David had deeded power to Solomon.

It was Adonijah who finally spoke. "We had all best scatter to our individual fate. The salt of our covenant has been spilled by Solomon, our uninvited, invisible guest, who holds the one covenant that matters."

"Long live King Solomon," Joab said with venomous sarcasm.

Striding from the tent, the brother of Solomon said mockingly, fearfully, "Yes, and long live King Adonijah."

Chapter Three

In the first few hours of his rule, Solomon was virtually ignored. The affairs of the empire had come to a standstill. Nothing official was brought to the attention of the new king over
Israel and its possessions.

Solomon was aware that the limbo into which the governing
process had descended was in deference to his father. All Israel
knew that he who had been the pride of the Hebrews for forty
years was dying, else David would not have consented to the
anointing of his successor.

Solomon passed the time reveling in the still fresh memory of
the coronation which, despite his misgivings, he had enjoyed.
The frustration of not having the opportunity to deliver his
speech publicly seemed of small import now. Perhaps it was just
as well. Speeches meant little unless they generated action. It
would be preferable, far more so, to demonstrate his policies with
deeds rather than merely speak of them.

He was amazed at how quickly he had accommodated himself
to his role as king, acknowledging that Nathan and Bathsheba's
arguments had been both persuasive and correct. The fact that
the coronation had not been marred by a single disquieting incident confirmed that God, using David as His instrument of
practical help, had indeed protected him. Solomon was seated in
the unostentatious, high-backed chair which served as David's
throne, set atop a small dais reached by creating a mound of six
worn, stained, yellow-carpeted steps. Stretching one long leg to
rest on a circular footstool, Solomon noted that the simple wood-
en chair was unsuitably rude for the power represented by the
throne of Israel.

The large room in which he sat was silent. The dynamism of

the palace had also come to a panting halt, like a hare weary of the chase. Once the king's royal audience hall had been the center of a whirling pageant, filled with the lyric and melody of singers and musicians, David frequently joining in and having the most pleasurable time of all the participants. Often there had been leaping maidens in rainbow-colored cloaks dancing in swirling eddies, the audience composed of David's copious retinue of wives, concubines, children, and court officials. Other guests invariably attending were David's mighty men, his leading officers from the outposts of Israel's dominions, who came to enjoy the entertainment and give the king the latest intelligence concerning their individual areas. They came also to pay David honor and deliver to him tribute in gold talents, other valuable metals, and produce.

The yawning void of the palace and the isolation of Solomon at last came to an end when Nathan entered.

"How is it with my father?" called Solomon.

The prophet bowed and walked heavily to the foothill of the dais. "At this moment," Nathan said quietly, "he is in a stupor. He wakes and sleeps. The physicians say the balm of Gilead will not heal him. Abishag, who is yet a virgin though she clings to the lord David like the soft skin of a kid covering fleshless bones, attends him. But the warm, undefiled body of the Shunammite nurse does not rid the king of his chills."

"Set a herald at David's door so that I may be informed at once when he is ready to receive me," Solomon replied. "A king has need to speak with a king."

"Reality must be faced," said Nathan, raising the tone of his voice. "Israel has but one functioning ruler, and King Solomon must act immediately with royal firmness against his enemies. We have no word as yet of Joab and Abiathar, but Adonijah is cornered. His fate awaits your decision. I urge you to dispose of him swiftly, for he would have dealt so with you if your positions were reversed."

"Surely, Adonijah is at rest with the heart of the matter and has no further ambition for the throne," Solomon said, somewhat astonished that the first problem presented to him concerned his brother. "Surely, there is nothing more to fear from him."

"While he lives, he is a threat. Adonijah is not without cleverness, resources, and friends. He covets the throne still. Already he begins a new plot against you."

"What proof does Nathan have?"

"Hear for yourself."

Nathan strode quickly to the door of the throne room and ushered in a nervous, squat, middle-aged man wearing a sweat-band and a filthy tunic. "I come from Gihon with a plea from Adonijah who bade me make it in his stead," the man said, dipping his frame in an arch of respect to Solomon.

"Why does not one son of David have the courage to come and speak directly to another son of David?"

"Adonijah fears for his life, and he claims the protection of the altar where my lord was made king."

"The protection of the altar," interjected Nathan, "may be claimed only by a manslayer. Has Adonijah repented and killed his cohorts, Joab and Abiathar, those treasonous dogs of Israel?"

"I know of no one he has slain." The squat man was clearly uncomfortable in his role as intermediary between nobles. "I am but a struggling mason, who labors long and hard for his bread. I lingered after my king's anointing, so fatigued was I from the excitement, and thus met the lord Adonijah briefly and by acci-dent."

"Nathan has spoken hastily," Solomon said. "The asylum of the altar may also be given to one who fears his own death."

"In his heart, Adonijah is a manslayer," Nathan interjected, "and his victim may yet be the timorous Solomon."

"What further message do you carry from my brother?" Solo-mon asked the mason.

"The lord Adonijah said, 'Let King Solomon swear to me that he will not slay his servant with the sword.' "

"I beseech you to send the executioner," Nathan insisted. "Otherwise your throne will not be secure."

Solomon pondered. Then he told the ill-at-ease emissary, "Say to Adonijah that if he shows himself worthy, not a hair of his head shall fall to the earth. But if wickedness is found in him, he shall die."

"I will repeat the king's command to the lord Adonijah," the mason replied, eagerly bowing his way out of sight.

"Solomon's first decision is his first mistake," Nathan said with disgust. "If you spare your wily brother, you risk your own life."

"Absalom defied David, but my father did not order his death. A king's inheritance includes the compassion of Yahweh."

Before Nathan could argue further, Solomon rose abruptly, strode down the steps and out of the throne room, leaving the prophet's mouth agape.

In his chamber, Solomon changed into a fresh cloak and went to his writing table. He felt a sudden urge to record the events at Gihon and all that had led to his coronation while they were still lucidly and sharply in mind. In the center of the table, his eye caught a papyrus. Solomon recognized the handwriting as his father's, David's familiar, irregular penmanship, bold upward swings and deep downward slopes, denoting unquenchable energy. But with what pain the generous number of lines must have been composed by his stricken parent. Was this David's dying blessing? Was it a testament of wisdom and instruction on how best to rule Israel, a testament from his father for which he had longed from the moment he had decided to accept the throne?

Across the top was written: A Psalm for Solomon. Carefully, the son of David read the jagged lines and the implications between the lines. As soon as Solomon's eyes touched the papyrus, he realized that David had lost none of the shimmering beauty of his style. The loveliness of his language artfully complemented the sublimity of his thoughts.

> Give the king your judgments, O God, and thy
>   righteousness unto the king's son.
> He shall judge thy people with righteousness, and thy
>   poor with judgment.
> The mountains shall bring peace to the people, and the
>   little hills, by righteousness.
> He shall judge the poor of the people, he shall save
>   the children of the needy, and shall break in pieces
>   the oppressor.
> They shall fear thee as long as the sun and moon
>   endure, throughout all generations.
> He shall come down like rain upon the mown grass: as
>   showers that water the earth.
> In his days shall the righteous flourish; and abundance
>   of peace so long as the moon endureth.
> He shall have dominion also from sea to sea, and from
>   the river unto the ends of the earth.

They that dwell in the wilderness shall bow before
him; and his enemies shall lick the dust.
The kings of Tarshish and of the isles shall bring
presents: the kings of Sheba and Seba shall offer
gifts.
Yea, all kings shall fall down before him: all nations
shall serve him.
For he shall deliver the needy when he crieth; the
poor also, and him that hath no helper.
He shall spare the poor and needy, and shall save the
souls of the needy.
He shall redeem their soul from deceit and violence:
and precious shall their blood be in his sight.
And he shall live, and to him shall be given of the
gold of Sheba: prayer also shall be made for him
continually; and daily shall he be praised.
There shall be an handful of corn in the earth upon
the top of the mountains; the fruit thereof shall
shake like Lebanon: and they of the city shall
flourish like grass of the earth.
His name shall endure for ever: his name shall be
continued as long as the sun: and men shall be
blessed in him: all nations shall call him blessed.
Blessed be the Lord God, the God of Israel, who only
doeth wondrous things.
And blessed be his glorious name for ever: and let the
whole earth be filled with his glory: Amen, and
Amen.
The prayers of David the son of Jesse are ended.

Solomon crossed to the window and stood transfixed, watching a scudding avalanche of clouds filter the light from the sun
over Jerusalem.

And for the first time since childhood he cried.

His tears were for the ocean of beauty and insight of David's
psalm. Solomon knew the cadence and rhythm of the words
were abundantly more than words.

His tears were also for the prophecy and promise embodied in
a father's sacred hymn to his son and to God.

Solomon cried for all things under the sun: the joys and sor-
rows of life; the beginning and end of things. He cried for the

inevitable destiny of men: *One generation passeth away, and another generation cometh: but the earth abideth for ever.*

His tears were for the poems that men wrote; for the poets whose verses would never be penned, lost inspiration drowned in wine, gluttony, torpor, and the limitless dissipations of body and spirit. Solomon wept for the folly of men and for the rare victories that men achieved. He cried for ambition buried before the tomb takes the body; for ambition realized by a few fortunate men drunk on the elixir and challenge of life, they, most blessed of all, who always had a new song to sing, a new dream to chase. His tears were for those who foolishly lived as though they would never die, leaving nothing behind except dust.

He shed tears for his own sublime opportunity to work for Israel. Between the rising and setting of the sun of life, while the wind yet curled south and north and the rivers inexorably emptied into the cup of the unfilled sea, there was much labor for the leader of Israel, and this was reason for joyful tears. For all this Solomon cried, sad and happy weeping induced by David's psalm of psalms.

His eyes were still tear-stained when he noticed Nathan, whose knock he had not heard, standing before him.

"Lord of the Hebrews," the prophet announced, gallantly disregarding the sight of his weeping sovereign, "Adonijah grovels in the throne room."

* * *

From his aerie atop the dais, Solomon stared hawklike at his half-brother. The cringing, scraping figure before him was an alien. The ivory complexion had turned sallow, the symmetry of his features pitted with gullies of terror. Solomon had never known Adonijah well; he knew more of him by reputation than through shared conversation and experience.

Not long ago this transfigured heap of flotsam cowering before him had been a high-spirited, sleek, charming young man who abjured learning and labor. Adonijah's one consuming passion was women. And the weakness was perhaps not entirely his fault. So handsome was he in countenance and body, so perfect a facade of masculinity did he project that it was easy to understand why countless women had succumbed to him. This would have been true if he had been a slave rather than a son of a king.

Matching Adonijah's animal attractiveness was his animal response, giving himself to any receptive maiden, comporting himself with unbridled lust instead of discipline and selectivity. He charged through endless bouts of passing sexual pleasure, which he substituted for the pursuit of God and the perilous shoals of self-examination.

While Solomon had been discreet and discriminating in his youthful forays with women, Adonijah had bragged rashly and publicly about his conquests. His humor and morality were fit for a soldier's tent, not a king's palace. Undoubtedly, this was one reason Joab had rallied to him.

Among Adonijah's female trophies were the accessible women within the wide circle of the court, women of high station from wealthy families who were not David's concubines. But according to persistent rumors, it had not stopped there. Adonijah also, and this was unforgivable, had taken several of David's women, an offense, if verified, punishable by death. Moreover, when Adonijah was bored, curious, or jaded, he sought unmentionable erotic delights and perverted satisfactions. He would commandeer the house of prostitution for an evening. The gaily garmented and finely ornamented women, wearing a blatant phallic symbol on their brows to indicate their profession, knew Adonijah's most intimate cravings. And he persisted in his relationships with the harlots although custom dictated such vice equalled infidelity to God.

"Our father's chair well suits my talented, brilliant, and courtly brother," Adonijah murmured from his nearly prone position.

Solomon was nauseated at the unctuousness of the remark from one who, at least in Nathan's opinion, would have exterminated him without blinking had his plot to usurp the throne succeeded.

The nausea was replaced by pity as Solomon ordered, "Rise and show yourself a man."

Adonijah scrambled to his feet, but his body remained stooped.

Menacingly Nathan challenged, "Where are the other conspirators? Bring us Joab and Abiathar."

"I know not where they may be. I swear it by Yahweh."

"Adonijah," Solomon said, "I long to know why you sought the throne as ardently as you seek your harlots."

"I sought not the throne for myself. I was beguiled by Joab and Abiathar. None of it was my own doing."

"He lies," steamed Nathan.

"Nathan judges you would have killed me if our father had sanctioned your anointing. Is that so?"

"I would have dealt with you as I implore you to deal with me—with mercy. My actions have been rash and I admit my defeat. But we are of the same blood and so I swear my loyalty to Solomon."

"Blood does not guarantee loyalty. Ask David if his rebel son, Absalom, was loyal. The land of Ephraim will clutch the bones for a thousand years of the sons of Israel who fell there because of Absalom's unnatural aspirations."

"Long life to King Solomon, for he is merciful," Adonijah whined.

"Mercy, my brother, is the partner of justice. So did I send you a warning that if wickedness instead of worthiness is found in you, justice will demand your death. The empire cannot stand if there is turmoil at the foot of the throne."

Solomon paused, a strong feeling of brotherly affection unexpectedly sweeping through him. For a moment, he allowed himself to think of how comforting it would be if Adonijah became a brother he could trust, who would stand beside him and be a strong, devoted, and loving friend.

"I shall prove myself worthy should my life be spared," Adonijah pleaded. "I will live blamelessly."

To Solomon, the words lacked conviction. Adonijah's eyes mirrored hatred and resentment, not love or honesty. Nathan's distrust of Adonijah was undoubtedly justified, and Solomon knew it was hopeless to yearn for his brother's comradeship. As with Cain and Abel, the gulf between them could not be spanned and the killing of one brother by the other was probable.

Nevertheless, Solomon said, his face hardening, "I seek only your promise that in all ways you will be faithful to the throne as the throne, if not to Solomon as king."

"It is given."

"Then you are free to go in peace, but I warn you again to avoid trouble and troublesome desires. The choice of living a long or short life is yours alone."

"Solomon is all-wise, all-merciful. Never again shall I covet anything except my life."

"All men have needs and ambitions above bare existence.

Only be certain that what you set your eye upon in the future is modest and attainable."

"Solomon is gracious. Bless his mercy," said Adonijah. He was still in his half-crouch as he retreated from view.

"We will hear more from that wretch," the unpacified Nathan said.

"I think you are correct. I think it was a mistake to show him mercy."

Solomon's frank admission of error puzzled Nathan. He asked: "Why not then be done with Adonijah now before he plows new furrows that will bring distress and possible disaster?"

"In my chamber," said Solomon, "you saw me crying. I was in tears because of a psalm my father wrote for me. He entreated me to judge with righteousness and to save the souls of the needy. Adonijah is needy."

"Though not, by your own assertion, deserving of mercy. You judged him with misplaced generosity."

"Nathan," Solomon concluded, "the sound of the people and the shophar yet rings in my ears. The oil of anointing yet clings to my head. A coronation celebrates life, not death. No doubt my judgment of Adonijah was not wise or righteous and was in fact too generous. But for a king's first day on the throne, it was a proper judgment."

Chapter Four

She was the rock, the olive and the desert, the bride of kings, and the mother of prophets.

Older than the time of Abraham, she was the core of the promise of the Promised Land.

A maiden alternately shy and proud, she could not be seen until the avid pilgrim crossed the chain of broken hills that masked her physiognomy. Then, within her parapets, she bade the visitor a stunning, many-layered welcome, unveiling herself with the mystery, allure, shyness, boldness, piety, and holiness befitting the queen city of the world.

She was called Jerusalem and Salem. Asaph, David's chief palace musician, retained by Solomon in one of his first acts of state, wrote of her:

> In Judah is God known: his name is great in Israel.
> In Salem also is his tabernacle, and his dwelling place in Zion.
> There brake he the arrows of the bow, the shield, and the sword, and the battle.

Joab had captured her for his king, and so she was also called the City of David. Because she was located on a high natural plateau, which made her virtually immune to attack, David made Jerusalem his capital and ordered the Ark of the Covenant to rest in her bosom.

Jerusalem became a city like no other, an ageless, matchless, spiritual beauty, the stronghold of Zion, the abode of Yahweh, and the heartland of the children of the Lord. *Thy holy hill,* David had said of her in dedicating Jerusalem to God.

In the eastern portion of the hallowed home of the Lord, near

43

the south end of a knoll, up which an occasional, salubrious breeze managed to climb, David had built his modest palace, already storied for its shame and its splendor. Here, from the roof of the palace one sultry night, David spied the tantalizing figure of a maiden taking her bath. Her name was Bathsheba and from their bittersweet union had come Israel's third king. Here in the palace's inner chambers David made the decision to kill Uriah. Here also he married the enticing Bathsheba and repented of his misdeed. And from here he had sped Solomon to coronation.

And now David was to add another chapter to the biography of the palace. To the amazement of his physicians, the old warrior suddenly regathered his vitality. Announcing he felt much stronger, David called for a two-day festival.

The palace again came alive, humming with resurrected energy, the throne room festooned with fresh torches and lamps, the stained carpet at the mound of the dais replaced. The walls were washed and the king's house completely combed of dirt and neglect.

The mood of excitement and celebration emanating from the palace reflected itself throughout the city, which was also throbbing with new vigor. Again Jerusalem became as a sea into which all the rivers of Israel and its dominions flowed.

With the exception of Joab, who was in disgrace and still in refuge, all the mighty men who led David's standing army of two hundred and eighty thousand hard-fisted veterans and all the mighty who were the first among their tribes came to David's city and his palace. Rough and untutored men, their strengths and passions were: love for the Lord, for David, and for the battlefield. Their weaknesses were jealousy and overweening ambition. But virtue outstripped flaws in these valorous men who had known the thunk of clanging armor. These leaders were only two generations removed from the dung of the pastures and they had been indispensable in helping the Israeli juggernaut to victory.

They swarmed into the throne room, these nerve ends of the empire, anxious to hear what they had been warned would probably be the farewell address of David, fearing that this would be the last time they would see their beloved slayer of Goliath. They were anxious, also, to measure the king in whose soft hands now reposed the ganglia of all the tribes and dominions.

"The mighty and valiant men will not be easily impressed with the new king of Israel," Nathan told Solomon. "It would be wise for my lord to present himself before them as unostentatiously as possible."

Agreeing, Solomon appended perceptively, "I am mindful that this day—this occasion—belongs to David."

And so Solomon and the prophet arrived virtually unnoticed, entering from a side door without fanfare. For a while they stood near the throne, Nathan adding names to all the strong faces who were the congealed summit of Israel's power.

Solomon calculated, too, as he began strolling through the overflowing audience hall, adroitly managing to convey the impression that he was a king above them yet a friend with whom they were equal. Nathan made introductions formally, and Solomon talked briefly and informally of inconsequential matters with the men whose names and tribes were a rollcall of the Hebrew legend, the ironsmiths who wielded the Hebrew hammer.

He met the ironsmiths of all twelve tribes.

Eliezer, leader of the Reubenites, who had fought with David against the Philistines.

Shephatiah of the Simeonites, the tribe that protected the southern flank of the kingdom. It held sway over more than eighteen cities whose epicenter was the venerable well of Beersheba from which Abraham had drawn water.

Overlord of the Levites, Hashabiah. His men specialized in serving David as judges and scribes. Their most important service was supplying the priests who traveled with the army.

Zadok, who spoke for the Aaronites, still proud of their descent from the elder brother of Moses.

The arid soil of the Judahites produced the hardiest men of Israel. It was David's own tribe and led by his brother Elihu.

The respected Omri (the mere mention of the name carried respect since it meant "worshipper of God") was the champion of the tribe of Issachar, which possessed the kingdom's richest lands, from Carmel to the Jordan.

The people of Zebulun, located to the north, claimed its men were second in valor to none. They had sent Ishmaiah.

Jerimoth represented Naphtali. Its boundary was the northernmost frontier of Israel. Without its constant, conscientious watch for invaders, none in the kingdom could sleep with assurance.

The children of Ephraim, whose tales could busy a hundred scribes for a thousand years, were symbolized in the person of their doughty chief, Hoshea. Carved from Canaan, one of Jerusalem's gates was named for fertile Ephraim, where David had fought Absalom. There Absalom once had a sheep farm and there he murdered David's eldest son Amnon for seducing his half-sister Tamar. The killing had touched off the quarrel that led to Absalom's rebellion against David.

Joel and Iddo had equal status among the tribe of Manasseh, which held the wooded mountain country near the Valley of the Jordan. Manasseh had joined David while he was a fugitive from Saul and contributed one hundred thirty-eight thousand soldiers to his army,

Iaasiel came for the Benjaminites, who had sired moody King Saul. Commercially and militarily, the tribe was extremely important. It held the strategic territory between Judah on the south and Ephraim on the north.

Azareel was dispatched from the tribe of Dan, whose men had been the rear guard during the exodus. They had also won their land from the Canaanites, and raised fierce, brawny sons, notably Sampson.

In his brief, polite exchanges with those who were the stewards over all the substance and possessions of the kingdom, Solomon was treated with outward respect. But none of these men were awed by him as were the people who had sent up hosannas at Gihon. These nobles were the comrades of David, who had helped him to gather in, acre by embattled acre, what had become the rich crop of empire. Their respect for Solomon was, for the most part, given in deference to David. Though David was no longer king, he was yet *their* king. In some measure, David would always be their king. Besides, for most of them, the transition had been too swift for easy adjustment.

"Do they accept me?" Solomon asked Nathan when they had finished their tour through the audience chamber and returned to the base of the throne.

"They are curious and some are skeptical. But that is one reason your father has assembled them. May God give him the strength to speak eloquently and quiet their fears so you may rule free of dissension."

Nathan's assessment was correct. Among some of the chiefs the polite but cool respect accorded Solomon had privately turned to grumbling and disquietude.

"He is winsome enough. Yes, Solomon appears engaging," said Iaasiel to Shephatiah. "But our Saul, though he became sorely beset, looked a king. Physically, he was a head taller than the rest of our people. Solomon is tall, though he appears more a stripling than a sovereign. Saul was strong until he became possessed. I would give a thousand talents of gold to know if Solomon has the strength to resist the unkind spirits that smote our son while he was king of the Benjaminites and Israel."

Elihu bristled to Joel, "Why was the coronation held in such haste? Why was not I, the brother of David, invited to the anointing? In the hills of Judah, say those who tend the flocks, that which is not seen, except for God, does not exist."

Hashabiah of the Levites had objections to Solomon on priestly grounds. He said to Hoshea, "This is a new way of kingmaking. It was the prophet Samuel who anointed both Saul and David. Howbeit that David has served us as king *and* prophet?"

Eliezer, Zadok, Omri, Ishmaiah, and Jerimoth made approving remarks about Solomon, best summed up by Iddo as he talked to Azareel, "It is done. Solomon is king of Israel and Manasseh. I pray that Yahweh blesses him."

All conversation came to an abrupt halt as two of David's Cherethites and two of his Palethites shouldered their way through the huge door, efficiently slicing a path down the middle of the vaulting chamber room.

In a moment, David appeared, half-sitting on his couch, borne aloft by four soldiers.

The valiant men of Israel quickly found their voices, and Solomon was impressed with the warm, loud, gruff, endearing greetings his father received, an unintentional but pointed contrast to his own reception by the same men.

David's litter was carefully placed beneath the dais of the throne. For a few long moments, seemingly helpless, he did not move. Then a deep gasp pealed from the throats of the mighty warriors as David, slowly, but with the muscles of a much younger man, succeeded in freeing himself from his couch. The gasp translated into applause and joyous, prayerful shouts of praise and encouragement as he struggled to his feet and stood erect.

Digesting the feast of so many friends, David's eyes choreographed every man in the room. Then he began to speak, his words forming out over his trident of wispy white beard, words addressed to his comrades in the high, rhythmic, and poetic language of the scrolls.

"Hear me, my brethren," he began tenderly, and his salute was silence and rapt attentiveness. "I had it in my heart to build a house of rest for the Ark of the Covenant of the Lord, and for the footstool of our God, and had made ready for the building. But God said to me, 'You shall not build a house for my name, because you have been a man of war, and have shed blood.'"

Solomon, the prisoner of peace, ached for David, who had been the captive of war. There was profound poignancy in his father's life. God had allowed him to build a nation, but not His temple, which had been David's fondest wish. Yet were it not for David, Abraham's covenant might never have been fulfilled. The Philistines, the Canaanites, the Egyptians, and all the other foes of the Hebrews could well have trampled the dream of the land of promise. By the sword David had made certain that Hebrew women were no longer raped by rampaging, invading armies. Hebrew cities were no longer sacked. And no king dared decree, as did the king of Egypt in the time of Moses, that Hebrew midwives kill every Hebrew manchild on the birthstool. David had been compelled to serve with the spear and maul and other body-sundering tools of war so that Solomon, hopefully, could serve with line and plummet, the tools of the peaceful builder.

"Howbeit," David was saying, "the Lord God of Israel chose me before all the house of my father to be king over Israel for ever: for he has chosen Judah to be the ruler; and of the house of Judah, the house of my father; and among the sons of my father he liked me to make me king over all Israel."

David's mind, Solomon reflected, was yet thorn-sharp. He was far from that simpering senility which must have activated Adonijah, Joab, and Abiathar into believing they could kidnap the throne without David's opposition. David was diplomatically reminding the men of might that Judah was the fourth son of Jacob, yet God had chosen him to father the pre-eminent tribe of the Hebrews.

"And of all my sons, for the Lord hath given me many sons," continued the peerless septuagenarian, "He hath chosen Solomon my son to sit upon the throne of the kingdom of the Lord over Israel."

Solomon could scarcely believe the words of the old king. David was asserting with even portions of obliqueness and obviousness that God had chosen not his oldest, but his most capable manchild to receive the anointing.

This was his father's first public statement concerning the succession, his personal acknowledgment to those who were still skeptical that David's throne was imperishably Solomon's throne. The declaration from David, because it also embodied his father's love, was as meaningful to Solomon as the poured oil from Zadok's horn.

The choice confirmed, David had no further reason to linger on Solomon's promotion, now an accomplished fact and accepted among the people.

The mightiest of Israel's mighty warriors then outlined the commission between God and himself that had accrued to Solomon:

"And He said to me, Solomon your son, he shall build my house and my courts: for I have chosen him to be my son, and I will be his Father. Moreover, I will establish his kingdom forever, if he be constant to do my commandments and my judgments."

David's next words were a challenge and a warning to the chieftains: "Now therefore, in the sight of all Israel, the congregation of the Lord, and in the audience of our God, keep and seek for all the commandments of the Lord your God: that you may possess this good land, and leave it for an inheritance for your children after you for ever."

The old king, who indeed had found the eloquence for which Nathan had hoped, next swept his gaze to Solomon, his thin arms reaching for his son. Solomon moved a few paces to his father's side. He could hear labored breathing as David touched a thin hand to his shoulder, met his eyes, and addressed him directly.

"And you, Solomon my son, know the God of your father, and serve Him with a perfect heart and with a willing mind: for the Lord searches all hearts, and understands all the imaginations of the thoughts; if you seek Him, He will be found by you. But if you forsake Him, he will cast thee off for ever. Take heed now; for the Lord has chosen you to build a house for the sanctuary; be strong, and do it."

David removed his arm from Solomon and raised it in a signal.

Eight soldiers, buckling under the heft of two oversized, double-handled chests, clumped into the chamber and put the chests to rest at the feet of David and Solomon with a booming thud. Solomon recognized the one-eyed Cherethite who had held the reins of the mule when he had embarked for Gihon. The soldier loosened the chains that bound the chests and lifted back the un-oiled, screeching lids.

Instinctively, all pressed in for a closer look, and what they beheld dazzled and puzzled them. One chest brimmed with gold, silver, and precious stones, and the other with scrolls.

As Moses in the wilderness had been shown a pattern for a tabernacle to God, David now showed the pattern for his temple to the Most High. Solomon and the congress of leaders saw on scroll after scroll the finely drawn, detailed plans for the house of the Lord. Even Nathan's face was a bubble of acclamatory shock. Such grandeur, Nathan knew, could emanate only from Yahweh, master of all architects.

It was all there on parchment, everything that was to go into the magnificent structure for the God who had guided the Hebrews from Ur to Jerusalem. Included were the plans for the temple's porch, the adjacent houses, the rooms of the treasuries which would hold gifts dedicated to God, the inner chambers, the mercy seat, the chambers for the Levite priests.

Now David weighed out gold and silver for the candlesticks of the temple, for the lamps, and for the tables which would hold the showbread, fleshhooks, bowls, cups, and basins. And he weighed out refined gold for the altar of incense and for the chariot of the cherubim whose outspread wings would protect the Ark of the Covenant.

"All this," said David, "the Lord made me understand in writing by *His* hand upon me, even all the works of this pattern."

David again directly charged Solomon with the sacred mission of building the temple: "Be strong and of good courage, and do it; fear not, nor be dismayed, for the Lord God, even my God, will be with you. He will not fail you, nor forsake you, until you have finished all the work for the service of the house of the Lord." David's veiny arm indicated every onlooker as he added, "The Levites, even they shall be with you for all the service of the house of God; and there shall be with you for all manner of workmanship every willing, skillful man, for any manner of service; also the princes and all the people will be wholly at your commandment."

In ladling out his gold and silver, David had proved to the princes of Israel that he had not squandered or lavished his wealth on personal indulgences. They could see he had stored great treasure for building the house of God. But the vast undertaking was not to be financed solely by David. All must have the opportunity to give an offering for the holiest of holy tabernacles. All must have the opportunity to show allegiance to God and join with Solomon in raising the temple for His glory.

David said:

"Solomon my son, whom alone God has chosen, is yet young and tender, and the work is great: for the palace is not for man, but for the Lord God. Now I have prepared with all my might for the house of my God the gold for things to be made of gold, and the silver for things of silver, and the brass for things of brass, the iron for things of iron, and wood for things of wood. Onyx stones, and stones to be set, glistering stones, and of divers colors, and all manner of precious stones, and marble stones in abundance.

"Moreover, because I have set my affection to the house of my God, I have of mine own proper good, of gold and silver, which I have given to the house of my God, over and above all that I have prepared for the holy house. Even three thousand talents of gold, of the gold of Ophir, and seven thousand talents of refined silver, to overlay the walls of the houses withal: the gold for the things of gold, and the silver for things of silver, and for all manner of work to be made by the hands of artificers. And who then is willing to consecrate his service this day to the Lord?"

The princes of the tribes of Israel offered willingly. They pledged to Jehiel, the priest in charge of the temple's treasury, five thousand talents of gold, ten thousand drams of gold, ten thousand talents of silver, eighteen thousand talents of brass, and one hundred thousand talents of iron. Also precious stones in abundance.

So great was the outpouring of generosity that David rejoiced and said before all the congregation, "Blessed are you, Lord God of Israel our Father, for ever and ever."

David had accomplished much in rousing himself from his sickbed to apostrophize Israel's mightiest. He had firmly sealed

Solomon to the throne and secured the future of the temple. Now his strength was draining rapidly, yet he sensed there was more to be said, that a last word, a bequest was expected.

Girding himself with his final ounces of energy, it was not the David filled with too many years, but the David of the lyre, the psalms, and the songs who spoke.

"Yours, O Lord, is the greatness, and the power, and the glory, and the victory, and the majesty: for all that is in the heaven and earth is yours; yours is the kingdom, O Lord, and you are exalted as Head above all."

David's vocal poetry embraced his comrades as a parting kiss between lovers, as a benediction between brothers who had fought and spilled blood together so that the covenant would not be lost, broken, or abandoned, but be preserved at all cost. His words were filled with grandeur and elegance.

"Both riches and honor come from you," David continued, speaking before his brethren while yielding himself to God, "and you reign over all. Now therefore, our God, we thank you and praise your glorious name."

He paused for breath, and his concluding words came in a climatic thrust:

"But who am I, and what is my people, that we should be able to offer so willingly after this sort? For all things come from you, and of your own have we given you. For we are strangers before you, and sojourners, as were all our fathers: our days on the earth are as a shadow, and there is none abiding.

"O Lord our God, all this store that we have prepared to build you a house for your holy name comes of your hand, and is all your own. I know also, my God, that you test the heart, and have pleasure in uprightness. As for me, in the uprightness of my heart I have willingly offered all these things: and now have I seen with joy your people, which are present here, offer willingly to you. O Lord God of Abraham, Isaac, and of Israel, our fathers, keep this for ever in the imagination of the thoughts of the heart of your people, and prepare their hearts toward you."

"And give to Solomon my son a perfect heart, to keep your commandments, your testimonies, and your statutes, and to do all these things, and to build the palace for which I have made provision."

And the last of David's last words to his brethren were:

"Now bless the Lord your God."

The congregation obeyed, bowing their heads before the Lord. Then they bowed their heads to David, the chieftains certain by now they would never see their king again.

A few moments passed quietly and then Solomon and all the assembly watched as David, after sinking to his couch in exultation and exhaustion, was carried out of the throne room.

Each of the mighty of Israel was left to his own thoughts.

Solomon's piercing thought was that if it had been required this day, David somehow would have found strength to slay another Goliath.

Chapter Five

"I go the way of all the earth."

David tripped his dying words out falteringly, almost imperceptibly, then lapsed into unconsciousness while Solomon desperately hoped that God would stay his father's final appointment.

David's chamber was suffocatingly hot, menorah-shaped flames leaping from the huge hearth. Heavy black curtains, swaybacked against the windows, kept the room protected from the near perfect weather outside, Jerusalem bathed by a gently gliding wind and incandescent under an orange sky.

Sitting beside the couch which held David's frail frame, Solomon marked the irony. The spark of David's life was slowly being snuffed out at the precise moment that the city was vibrating with the celebration of a new beginning. The City of David was vital and virile while the king for whom the city was named was comatose and feeble.

The young king had awakened early to the blast of trumpets swirling in through his open window. This time it was a massed orchestra of booming, blasting music composed of divers instruments that screamed, caroled, and hymned over Jerusalem and onward to the neighboring valleys. This time the rending noise exceeded a thousand-fold the rumblings of the shophars that had lofted through the city on the day of Solomon's anointing.

Everyone in Israel, it seemed, had crowded into the rock-olive-desert capital that more than ever—because Solomon had been crowned within its periphery—was the capstone of the empire.

Streets, buildings, mountains, little hills, and the altar of the tabernacle were honeycombed with dancing, shouting, Godmagnifying people. The celebrants were there for Solomon's second anointing, which David had arranged as a witness before all Israel to re-emphasize his chosen son's title to the throne, and as the apex of the two-day convention of the chiefs from Dan to Beersheba.

The festival had been underway since dawn, but Solomon had not made his expected public appearance, preferring to remain in his quarters, waiting for a summons to his father. Nathan told him the audience would come the moment David was lucid enough to speak.

"Our lord has one final charge to convey to the king before he sleeps with his fathers," the prophet had confided.

At last a servant hailed Solomon to David. When he came into his father's presence, his nostrils were assaulted by the mingled smell of variegated medicinal ointments.

Nathan, Bathsheba, Abishag, and the physicians attending David withdrew quietly at Solomon's appearance.

Solomon gazed with anguish at his father, knowing that everything that could be done for David had been done.

Physicians summoned from all corners of the kingdom had ministered to him. But their treatments were ineffective and contradictory; the only consistency, was failure to cure his infirmities.

Mandrakes and amulets had been tried. On the advice of one physician from Simeon, David's couch was moved to a balcony and, despite his marrow-deep chills, he had slept two nights in the open air in the belief the moon would make him well.

David had ingested quantities of medicinal herbs. His skin had been coated with other aromatic herbs, aloes, cassia, and cinnamon, which did not heal. Nor had Gilead's oily balm, or leeches.

A physician from Manasseh, observing that David's blood did not warm him, prescribed more blankets of the heaviest sheep wool. When the blankets brought neither warmth nor improvement in David's health, the physician suggested, "Let there be sought for my lord the king a young virgin, and let her wait upon the king, and be his nurse. Let her lie in your bosom, that my lord the king may be warm."

David had wearily assented.

Israel was combed for the kingdom's most voluptuous maiden. She was found in Shunem, in the rich, lush land of the tribe of

Issacher. Abishag, full-breasted, tapered of leg, and flawless of feature had been brought posthaste to the palace.

David was pleased and he made her his concubine as well as his nurse. Some in the palace whispered he had summoned a priest and secretly married the captivating Shunammite.

Abishag had taken up her responsibilities for David's care with enthusiasm, enveloping herself under his blankets, seeking to transfer her radiant vitality to him. She sought, also, to excite and mate with David.

When David found he was incapable of knowing her sexually, he reluctantly, yet with some feeling of relief, decided the time had arrived for the king to step aside. Since he could not recoup his vigor, the strength of Israel was threatened, for it was widely believed that the impotence of the king would be visited on the kingdom. The fertility of women, the tumesence of men, the breeding of cattle, the growth of crops—all were considered in danger so long as he remained on the throne.

David was tired, stricken beyond endurance with the burdens of rulership. It was an auspicious moment to hand power to one of his sons. And so he had listened to the case for Solomon, argued before him by Nathan and Bathsheba in the presence of Abishag. Although David was reminded of his oath at Solomon's birth to make him king, he selected Solomon primarily because he had been inspired by God and because Solomon had shown intelligence, restraint, and respect. David felt grossly insulted by the actions of Adonijah, his over-anxious, would-be heir. The affrontery of Adonijah declaring himself king without his consent, consultation, or approval rankled David. Could the nation that he had planted with a lifetime of sacrifice be reaped by a son who had sown nothing? A son who considered his father only a cripple in mind and body? Healthy or not, the king of Israel was more than a sovereign—in the eyes of God and the people he was sacred. Such high position must be earned and not taken for granted, nor casually and audaciously usurped. As he had opposed Absalom, he would oppose Adonijah.

Since his anointing at Gihon, Solomon had deduced much of David's thinking and learned more of his father's feelings from Nathan and Bathsheba, who visited with him often and repeated his conversation.

Still staring down at David, couch-ridden and sallow-faced, a shadow of the articulate visionary, prophet, and preacher he had been only yesterday before the leaders of the tribes, Solomon found it difficult to believe he was the same man. One side of David's face had collapsed, and even in sleep he looked uneasy and in pain. Every few moments his body shivered—he could find no warmth.

But Solomon would not permit his skein of hope to run out. He wanted his father to live and serve with him as co-regent. David, though he might be handicapped by age and illness, could help his reign enormously. The lion of Judah could yet fend for the lambs of Jerusalem.

Solomon heard the muffled blare of trumpets and other instruments invading the curtained chamber from somewhere near the palace. The music was a call to glory. Solomon, however, remained beside David, unmoving. The room had grown warmer, almost unbearably stifling, the raging blaze in the hearth fireball-hot.

Solomon had no idea how long he had been with his sleeping father when David, coming suddenly to consciousness with a suggestion of recovered stamina, said again, "I go the way of all the earth."

David struggled and succeeded in balancing himself on an elbow. "Solomon, my son," he declared emphatically, "be strong, and show yourself a man."

"How best does a king show himself a man?"

"Keep the charge of the Lord your God," David answered in almost the same devotional inflection he had used during his occasional visits with Solomon when he was a boy. "Walk in His ways, keep His statutes and His testimonies, as it is written in the law of Moses, that you may prosper in all that you do and wherever you turn."

"In all ways will I obey the Lord," Solomon promised.

A new expression—ominous as the gathering of thunderheads—stormed across David's face. He leaned the pale cloud of his head closer to Solomon and rained out the words, "You know what Joab did to me, how he murdered Abner and Amasa, two of my finest captains, avenging in time of peace blood which had been shed in war, putting innocent blood upon the girdle about my loins, and upon the sandals of my feet."

David paused, gulping for air. As Solomon adjusted his blankets he thought that the killing of Abner and Amasa were the least of Joab's manslayings, if murder could be weighed by degree. He wondered why his father had not first condemned Joab for slaughtering Absalom in express defiance of his orders. And why hadn't he condemned his savage general for his part in the conspiracy to steal the throne?

"How does my father wish me to deal with Joab?"

"Act according to your wisdom, but do not let his head go down to the grave in peace."

David's face now was a poisoned well that had not yielded all its bitter water. "There is also Shimei, the Benjaminite, who cursed me on the day I went to Mahanaim, but when he came down to meet me at the Jordan, I swore to him by the Lord, saying, 'I will not put you to death with the sword.' Now, therefore, hold him not guiltless, for you are a wise man, and know what you ought to do to him, and you shall bring his dead down with blood to the grave."

Though Joab and Shimei deserved vengeance, the prospect of carrying out David's direct commands for their executions troubled Solomon deeply. The prospect of ushering in his rule with blood contravened the line-and-plummet mood he wished to set for his reign, the mood already instituted with the mercy he had shown Adonijah. How could a man named for peace, carry out two executions?

No simple answer occurred to Solomon.

His father drifted off to sleep once more as Solomon struggled with his tangled legacy. David had told him to keep the statutes of Yahweh, and he considered none of God's laws more sacrosanct than the commandment. *"You shall not kill."* Yet was not David telling him clearly; "You shall kill"?

David did not rouse himself for a long while. Then, unexpectedly, he bolted to a sitting position on his couch, looking straight ahead, oblivious to Solomon. In a clear voice he intoned:

"The Spirit of the Lord speaks by me. His word is upon my tongue. The God of Israel has spoken, the Rock of Israel has said to me: 'When one rules justly over men, ruling in the fear of God, he dawns on them like the morning light, like the sun shining forth upon a cloudless morning, like rain that makes grass to sprout from the earth.'

"Yes, does not my house stand so with God? For he has made with me an everlasting covenant, ordered in all things and secure. For will He not cause to prosper all my help and my desire? But godless men are all like thorns that are thrown away; for they cannot be taken with the hand. But the man who touches them arms himself with iron and the shaft of a spear, and they are utterly consumed with fire."

David sank back to his couch, drifting immediately into what solace he could find in his shuddering sleep. His body tossed spasmodically like a wind-caught feather.

Having listened closely to David's peroration, Solomon understood that his father had given him the answer he sought to his dilemma: *Godless men are all like thorns that are thrown away . . . the man who touches them arms himself with iron and the shaft of a spear, and they are utterly consumed with fire.* Men who defied God forfeited their own lives, and Yahweh, not the king, meted out the sentence of death.

As he stepped from the chamber for a whiff of cooler air, Solomon did not know he had heard David's last words. Nathan was waiting in the corridor. "Our lord has given you his charge?"

Solomon nodded.

"Then you had best go to the altar of the tabernacle, where the trumpets and the people cry for you. I will see that your father is well attended."

The altar had a commanding view of the city. Formerly a threshing floor owned by Araunah the Jebusite, David had purchased it for fifty shekels of silver. It was to be the site of the new temple.

Pillars of smoke curled from an irregular circle of countless fires where the burnt offerings had been prepared according to ritual. A thousand bulls, a thousand rams, and a thousand lambs had been slain, their throats slit and blood drained. The carcasses were then skinned and dressed. The fat of the entrails and kidneys were placed on stones for the offering, the remainder of the meat chopped in pieces and cooked separately for eating.

Never had Jerusalem seen so vast a sacrificial feast. A thousand drink offerings had also been provided by David to consecrate the ceremony of Solomon's second anointing.

The people went into a renewed frenzy after Zadok again poured oil on Solomon. They rejoiced before God, once more shouting pleas that the new king would enjoy long life and blessings from Yahweh.

But the twice-crowned king could not with a full heart join in his own celebration. His thoughts were still with his father. Then Solomon saw Nathan approaching, and read the set features of the prophet before he reached his side. The announcement was an anti-climax.

"Our lord David sleeps with his father," Nathan said calmly. "Weep not, my king. He died in a good old age, full of days, riches, and honor."

What now, Solomon pondered as he struggled with his grief, could be said of the anointed sheepherder who had lived fully, furiously, and with the avenging, conquering sword of survival in one hand, while the other held fast to God?

He had been a man of simplicity and complexity, an adulterous murderer who was yet the honored of God, a poet and musician who bound together an empire. Above all, he had been human, hence flawed.

So diverse was his life that no man could easily write an epitaph for David. But the sweet psalmist of Israel had written his own on a night long ago in the high desert. It was a night when he was uncertain of victory in the next day's battle, although completely certain of victory before God. David's lyrical, reverent letter of love to Yahweh and Israel would more than suffice as his epitaph.

> I will lift up mine eyes unto the hills, from whence comes my help?
>
> My help comes from the Lord, which made heaven and earth.
>
> He will not suffer your foot to be moved: He that keeps you will not slumber.
>
> Behold, He that keeps Israel shall neither slumber nor sleep.
>
> The Lord is your keeper: the Lord is your shade upon your right hand.
>
> The sun shall not smite you by day, nor the moon by night.
>
> The Lord shall preserve you from all evil: He shall preserve your soul.
>
> The Lord shall preserve your going out and your coming in from this time forth, and even for evermore."

Soon news of David's death would spread throughout Jerusalem, and men would journey from the far places of the earth to his burial site at the southern end of the city, not far from the palace. The new tomb, hewn out of vertical shafts of rock, had recently been selected by David himself. Knowing oncoming sleep was near, he had ordered construction of his sepulchre.

Solomon's gaze encompassed the panorama beneath him.

The earth shook with the percussion of voices and musical instruments.

"I will lift up my eyes ... my help comes from the Lord," Solomon repeated from David's prayer of praise to the Lord.

Then Solomon saw the sky burning with a dark cloud of mourning for the dead king and he also saw the sky billowing with the pure cirrus of promise for the new king.

As the earth trembled and the sky burned, the City of David, though it would forever be called by his father's name, was now the City of Solomon.

Chapter Six

Bathsheba, alone in the spacious bedchamber of her handsome, high-ceilinged palace apartment, was still awed by Solomon's decree of a thirty-day period of national mourning for David, a tribute unprecedented since the death of Moses and Aaron.

She had hastily and gratefully concurred when Solomon suggested that the official bereavement be four times as long as that which was customary for the average citizen. David's life was at least four times more exalted than any other man in Israel. As no other, he had consecrated himself to Yahweh and the nation. The descendants of Abraham had not seen his like in courage, dedication, piety—and achievement—since Moses died within sight of the Promised Land.

More than most knew or suspected, David had confided in Bathsheba, though she was troubled and perplexed by much of what he said, particularly his explanations of the underlying motives for his ceaseless wars. She was, of course, a Hebrew, a daughter of the oath, and as such fathomed the uncompromising necessity of an inviolate homeland. But why so much shedding of blood? Why all the foreign conquests—did a Philistine or Moabite mother feel less grief than the mother of a dead Hebrew son? Why must the souls and hair of so many mothers be grayed when the young fruit of their wombs fell as casualties of conflict? She understood neither the abrasive need for war nor the subtleties of peace, the endless political intrigues among the contending desert nations and, most enigmatically of all, the competition of Israel's feuding tribes. She had long since given up coping with such anomalies.

Yet she had shared much with David. In addition to the adventure of the couch, her strong will often instilled confidence in him when he reached a decision on a vexing problem and yet doubted if his judgment was correct. Her life was David's life. Out of an unselfish heart, she had given him loyalty, stability, inspiration, tolerance, humor, and a relaxed atmosphere where he could be whatever his mood dictated. He could be the Judean sheepherder of his youth, the ardent lover, the troubled king, or the incomparable psalmist.

Always she had offered a willing, appreciative, and appraising ear, her delight never greater than when David recited his poetry. He had composed some of his most magnificent verses in her chamber.

It was she, Bathsheba remembered warmly, who had watched David deftly run his reed pen over the papyrus, swiftly composing the thrilling psalm celebrating the capture of Jerusalem.

"I was glad when they said to me,

'Let us go into the house of the Lord.'

Our feet shall stand within your gates, O Jerusalem.

Jerusalem is builded as a city that is compact together:

Whither the tribes go up, the tribes of the Lord, to the testimony of Israel, to give thanks to the name of the Lord.

For there are set thrones of judgment, the thrones of the house of David.

Pray for the peace of Jerusalem: they shall prosper that love you.

Peace be within your walls, and prosperity within your palaces.

For my brethren and companions' sakes, I will now say, 'Peace be within you.'

Because of the house of the Lord our God I will seek your good."

As inamorata and wife, Bathsheba knew she had, in the years of their turbulent and tender relationship, shown David love, respect, admiration, and understanding. And now Solomon displayed the same qualities by his public declaration for a month of homage to his departed father.

Twice now she had donned widow's sackcloth, remembering still with a deep edge of sadness the ill-starred Uriah. She had mourned him, too, after David gave the order for his certain death and Joab sent him on the suicidal sortie against the besieged Ammonite capital of Rabbath. Uriah had advanced, so one of the survivors of the battle later told her, as far as the gates of the city when he was killed, a pathetically vulnerable target caught in the open by an arrow from an archer shooting down from the heavily fortified wall.

Uriah, however, had died a distant death on a distant plain of war when she had been a bride only a short time. His death seemed almost totally impersonal and she had mourned him in absentia. Joab did not send his body back to the capital for an honorable burial, and the impatient David, who wanted her for his wife as soon as possible, would allow her no longer than seven days to express her remorse.

In contrast, the demise of David was intensely personal and painful. Her marriage to Uriah had been brief, their emotional understanding of one another superficial, their mingling ascetic. But with David there had been long and profound intimacy, spiritual as well as sexual. She remained steadfast to David no matter what the circumstances or provocation, sharing his repentence for their adultery and quenching her jealousy when he visited his other wives. And her loyalty did not cease when Abishag entered the palace maelstrom. Her fondest hope was that the Shunammite beauty could somehow revive David's health.

Despite Abishag's ubiquitousness, she had spent many moments alone with David during the last stages of his illness. When he was feeling well, he would dismiss his new maiden, who had loveliness but not maturity of years or mutual experience in common with David. Then they would talk, laugh and sometimes argue zestfully—as of old. And David had reassured her verbally and by act—Solomon's succession—that she was still his favorite.

And so she had girded herself in coarse sackcloth and dragged her way along heavily at the front of the long funeral procession, Solomon and Nathan supporting and comforting her as she wailed, "Ah, my husband!" and "Yea, my beloved!" She struck herself so ferociously that her fingernails drew blood from her cheeks and arms. She cried sincerely and unreservedly in her sorrow, unable to control herself even when the cortege entered the marble-columned limestone tomb and Solomon placed David's crown on his gold coffin.

* * *

The period of mourning was now over and activity in the royal residence and throughout the kingdom had resumed.

Drained of sadness, Bathsheba looked expectantly to the future. Solomon, she noted with satisfaction and mother's pride, sat firm on the throne. And her son had honored her greatly, cleaving to the fifth law of Moses. He had caused a seat to be placed for her at his right hand, which gave her the dignity and prestige that David never accorded her publicly. She became in fact as well as name the queen mother. She was put in charge of the harem. And she was particularly jubilant that Solomon had also put her in complete command of running the maze that was the palace household. This task alone would more than fill her time with important work.

Before her mirror, Bathsheba repaired the still-visible damage to her cheeks with powder from her cosmetic palette and applied a light henna stain to her nails. Though shards of white had appeared in her hair, she felt it unseemly to use dye. She avoided this as she did the heavy black eye paint worn by Jerusalem's prostitutes. She heartily disapproved of this recent fad among Hebrew women. Too amorous girls utilized the extract of antimony to attract suitors, and wives sluiced it with broad, unashamed strokes above their lashes in the belief it heightened femininity and the passions of their husbands.

Bathsheba was not without vanity, but she preferred to cover the unwelcome gray in her black curls with a loose-fitting wool shawl, hemmed with soft purple. Her only jewelry was a silver bracelet given to her by David.

Her beauty, she decided, had best be the resplendence of regal restraint.

As she completed the last of her make-up, a servant scurried in, a usually talkative girl who, to Bathsheba's annoyance, now stood mutely before her, gesturing toward the door.

"Silence and consternation do not become you," the queen mother said tartly.

With reluctance, the open-faced girl from a pious family in

Zebulun said succinctly, "The lord Adonijah wishes to speak with you."

The cub of Haggith? Bathsheba was taken aback. Her visceral reaction was to refuse the audience. Bathsheba was David's eighth wife, Haggith his fifth. Haggith had married David and borne him Adonijah at Hebron long before Bathsheba had come to David at the height of his glory in Jerusalem. Now she and Solomon held power, if not seniority, over Haggith and Adonijah.

Haggith had shown little but snarling, unconcealed resentment toward Bathsheba, even prior to Solomon's triumph over Adonijah. But Haggith had grown old and had little left to comfort her except the doubtful joy of a son who all but ignored her to indulge his own pleasures. Bathsheba knew that Solomon had given Adonijah his freewill choice of life or death and she had seen nothing of him since, except to catch a fleeting glimpse of him at David's funeral. Bathsheba sighed and decided that her responsibility over the palace required her to meet with Adonijah. Perhaps he brought a request from his mother that she could grant to show her generosity and prove that her elevation had not made her arrogant. "Have him enter," she told her nervous servant. A moment later, Adonijah slithered in like a prowling animal and hunched himself into a short-legged, wide-backed stone chair cushioned with a downy, embroidered green pillow.

"Do you come in peace?" Bathsheba asked at once, determined to demonstrate she harbored no ill will for the events of the past.

"I come peacefully," he replied without truculence, though Bathsheba missed the insincerity in his tone. "Moreover, I have something important to say to you."

"Say on," Bathsheba answered lightly and with relief. She assessed Adonijah's manner as respectful.

"You know the kingdom was mine," Adonijah said, "and all Israel expected me to reign. However, the throne has become my brother's." Bathsheba made no comment. Then Adonijah added, and again she failed to discern the insincerity, "The crown was Solomon's from the Lord."

"That is true, and bless Yahweh for it," Bathsheba said ingenuously.

"Now I have one request to make of you. Do not refuse me." Somehow Bathsheba could not help but enjoy the abject position in which Adonijah found himself. "Speak, I beg you," he said, "to Solomon the king, for he will not refuse you. Ask him to give me Abishag the Shunammite as my wife."

Since David's death, Bathsheba had modified her attitude toward Abishag. She had readily accepted her as David's nurse, but otherwise she had considerable reservations concerning the exquisitely attractive girl. Abishag was a potential source of trouble, and had little to offer aside from her incredible beauty. She particularly lacked charm and wit. Still, her beauty was towering enough to possibly entice Solomon into marriage! The thought was extremely distasteful. But what if Solomon did take Abishag as his first wife? The king of Israel had foremost priority to the nation's ranking beauty. The mere possibility of Solomon marrying Abishag petrified Bathsheba. Her son should wed a Hebrew girl of exalted rank who would bring him a great dowry, many children, and by her very presence enhance his stature. Abishag was poor in everything but consuming comeliness. And that, Bathsheba determined, was not enough, not nearly enough. Solomon's future would be protected by removing Abishag from his sight . . . into the arms of another, thus ending the possibility of an extremely unsuitable marriage.

Bathsheba congratulated herself for recognizing an opportunity to help Solomon by acceding to Adonijah's plea, which would ward off what could be a catastrophe.

"I will speak to the king in your behalf," Bathsheba said.

Adonijah thanked her profusely.

But as Bathsheba rose and made her exit she did not see the smile on Adonijah's lips.

* * *

Solomon greeted Bathsheba cheerfully as she entered the audience hall and walked to her small throne near the dais. She noted how handsome Solomon was, how nobly he filled David's chair, reinforcing her belief that it would be a tragedy for one such as Abishag to share his glory.

"I have a petition of small consequence to present to the king. I pray you will not deny my plea," Bathsheba said idly, though inwardly she was ruffled. Why had she shown more composure with Adonijah than she felt now before her own son?

"Ask on, my mother. You know I will grant you any wish."

"Then permit Abishag to be given to your brother, Adonijah, as his wife."

Solomon's face darkened and his eyes narrowed. "Why do you ask only that Abishag be given to Adonijah? Why not ask me to present the entire kingdom to my beloved brother?"

Bathsheba, astonished at Solomon's sarcasm and anger, left her chair and climbed three steps of the dais, spreading her hands to her son in supplication.

"Adonijah has asked only for a wife. He said the kingdom is yours from the Lord."

Still furious, Solomon replied, "Through Abishag and my mother, Adonijah asks far more than a wife. He petitions for the throne itself!" Noting that his mother was yet uncomprehending, he raged, "Nathan, Benaiah, and others have told me that Adonijah still plots with Abiathar and Joab for the power which has been bestowed on me. My enemies have become unclean jackals with appetites that cannot be sated. Now Adonijah has committed a crime that not even a king can forgive."

"And what is the nature of your brother's dastardly crime?" Bathsheba asked, helplessly confused.

"For myself, I care nothing for the dull-witted Shunammite. But my mother has either forgotten or chosen to ignore the long-established tradition of the royal house of Israel that he who inherits a woman of the dead king inherits the throne. Though the custom is outmoded and unworthy of serious thought, it is fervently believed by the priests and people. We are a nation committed to the acumen of Yahweh, yet there is much foolishness in our ways. But the greatest insult to me is that you have been used and deceived."

"In what way?" Bathsheba was still struggling to grasp the implications of Solomon's livid outburst. "I have spoken to you only with a mother's love. I would not see you harmed."

"My enemies," Solomon explained carefully, "count on my not denying you any request. By sending you to me with Adonijah's clever petition, they believe they have put me in a quandary without solution."

"Which is?"

"I have no doubt Adonijah already spreads the news to his cohorts and through them to the entire city that the mother of the king has agreed to seek for him a woman of the king—and therefore Adonijah, not Solomon, is the rightful sovereign of Israel."

Bathsheba stumbled back to her seat, near collapse. She was reluctantly engulfed at last by understanding ... and humiliation. She had underestimated the wiliness of Adonijah who had not, after all, come to her in peace, but callously and cynically used her as an instrument in his continuing war for the throne. She castigated herself for the stupid presumption that her son would so much as consider marrying Abishag. She had underestimated both Adonijah and Solomon. Her dejection would have been total except for the buttressing realization that God had blessed her son with remarkable insight, every bit of which he would need to hold the throne.

"How do you plan to deal with your brother?" Bathsheba asked with fatigue.

Solomon came to his mother and put a comforting hand on her shoulder. His voice, however, was a threnody. "With this treason Adonijah has forfeited the mercy I have shown him. Because of this conspiracy, I have no alternative but to put him to death—today!"

* * *

After hastily running from the throne room to her apartment, the past roared back to Bathsheba, questions slashing through her mind that challenged the meaning of her entire life.

What if David had not seen her bathing that night from the palace roof? Would everything have been simpler and happier if she had had the courage to refuse the king? Yet she had immediately felt true love for him.

Even after she had submitted, would it not have been better to have compounded her sin? She could have continued her illicit relationship with David while insisting she remain married to Uriah. Such an arrangement was made by other Hebrew women. Had she so acted, Uriah's death might have been avoided. Avoided, too, would be the guilt she still bore of being an accessory to her first husband's death, although she did not know David planned to have him killed.

What if she had never met David, mothered a king, become a queen?

Was the blood that Solomon must spill to keep the throne worth the throne?

A flashback of shock and sorrow over David's demise overcame her. Had David been wiser than her son in insulating her from the cares of rulership? She had conspired and cajoled to give Solomon David's crown. *Why?*

Why had she not preceded David in death?

Bathsheba fell to her knees, beseeching God for answers.

Chapter Seven

Godless men are like thorns . . . they are utterly consumed with fire.

Under his raven-dark hair, Solomon's brow furrowed as he summoned to mind the final admonition of David. Absentmindedly, he ran his hand across the fresh stubble on his chin. Out of respect for his father, he had followed tradition and cut his beard when David died.

Solomon thought of the four godless men who had defied the will of Yahweh and betrayed his father, the four who would have him wear a crown of thorns.

For him, vengeance and violence were hard, alien taskmasters, but he had been maneuvered into a position where he could do no less than consume Adonijah, Abiathar, Joab, and Shimei with David's legacy of fire. However reluctant he was to deal harshly with his foes, however strange and disturbing he found the task of meting out punishment to fellow human beings, disposing of his quartet of enemies was an absolute necessity. Too much was at stake for him to act otherwise.

There must, finally, be an end to internecine strife at the foot of the throne. Power must, finally, be consolidated in his hands so that he could get on with the ambitious plans that were already boiling inside him.

All the land that God had covenanted with Abraham was in Israel's possession. But the Hebrews had been at war almost continuously for three hundred years, until his father's conquests brought a tenuous peace. Solomon knew this peace could be shattered at any moment by the discontented within the empire and by predators outside the empire. Egypt especially posed a perpetual threat. Thus old alliances with the conquered nations

73

must be reinforced and new alliances with neighboring nations, all potential foes, had to be forged.

Internally, Israel was still crude, boasting raw power with few of the distinguishing characteristics of a truly civilized country. Moreover, the kingdom was too loosely united, held together in part by a common inheritance of struggle, but held together essentially by a common love for Yahweh. Solomon was certain that the tie between the tribes would be loose until the temple was built. The temple, a shrine of thanksgiving to God, would also serve as a unifying force for the leaders and people of Israel.

Also needed for a still war-scarred, war-threatened Hebrew citizenry were new defense fortifications and honorable, meaningful labor to breed a new kind of pride and love of country. The result would be increased wealth for the individual Israelite and the nation. This could best be accomplished through a vast building program, trade, and development of the nation's most valuable resources—the yield of the mind as well as the mineral and agricultural bounty of the soil.

As the kingdom went, Solomon realized, so went the empire. For Israel to grow, prosper, and gain greater influence and prestige throughout the world, a magnificent palace for the king had to be erected. Court life must flourish with spectacle and sophistication so unmatched hospitality could be offered to the Hebrew mighty and to foreign princes.

Hard work, craftsmanship, architecture, the study of philosophy, the pursuit of all culture, the spread of commerce, and preaching the verity of the one true God must be expanded on a breathtaking scale to achieve peace within and without the borders of the kingdom and the empire.

Only four men stood in the way of this flow of blessings, and so they must be dealt with swiftly, each to be punished in deserving measure.

Hearing a scurry of feet, Solomon looked to the entrance of the throne room and saw Abiathar in the escort of four Pelethites. The face of the tall, gaunt priest was as chalky white as his finely woven conical cap, the most distinctive of his vestments.

After dismissing the soldiers, Solomon declared, "Abiathar, you are worthy of death for your part in the conspiracy to steal the throne."

Abiathar thought his life not in danger. The king himself could not summarily order his execution since as a priest he was under the special protection of Yahweh. From that strength, Abiathar spoke forthrightly to Solomon. "Adonijah is the eldest of David's sons and he yet merits the crown."

"True, he is the eldest. But where is his merit? Is there merit in disobeying Yahweh?"

"Adonijah acted only in accordance with the wishes of Yahweh."

"Was it Yahweh's wish that Adonijah's actions aggrieve my father's last days? Was it the wish of the Most High for my unscrupulous brother to viciously misuse and take advantage of my mother's trust so that he could further his ambitions?"

"Does the new king of Israel maintain he has no ambition?" Abiathar asked cannily. "Let him then give his place to Adonijah."

"Unlike my brother, I did not declare myself king. I had no unnatural ambition. Nor is my taste for women unnatural. I did not lust after the forbidden Abishag. After tiring of the Shunammite beauty, Adonijah as king would surely open the palace to every prostitute in Jerusalem, thus shaming the throne."

"Is Solomon beyond the temptations of women? If that be the case, then Solomon is unnatural."

"You tempt the executioner, Abiathar," the king said sternly. "Solomon admires women, but that is not all Solomon admires. You misunderstand the use of women. For a king, wives and concubines are indispensible vessels of diplomacy. Each woman a king receives into his palace brings a dowry of peace or an end to a nettlesome problem. The fathers of the king's women are not likely to cause war or trouble. Why else should the sovereign of Israel support a generous establishment of women? A king is no different than the poorest camel driver. One loving wife can satisfy his needs. But he who wears the crown of the Hebrews has women in abundance only because they serve us in matters of strategy and statehood. Nonetheless, women should not be objects compelled to endure a monarch's lust. They should not be forced companions in the sinful pleasure of the orgy."

Abiathar would not be dissuaded. Persistently he plunged down a new course. "With Adonijah on the throne, the old tribal laws would be kept. He has promised that he would rule hand-in-hand with the high priest. The high priest would not be a servant, but a partner of the king."

"Saul ruled above the priests, David ruled above the priests, and I will rule above the priests, though I will take counsel from the priests and Nathan. But it is the king, who also is counseled by God, who must bear the responsibility for making final decisions. Such is the core of rulership."

"Yahweh would wish it otherwise. The prophet Samuel warned the children of Israel against giving allegiance to kings."

"Yet it was Samuel, when the Philistines threatened to overwhelm us, who anointed Saul and then my father. It was primarily the kings of Israel, not the priests or prophets, who defeated the Philistines and brought the covenant to fruition and gave us a nation and an empire. Your goal, Abiathar, is not to be a partner of the king but to make him your subordinate. Such unorthodox questing for position has blinded you to reason and God's truth."

"Howbeit," said Abiathar with unrestrained boldness and sarcasm, "that our young king comes to us without flaw or imperfection? Howbeit that he is all-wise?"

"Virtually the first lesson I learned from my father is that flawlessness and perfection belong only to God. I do not claim I am all-wise, for that is impossible for anyone except Yahweh. I claim only that I am king of Israel."

"By a stroke of luck!" Abiathar bridled.

"I did not come to the throne by the wish of David alone. How strange that a priest would interpret Yahweh's action as mere chance." Solomon's indulgence of Abiathar's insolence and ungodliness was wearing thin. "You have strayed far from your oath by seeking to make the king your puppet. You have acted from worldly motives, dishonoring your vestments and vows. You have acted out of jealousy, not satisfied to share the office of high priest with Zadok. Now Zadok alone is my high priest."

"If you take my rank, you may as well take my head." The bravado was gone from Abiathar's voice as soon as he heard what to him was the harshest judgment Solomon could render.

The king answered: "You are the last of the house of Eli, and in Shiloh the word of Yahweh was spoken that your house would fall. Saul slaughtered your father and eighty-three other priests for remaining loyal to David when he and Saul became enemies. But because you served David in his wanderings and supported him during Absalom's rebellion and aided my father by guarding the sacred Ark of the Covenant, I will spare your life, despite your disloyalty in supporting Adonijah. You are to go to Ana-thoth, and there tend your fields. You are banished from the court and the royal shrines."

Shattered, Abiathar said, "Exiling me to my ancestral proper-ty in the rocky land north of Jerusalem, stripping me of my authority, and removing me from the heart of the kingdom is not only demeaning, it is beyond vengeance. It is a living death for one who has been the high priest of David to suddenly be no more than a farmer."

When he saw that Solomon was unmoved by his plea, Abia-thar, clinging to a final hope, inquired of the king, "How fares it with Adonijah?"

"Hear for yourself," Solomon said, sighting Benaiah at the entrance to the throne room. Square shouldered and trim, with the stiff bearing of a perfect military man, Benaiah strode toward the dais. He was accompanied by Nathan.

"Abiathar inquires after the welfare of Adonijah," Solomon said.

"As my lord commanded, Adonijah is dead, slain by my own sword," Benaiah declared.

"He was found on his couch, coupled with a street whore," Nathan added with disgust. "To her no harm was done. She fled in hysteria, shouting for God's charity and loving-kindness, promising to renounce her life of sin."

"Adonijah remained true to his nature until the last," said Solomon to Abiathar.

Crushed, Abiathar walked from the audience hall. Before he was out of sight he removed his conical cap, the painful gesture of abject defeat.

"Abiathar goes to his exile, and my brother is slain," Solomon said, "but I fear there is more work for Benaiah's blade. What news of Joab?"

"He was discovered at the tabernacle of the Lord," Nathan answered. "He clings to the altar, claiming sanctuary. He begs for his life."

"I told him," Benaiah recounted, "the king commands that he leave the altar. But Joab said, 'No, I will die here.'"

"Then give him the punishment he demands," Solomon or-dered.

"I am to slay him on holy ground!" Benaiah was clearly re-pelled and frightened by the consequences of an execution at the

Lord's shrine. "My fidelity is to my king, yet I have no desire to displease Yahweh."

"Until now," Solomon answered, "you have been general of my father's twenty-four thousand Cherethites and Pelethites. Because of your valor and your devotion to the throne, I name you commander-in-chief of all the armies of Israel!"

"My lord does me great honor," Benaiah said. "I am grateful, but I cannot slay Joab at the sacred altar."

"Joab is clever," Nathan pointed out. "He has sought the altar because he believes he is safe from punishment there. But the tabernacle was not meant as the final refuge of an unprincipled man who has disobeyed God, yet uses His holy place as a shield. The altar is despoiled when it becomes a refuge for a murderer."

"Nathan is correct," Solomon said, fearing that Benaiah had interpreted his promotion as a bribe instead of a well-deserved reward for past service and present loyalty. Benaiah was a heroic and famous figure throughout the kingdom. Single-handedly he had slain two ferocious Moabite warriors and killed a spear-wielding Egyptian while armed only with a staff. When David was bogged down by snow during the war against the Philistines, he had also proved his valor by fighting a lion, killing the beast in its own lair.

"Among my father's dying words," Solomon continued, "was a charge to me that Joab's head should not go down to the grave in peace. Because Joab hurled three deadly javelins into Absalom, against my father's orders, David could never forgive his crime. He was inconsolable. Therefore did he cry, 'O my son Absalom, my son, my son Absalom! Would God I had died for you.' Joab was also the slayer of Abner and Amasa, two captains better than he. Their blood must be avenged. So did my father command. You are to execute Joab where he stands."

Benaiah no longer hesitated. Nathan and Solomon had rationally swept away his objections. The general bowed and declared, "I will attend to Joab as he deserves. It is Yahweh as well as the lords David and Solomon who have decreed his death," he said as he left.

"And now let us put an end to this wretched task of retribution," Solomon told Nathan. "Have the Benjaminite, Shimei, brought to me."

The genuflecting, porcine presence of Shimei was quickly hastened to the dais.

"I mistrust you," Solomon began bluntly. "You are an enemy of the house of David."

"My lord, how have I harmed the king?" The oval face of Shimel was an ill-fitting cloak of innocence.

"You cursed and cast stones at my father during Absalom's insurrection," Solomon said, annoyed that the shrewd, unctuous stave-shaped man before him would choose to forget what was unforgettable. "You stained David with undeserved bloodguilt."

"When your noble father crossed the Jordan, I threw myself at his feet and repented of my foolhardiness. He forgave me as Yahweh forgives all who virtuously repent a rash mistake. Did not Yahweh forgive the rashness of the venerable David's amorous relationship with Bathsheba?"

The indelicate remark turned Nathan splenetic. "This Benjaminite animal insults the king's father and mother," he declared to Solomon. Then the prophet turned to Shimei with loathing. "David's contrition for his conduct with Bathsheba thrusted itself forth from the despair of a holy heart. Your repentance was false. It was the repentance of expediency, as David well knew."

"And yet, in spite of your lying tongue, my father showed you compassion at the Jordan," Solomon added. "But I say in truth, in his last hours David called for your death."

"The noble David's illness was as long lasting and deep as it was unfortunate. The mind of the noble David, perhaps, was not his own," Shimei replied with an innate craftiness which managed to straddle the knife-thin difference between insolence and respect. "What purpose would be accomplished by taking the head of one who adored David and adores my lord Solomon?"

"If Shimei is filled with adoration for the crown," declared the unconvinced and unappeased Nathan, "why do persistent reports come to the palace that you maintain friendly and intimate relations with the king of the Philistines?"

"It is not so!" Shimei said indignantly. "I swear my loyalty to Solomon by Yahweh and by all my lands and servants."

"You speak of servants when you have the reputation of a brutal slavemaster," Nathan charged.

"My servants are as my children," insisted Shimei. "And to them I am a kind and generous father."

Solomon turned impatient at the bickering. If Nathan could prove Shimei's alliance with the Philistine king, he would have eagerly revealed his evidence. And Shimei's treatment of his slaves was probably no better or worse than that accorded by other wealthy Hebrews to those held in bondage.

"Even as my father showed you mercy," Solomon said, anxious to bring the confrontation to a close, "I, too, will be merciful, although by doing so I defy David's wish. Remove yourself from your house on the road to Jericho, and build a dwelling in Jerusalem. If you remain within the gates of the city and travel no further than the brook of the Kidron your life will be safe and you may spend your remaining years in peace." Solomon shot an iron glance at Nathan, an unspoken command for him to keep silent. "Shimei, remember my warning. If you leave the city, your blood will be on your own head."

Nathan managed a deep grunt of disapproval.

"The verdict is just and I will obey," said Shimei nimbly, relieved that his punishment was nothing more than confinement to the capital. Smiling inwardly, he assessed Solomon as a weakling and too inept to carry out his father's dying directive that he be put to death. Solomon was probably as much a liar as he was limp of will, he thought. And except for Nathan's insistent accusations, Shimei was certain he would not have received even this slight penalty. As quickly as he could feign decency and respect for Solomon, Shimei fled the throne room.

That night in his chamber the king received a Cherethite messenger sent by Benaiah. "My lord, Joab is dead," the soldier reported, "and General Benaiah personally attends to his burial."

Solomon gave thanks to Yahweh for the strength—and restraint—he had displayed in vanquishing his opponents. Instead of instigating a bloodbath, and slaying every supporter of Adonijah—whose partisans still were numerous—he had been compelled to order the executions of only his brother and Joab. Without leadership, those adhering to the cause of Adonijah were helpless. Hopefully, they would come to accept him as king without further contention.

He preferred not to linger on the executions of Adonijah and Joab, finding solace in contemplating the leniency he had shown Abiathar and Shimei.

Two lives taken and two reprieved was not too costly a price to keep the throne.

Solomon realized how different he was from his father, shud-

dering at the memory of David's excesses, even when his enemies were helpless. He had never understood why David allowed Joab to preside over the six-month slaughter of every male
in Edom after victory had been assured in the battle of the Valley
of the Salt. The massacre of the lame and the blind in the capture
of Jerusalem had also been wildly excessive. So, too, was the
decimation of two-thirds of defeated Moab. Solomon knew he
would be incapable of such wholesale vengeance, no matter what
the provocation.

He went to the low stool before his six-legged couch and lifted
himself tiredly onto his canopied bed covered with linen sheets.
A soft wind sifted through the open window, but it did not lull
him to sleep.

The generation of David had in fact passed and his own generation had come. He should have felt elation now that he was the
unchallenged ruler of the empire but as he rummaged through
his emotions Solomon had no sense of jubilation. And tired as
he was, slumber continued to elude him.

He felt a void in his spirit, a deep sense of being incomplete.
More than the throne itself, he yearned for a personal meeting
with the Lord. His hunger for the Most High was so great that,
until it was sated, Solomon was certain he could never rest.

Chapter Eight

Here stood Gibeon and here stood Solomon. He was not the first ruler of Israel to enter the gates of the inspired and blooded city, but the first to come in peace.

Here Solomon sought direct communication with the Lord so that he might unburden himself. His longed-for meeting with the Highest of the high had become a fixation, haunting him now in his waking hours as well as in sleep.

Would God speak to him as He had spoken to Abraham and Moses? Would God speak and act for him here in Gibeon as He had for Joshua?

Sensing his responsibilities too large and feeling ill-equipped for the throne, Solomon had worked himself into a mood of profound despair. He felt a void which he knew only the Lord could fill.

His despair was bordering on panic, so much so that if the Lord did not visit him, he might abdicate his nearly virginal throne. Of what use was his power without the personal guidance of the Lord? How could he reign wisely without divine, intercessory sanction? If the Lord came to him and blessed him, he could move forward with supreme confidence. If the Lord chose not to come to him, he would be lost and would know with certainty that he and his ambitions for Israel had been repudiated.

Gibeon was spread before Solomon like a rumpled cloak tinted white and sea-green. From his promontory at the altar two hundred feet above the city, which lay athwart the main road from Jerusalem six miles to the northwest, the king could see Gibeon's rippling, running springs and the terraced vineyards, laved by Hebrew gore.

Gibeon was the bittersweet Hebrew battleground and the setting for an unprecedented wonderwork of the Lord.

Here the Lord fought for Israel in the time of Joshua, the fiery successor to Moses. After an all-night march, Joshua and his followers had swooped down in a surprise attack against the armies of five Amorite kings who had the stronghold surrounded. More of the quickly defeated Amorites died from hailstones flung from the sky than the children of Israel slew with their swords. While there were yet more Amorites to kill, Joshua, in perfect faith, declared in the sight of Israel, "Sun, stand still upon Gibeon!"

And the sun had stood still.

No day was like that before or after, the Lord hearkening to the supplication of a righteous man, aiding the Hebrew victory with an astounding miracle.

Here in Gibeon was the horrendous field of the sword-edges. By the large pool, twelve men of David's army had confronted twelve soldiers from the host of Saul. The twenty-four warriors, selected for their strength and ferocity, were all killed in the brief, spectacular combat—a gruesome, unnecessary prelude to David's triumph when both sides clashed in full force a few hours later.

Here in Gibeon, by the great stone, Joab took the trusting Amasa by the beard with his right hand as if to kiss him. But with his left arm he riddled his blade into the fifth rib of David's nephew, shedding his bowels to the ground. It was one of the vicious deeds for which Joab incurred the unforgiving enmity of David.

But Solomon came to this battleground primarily because of Joshua's experience with the Lord at this site. The city, part of Benjaminite territory, was assigned to the Levite priests, and the sixteen-acre plateau atop the hill offered a worthy, spacious arena for a king to worship.

Though he had brought a sizeable entourage from the palace, including Nathan, Bathsheba, Zadok, and Benaiah, Solomon completely ignored them, his mind buried deep in the pit of his own thoughts.

He had come to Gibeon as an explorer, uncertain if the journey would quell the undefined but massive misgivings coursing through his soul. He could not give a name to the deep apprehensions that had swallowed him. No doubt to others he appeared superbly self-assured, a young king who was completely fearless and confident. All Israel knew he had dealt forthrightly with his enemies, and his throne, apparently, was no longer in jeopardy. Seemingly, he was the most envied of men. Ahead of him stretched long life and a long reign. He had power, riches, youth, and freedom to work his will.

Yet here he stood in Gibeon—solitary, aloof—as much a seeker as the humblest penitent in Israel.

Solomon gave the signal for the sacrifices to begin, and the day was spent in presenting to Yahweh a thousand burnt offerings. Solomon insisted it be a *whole* offering, that neither priest nor layman should partake of a sliver of meat from the slaughtered animals. He wanted his sacrifice to be entirely a gift to God.

As one animal after another was herded growling, bleating, lowing to the altar for throat-cutting, Solomon's ardor for the Lord grew. He watched the flaming hides emit smoke trails to the opal-daubed skies. By nightfall he was in a private ecstasy, and was unaware of Nathan and Benaiah leading him to his tent and placing him on his couch.

When the seeker who had come to storied Gibeon was alone, he closed his eyes, the totality of his being kidnapped by the all-engulfing exultation of holy fervor. For a few moments there was only the sound of his thumping heart. Then suddenly there was a sound more musical and beautiful than David's lyre.

"Ask what I shall give you," God said.

The pilgrimage had not been in vain!

Solomon answered from a thirsty, grateful heart: "You have showed your servant David, my father, great mercy, because he walked before you in faithfulness, in righteousness, and in uprightness of heart. And you have kept for him this great and steadfast love, and have given him a son to sit on his throne.

"And now, O Lord my God, you have made your servant king instead of David, my father, although I am but a little child. I know not how to go out or come in. And your servant is in the midst of your people which you have chosen, a great people, that cannot be numbered nor counted for multitude.

"Give therefore your servant an understanding heart to judge your people, that I may discern between good and evil: for who is able to govern this your great people?"

That Solomon had asked this of Him pleased the Lord.

God replied, "Because you have asked this thing, and have not asked for yourself long life or riches or the life of your enemies, but have asked for yourself understanding to discern judgment, behold, I have given you a wise and an understanding heart. So that there was none like you before, neither after you shall any arise like you.

"And," God said further, "I have also given you that which you have not asked, both riches and honor, so that there shall not be any among the kings like you all your days. "And if you will walk in My ways, to keep My statutes and commandments, as your father David did walk, then I will lengthen your days."

Solomon's eyes opened. Again he was alone in the tent. But now all his misgivings and apprehensions had fled. He felt tranquil beyond measure. The God of Abraham, Moses, and Joshua was his God. The Lord had come to him, as He had to his predecessors, in an hour of need.

I have given you a wise and understanding heart.

The wisdom given to him by the Lord during his waking dream was an overwhelming gift. More could not be asked from God, and more could not be granted from Him. For if a man was given wisdom, many other blessings would inevitably flow.

Once more Solomon closed his eyes, slipping into slumber smoothly, and for the first time in weeks he slept through the night like an innocent child.

* * *

At Solomon's order, his party returned the next morning to Jerusalem, not to the palace, but to the Ark of the Covenant. The benefaction entrusted to him at Gibeon must be further acknowledged.

Standing before the Ark, Solomon presented more burnt offerings, offerings of peace and gratitude to the Lord. Then he commanded a citywide feast for the next day, declaring it a sacred meal, in which God should be magnified.

On his way back to the palace with Nathan and Benaiah, Solomon surmised that the Lord's visit had come at a propitious moment. The Lord had appeared not alone in answer to his prayers, but to prepare him for a decision regarding a transcendently important matter. He assumed the first test of his newly-granted wisdom would be one of prodigious purpose, requiring the mobilization of all his faculties and power as emperor. It would be a test that perhaps would affect the welfare of the entire nation.

He was surprised, therefore, to find two women waiting for him in the throne room, one of them holding a baby. The black eyepaint of the women, their garish head ornaments and tightly belted cloaks instantly identified them as harlots. So soon after the grandiloquent experience at Gibeon, Solomon did not expect an encounter with pariahs.

He climbed to his chair and scrutinized the unlikely threesome. The dozing infant was in the arms of the shorter woman, who was fair-haired and completely composed, betraying no fear. The other harlot was black of mane and uneasy, twisting her hands in nervous, endless circles.

Both were younger than himself. Though the punishment was rarely meted out, every prostitute in Israel knew the ultimate danger of her profession. Under the law the king could order a prostitute stoned to death. Yet by their very presence in the royal audience chamber, the harlots made it apparent that they were oblivious to any dread of punishment.

The huge room was an icicle of silence until Solomon said, "For what reason do you appear before the king?"

The dark-haired harlot spoke first. "My lord," she said fretfully, "I was delivered of a child while this woman dwelt with me in the same house. On the third day after my son was born, she also was delivered of a son. We were alone in the house. There was no stranger with us. Then this woman's son died in the night, smothered by her own body. And she arose at midnight and stole my son from beside me while I slept. Then she laid her dead son in my bosom. When I rose in the morning to nurse my child I looked at it closely and saw the dead child was not mine."

"No," declared the other woman firmly, tucking the baby closer to her. "This living child is my son, and the dead infant is hers."

Still twisting her hands, the dark-haired harlot turned to her adversary and said with anguish, "The dead child is yours; the living child is mine."

Nathan was vastly annoyed. He flounced to the infant and inspected it carefully. "The child resembles both women and resembles neither," the prophet said to Solomon. "Let us keep it in the palace until these accursed females are through making sport of the king. Only Yahweh knows which of them lies and which tells the truth. It is an impossible decision for the king."

Concurring, Solomon said, "The decision does seem impossible. Therefore, Benaiah, take your sword and divide the living child in two, and give half to each of the women."

The first harlot who had addressed Solomon screamed: "My lord, give her the living child, but do not slay it."

The other harlot responded with a contemptuous glance at her rival, saying, "The child shall be neither mine nor yours." She stepped to Benaiah and thrust the infant into his hands. "Divide it!" she said with apparent unconcern.

Benaiah raised his sword.

"Spare the child!" Solomon ordered. "Give it to the woman who would not see the infant slain, for she is the mother."

The face of the fair-haired harlot drooped. With a start she realized her hasty words had convicted her—a loving mother would suffer any alternative other than permitting the son of her womb to be killed.

Benaiah transferred the child to its rightful mother. She bowed before Solomon and said, "May all Israel hear of the judgment which the king has rendered and stand in awe of him, perceiving that the wisdom of God is in him to render justice."

After the women left, Nathan peered at Solomon with new respect. The prophet burned with curiosity. "What if both women had allowed Benaiah to slay the child? My lord would have been responsible for the death of a guiltless, helpless infant."

Solomon smiled and did not reply, contenting himself with the remembrance of God's pledge at Gibeon . . . *I have given thee a wise and an understanding heart.*

PART II

"Except the Lord build the house, they labour in vain that build it: except the Lord keep the city, the watchman waketh but in vain."

—Psalms 127:1

Chapter Nine

The hounds and jackals game board was spread on a waist-high cedar table between Solomon and Bathsheba. The king was in his mother's apartment to idle away a rare hour, consciously seeking relaxation before facing the fury he knew would soon explode around him.

The attempt to distract himself was not completely successful, but Solomon gave as much attention as he could manage to the spirited competition that always ensued when he played the game with his mother. The pastime was Bathsheba's favorite diversion.

Solomon picked up and threw the sheep-ankle dice, letting loose a shout of glee when he read his number. Then he marched his slim, ivory, dog-ended peg three holes forward, exactly the amount required to divest his mother of her last jackal-headed peg.

"Another contest," Bathsheba insisted. "King though he is, Solomon must lose at least once."

Solomon laughed as his mother reassembled the ten pegs. Much to Bathsheba's annoyance, he had won the previous four games. She played at hounds and jackals with the same ferocious urge to win as men at war.

Forcing lighhearted conversation, Solomon asked, "What mischievous gossip issues from the harem?"

"There is more consternation than gossip. The harem grows larger each month. Most of the women are comely and their fathers are rich and influential. I sometimes tire of counting and seeing to the comforts of the fairest women any king possesses. But the women wonder, as do I, why Solomon has more than a hundred concubines, yet seldom calls for one of them to warm his couch."

"The shallow pleasures of the flesh, the foolish reason most men support a harem, holds slight interest or satisfaction for me," he replied. "But the harem will grow larger because it is indispensable to Israel. For myself, I soon will have no physical need whatever for a concubine."

"Then it is as I expected. Solomon plans a marriage! Thus have I excused your reluctance to fully enjoy your women." Bathsheba's face was aglow with anticipation. "A royal wedding is overdue. Who shall be your queen?"

Had he hinted his plans too broadly or was his mother's intuition inexplicably uncanny? She had guessed correctly, but he chose to say nothing about his pending marriage. The bride's name would launch an immediate tirade from Bathsheba, and for the time being he preferred to avoid a quarrel.

"Patience, my mother. Tonight you will learn who is to be the queen of Israel."

To Bathsheba's repeated pleas for the identity of his wife-to-be, Solomon good-naturedly but firmly avoided an answer.

He threw the dice again, this time casting a seven, a number considered sacred and a good omen. Solomon took what small encouragement there was from the approving talisman. He continued to play the game rigorously, but his mind was elsewhere . . .

The first three years of his reign were being hailed throughout the kingdom as Israel's golden dawn. Nathan and other trusted confidantes told Solomon the vast majority of priests, princes, and people approved the pathfinding decisions he had made. His steady, untiring labors were preserving the kingdom and empire from within and without. Even so, what had been accomplished was only a burnished beginning.

Now Solomon was readying a bold, breathtaking proclamation that would galvanize the nation, empire, and world. The announcement was the result of long, delicate, and finally encouraging correspondence with no less a plenipotentiary than Pharaoh, which had led to direct discussions between Benaiah and court officials of the monarch of the Nile. Solomon had confided his new diplomacy only to Benaiah, sending him to Egypt as his secret ambassador. A mutually beneficial agreement had been hammered out, and Solomon had made a difficult decision, electing to swim in the riptide of an alliance with Israel's ancient enemy.

He knew that the provisions of the alliance might cause the earth of Israel to shiver. One part of the compact in particular would touch the most sensitive nerve of his countrymen. The risk he was taking was fraught with danger and he could not predict the reaction of his intimates and the people. An extremely negative reaction could topple his crown and lead to his death. At the least, the alliance would cause dissent and be passionately debated. But the treaty of intimate friendship with the sun god whose forebears had held his ancestors as slaves had to be consummated because it was absolutely necessary to guarantee the preservation of Israel and its conquered territories by peaceful means.

The time was ripe to act; there probably would never be a more favorable moment. The crop of gold he had reaped thus far in his brief reign allowed him to look beyond the horizon of the kingdom, to let his shadow fall beyond the empire. It was a luxury he could afford only because Israel was internally secure, although that security was volatile and always in jeopardy.

The nation that had not been a nation at his coronation had been swiftly woven into a united, cohesive force, a goal achieved with so little opposition that he had been buoyantly surprised. Since the beginning of Hebrew history, when the Lord had said to Abraham, "I will make a great nation from you," the promise could be equated with reality.

By persuasive reasoning rather than edict, Solomon had convinced the tribal leaders to accept several internal reforms that swiftly bred the molding of Israel into a solid, united force from Dan to Beersheba. He had fulfilled his goal of giving the princes and people a new sense of soaring dignity, brotherhood, and common purpose, and the dream of a boundless future. He had taught, implored, and convinced Israel that continued strength and survival could be achieved only through the unity symbolized and embodied in the central authority and prestige of the throne.

He had cautioned the Benjaminites, the Naphtalis, and the ten other tribes that each alone was a stray lamb separated from the fold and prey to the wolf. But together, united under God and the crown, they could be invincible.

His arguments and wisdom prevailed and tribal overseers,

speaking for themselves and their kinsmen, pledged their faith, loyalty, and cooperation to the throne. Each committed itself to the reality that all would survive and prosper or none would survive, much less prosper.

Solomon accomplished this without confiding to Israel's mightiest men many of his doubts concerning his father. They would resent the slightest besmirchment of David's reputation. But his love and admiration for his father did not blind him to David's weaknesses.

Under David the captured lands that were the protective buffers of the empire were ruled by restive and untrustworthy vassal kings, each ready to rebel if given any indication of hesitation, indifference, or cowardice from the palace in Jerusalem.

The kingdom itself, because of David's makeshift method of decision making, had emerged from the bestiality of all the tumultuous wars as an extremely loose confederation of almost totally independent states. David's greatest weakness as a ruler had been lack of ability (or interest) in creating a dependable, efficient, second tier of capable men to intelligently administer what had been bought with a sea of blood. On ascending the throne, Solomon quickly rectified this by appointing men of unquestioned merit to serve as his court officials and in the new posts of provincial governors.

Waging peace, Solomon quickly discovered, was more subtle and difficult than waging war.

In pursuit of greater homogeneity, he instituted changes that significantly tipped the balance of power from individual tribes to the throne. The changes were met with grumbling and gestures of rhetoric from the chieftains. But once they were swayed into accepting the manna of unity, they could not logically stand in the way of its implementation.

It had been clear to Solomon from the beginning of his reign that time-honored tribal boundaries insulated Hebrews from each other as well as from their enemies. He knew the old borders made little geographic sense and worked against the welfare of the kingdom, breeding suspicion, envy, petty disputes, and throttling commercial growth. And so Solomon rearranged the traditional borders, stripping land from each tribe and distributing it anew. The tribes were now separated by natural rather than artificial barriers. The new frontiers also made the nation easier to organize and govern. More importantly, the move served as a royal demonstration that tribal holdings were not inviolate, that only the kingdom was inviolate.

With this one daring reform, Solomon destroyed more than four centuries of outmoded custom that had decreed primary loyalty to the tribe.

Now the twelve tribal rivers all had their confluence at the throne.

The realignment of lands resulted in the concept of province rather than tribe. His new governors, reporting directly to him, were each in charge of one province. To tie the provinces closer to the throne, he made each responsible for supplying his burgeoning household with fine flour, meal, fat oxen, sheep, harts, roebucks, fallow deer, and plump fowl. It was a simple, efficacious procedure, carried out according to the calendar. The twelve provinces, under the guidance of their governors, were in turn obligated to supply his bread and meat for one month of the year.

He was careful to instruct his governors to diplomatically supplement, not replace, the influence of the tribal chieftains, who were sensitive men filled with hard pride that often became arrogance. Thus far the arrangement had worked extremely well.

His next step was even more revolutionary, one that was already piling up undreamed wealth for Israel. He convinced the tribal leaders, who then convinced their people, to abandon the practice of dwelling inside their fortified cities. Previously, the farmers and sheepherders left their protected strongholds during the day, going out past the guarded gates for only short distances to tend their fields and flocks. For security, they returned at night. The inept system, Solomon reasoned, was a product of fear. And it kept agriculture in a primitive state of development. The farmers and herdsmen produced only enough food, wool, and meat for their personal needs plus a small amount for sale at the marketplace. The result was that most of the population was undernourished, and what food could be purchased came at a high price in barter or shekels. Unless the system changed, most of Israel would always live at the edge of hunger. He, therefore, instituted a policy of safety for every man under his own vine and fig tree, ordering the army to patrol the countryside, to be always in sight and accessible. Reassured they were safe from bandits and marauders outside their fortresses, the farmers quickly spread across the land. There they built homes and raised families away from the cities, enjoying, loving, and cherishing their soil in a way they never had before.

Surplus instead of shortage, prosperity rather than poverty, were the rewards. Despite the grudging, arid desert and perpetual shortage of water, Israel was beginning to produce a bounty of grain, olives, flax, dates, figs, pomegranates, lentils, beans, chickpeas, cucumbers, onions, leeks, and garlic. The herds of sheep, oxen, and cattle grew large.

Now Israel was indeed becoming a land of milk and honey, its desert blossoming as a rose. The dream of Moses was in sight: "And the Lord shall make you plenteous in goods, in the fruit of your body, and in the fruit of your cattle, and in the fruit of your ground, in the land which the Lord sware unto your fathers to give you."

The plenitude would soon allow Solomon, if all went well in his alliance with Pharaoh and in his planned renewal of David's bond of friendship with the sea-faring Phoenicians, to begin a massive program of trade. His caravans would carry the surplus of Israel's soil to merchants and kings of surrounding nations, including Egypt and Tyre. Eventually his ships would sail to exotic ports, some of which could be reached only by three-year journeys across the endless oceans.

Peace!

Trade!

Vine and fig tree security!

Prosperity!

And that which more than anything else would prosper and bind Hebrews one to another—his sacred charge to build the holy temple!

A gigantic game of hounds and jackals, Solomon thought, the stakes all that had flowed from the covenant, and all that was yet to flow from the agreement between God and Abraham. So much of the Israeli future depended on how skillfully he could develop non-warring relationships with other sovereigns. For a while he mused at how simple his problems would be if Israel was an island set in lonely luster in an impenetrable desert, free to grow internally without concern for its neighbors and the rest of the world. But such isolation would probably produce stagnation. Without the clash of competition, growth and accomplishment were unlikely. In any case, Israel was an island only in a special way. Amid a sea of uncircumcised idolators, Israel alone was God's island.

Sitting at the junction of empire, Solomon as no one else was aware that the security of Israel rested on a delicate, interconnected set of domestic and international circumstances. Though Israel's own house was in order, the nation was at once powerful and weak, hardy and frail. If the kingdom and empire were not tirelessly watched, if he did not consolidate and augment his inheritance from David, all could tumble like the dice which he rolled. Then foreign hounds and jackals, the ambitious kings who once had snapped at Israel's vitals, would again be set free to encircle and ensnare Zion. His neighbors might amalgamate against him. That initiative must be taken from them, otherwise his reign would be little different than David's, pocked by unceasing wars, with Israel probably the ultimate loser.

Yet for Solomon, there was no compromise, no middle ground, between war and peace. He had chosen peace because war in all its manifestations, except when raw survival and the honor at Yahweh were at stake, was wasteful. He had chosen a complicated and sophisticated course, continued life and progress for Israel minus the sword. But he was an enlightened realist, addressing himself directly to the imperfect world in which he found himself. Though he abhorred war, the danger of armed conflict was ever-present. Until the coming of the promised Messiah, the earth would be full of war and sin. Only a king blind to reason and with a hopelessly romantic view of the world would believe otherwise. Solomon considered himself neither blind nor a romantic in either internal or external policy.

On the game board of nations, he was locked between two sinewed giants—Egypt to the south and Assyria in the north. Egypt was by far the greater threat; Assyria a hovering but lesser danger, its star waning because it was embroiled in civil and foreign dissension. However, an attack by the Assyrians could not be discounted.

Israel was ostensibly the brawniest nation among its neighbors. Its army was unmatched in numbers by any other power. Still it could be defeated. Manpower by itself would no longer guarantee victory. A cold chill had swept through Solomon when Benaiah informed him of Egypt's new weapons for which the host of Israel had no certain defense. Benaiah could not say with certainty if Pharaoh realized the enormous potential of his strength, but Solomon proceeded on the assumption that Egypt's ruler was not unaware of his power.

Complicating matters were two leprous spots that smoldered within the empire. Neither the bastions of Caananite Gath nor Philistine Gezer had been completely pacified by David nor reconciled to Hebrew rule. Momentarily, either or both could cause a contagion of trouble with might proliferate into war.

Solomon would pay a high price to avoid a major or minor war, but he would not pay any price for peace. He was sworn to keep intact all that Israel owned, and among its dominions he included Gath and Gezer. He would not hesitate to quell with force an internal rebellion or outside invasion, yet he would first explore every other alternative. The art of peace was neglected; the thunder of aggression well studied and extensively practiced. War was a failure of reason and wisdom, but loss of any Israeli territory would lessen his throne and Israel, which were indivisible. His entire strategy was centered around an intricate tactic designed to avoid the disaster of war while shepherding Israel to peace and a vaulting destiny—the spiritual, cultural, and commercial leader of the world.

Therefore an alliance with Egypt, no matter how shocking it would at first appear to his court and to the people, was a small concession for holding the miracle of Israel intact, for extending the influence of a kingdom born of divine will.

"I will make a great nation from you" was not a promise Solomon treated lightly.

* * *

Bathsheba, to her delight, had lost none of her pegs and captured all but two of Solomon's. Swooping in like a predator for the kill, eagerly anticipating her son's defeat, she turned reluctantly when she heard the voice of one of her servants. "General Benaiah requests an immediate audience with the king," the girl said.

Testily Bathsheba asked, "Cannot the general practice patience? Tell him the king is at his leisure. Have him wait, if only for a few more moments." Bathsheba looked greedily back at the game board.

The perplexed servant added, "The general declared it an urgent matter."

"I concede victory to my mother," Solomon said, barely able

to suppress a grin at Bathsheba's fanatic attachment to the frivolous amusement.

"Concession is not the same as a victory honestly earned," she said with a frown of displeasure.

"A victory, my mother, should be prized whenever it is honestly earned," Solomon observed. Then he told the girl to admit Benaiah.

Solomon knew his general would not disturb him in the privacy of Bathsheba's quarters unless his news was imperative. Benaiah had proved himself an energetic, understanding, and reliable friend. His mission among the Egyptians had been highly successful, and his rule of the army was skillful. If aroused, Benaiah could be as savage as Joab, but he also had mercy and idealism, qualities which had been absent in the character of his father's commander-in-chief.

Benaiah entered, impervious to Bathsheba's disapproving stare. "Shimei has broken his vow to the king," he announced. "The piggish Benjaminite returned to Jerusalem several hours ago after journeying from the city in bold defiance of my lord's injunction."

Solomon was startled. He remembered how sternly he cautioned Shimei not to leave Jerusalem if he valued his life. With wealth, land, and slaves, a fine house and a full harem, Shimei had every reason to remain confined to the capital, which Solomon still judged was a mild punishment for one condemned to death in the last spasm of David's life.

"You are certain of Shimei's disobedience?"

"One of his slaves he had lashed too often reported his journey to one of my most trusted captains."

"For what purpose would Shimei ignore my warning not to cross the Kidron?"

"He did not pass over the brook. He went in the opposite direction, to Gath."

Gath!

So recently on his mind, the name sent an alarm through Solomon.

"Shimei's supposed mission," Benaiah continued, "was to recapture two of his runaway slaves."

"You doubt that?"

"He is old and fat. He took no other men with him. It would be impossible for Shimei to bring back two young, strong slaves by himself. The matter was prearranged. There is a conspiracy afoot against my lord."

Solomon recalled Nathan's charge against Shimei, that he was unduly friendly with the Philistines. Nathan and Benaiah were right. Shimei's scheme was now as transparent as it was audacious. In Gath he must have met with Achish, the ancient Philistine fox that his father had left in control of the city after conquering it. Achish was one of the restive vassal kings perpetually on the verge of mutiny. As for Shimei, though he was not allied with Adonijah and his supporters, he had no love for the house of David. He led a small but powerful faction that would revel in the downfall of David's son. A plot between Achish and Shimei could conceivably kindle widespread insurrection in the empire. The fire of rebellion must be tamped immediately. Shimei had been given his opportunity to live, but his ambition and intrigue, his defiance of the order to remain inside the walls of Jerusalem, were inexcusable.

"Give Shimei to the executioner," Solomon declared. "Then send your finest captain with a thousand men to Achish and tell him of Shimei's fate. That should end whatever plot the Philistine conjures against us."

Again he had ordered the death sentence with reluctance. And again he felt betrayed by his power. Though he knew Shimei deserved his fate and the Benjaminite could only blame himself, the thought did not minimize Solomon's feeling of guilt. Was ordering a man to be killed too much power for even a king?

It occurred to him that power brought a paradox. Instead of the king directing the throne, the throne often molded the actions of the king. There was no choice but to end Shimei's life, however unworthy a life it was. The throne itself and by itself was in part a force that could not be totally subdued or controlled by the ruler who occupied the royal chair. Like the new nation he was seeding, the throne in large part had an independence and a life of its own. Often it was only a detail as to who was king since supreme earthly power frequently dictated unavoidable, automatic decisions.

* * *

Solomon dined that evening with Nathan, Bathsheba, and Benaiah. Before the wine was served, the general said, "Shimei has been executed, and the thousand men speed on their way to Achish."

He guessed that his prophet, his mother, and his general expected him to say something in regard to the death of the traitorous Benjaminite. Instead, Solomon announced, his voice sailing through the room like an arrow hurtling to a target, "I have made affinity with Pharaoh."

Nathan immediately demanded: "In what way?"

Now there was no holding back the storm.

Solomon paused, caught his breath, and added, "I am to marry the daughter of Pharaoh."

"Impossible!" Nathan's horror was as genuine as it was predictable. "Such a marriage is utterly, completely, totally impossible."

"The prophet hurries to a conclusion before he gives consideration to the circumstances," Solomon countered.

Nathan swept on, ignoring Solomon's mild rejoinder. "I cannot believe that he who is our king, and second only to Yahweh, so much as considers the notion of marrying an idolatress. She is the spawn of the ungodly ruler of the uncircumcised Egyptians. 'Thou shalt have no other gods before me' is the first and foremost of the laws. Flouting it is punishable by death. I will gladly cast the first stone at Solomon."

Though he had anticipated Nathan's charge and outrage, Solomon heard himself answering more bluntly than he intended. "Is breaking the first commandment more evil than simultaneously breaking the sixth, seventh, and tenth laws received by Moses? Did Nathan cast the first stone at David when he committed murder against Uriah after taking my mother in adultery? Violation of those laws are also punishable by death. Did Nathan cast the first stone when my father coveted his neighbor's wife in defiance of the tablets?"

"Solomon," screamed Bathsheba, "profanes the memory of his father and reviles his mother to her face. Another of the laws of Moses claims honor from a son to his parents."

It pained Solomon to see the obvious torment in his mother's face, but he felt impelled to place the serious accusation of violating one of God's fundamental laws in perspective. Moreover, he had no wish to be judged guilty of an uncommitted sin.

"God," Nathan was saying," owes no explanation to Solomon for expressing His will and granting David forgiveness in ex-

change for his repentance. I pray that God will be as merciful to
you."

"Though I marry Pharaoh's daughter," Solomon answered,
"there will be no need for me to ask repentance and seek forgiveness."

Nathan snorted, "Has Solomon then renounced the Most
High?"

The arrow came to its target as Solomon said, "Pharaoh's
daughter will embrace Yahweh. She will leave her idols in Egypt.
She will worship as we worship."

In addition to the unthinkable marriage, Nathan was humili-
ated because Solomon was obviously in communication with
Pharaoh, which was disgraceful enough, but the contacts had
been made without his being consulted. The prophet asked, with
sarcasm scathing, "Why did not my king and my pupil take me
into his confidence before suckling himself before Pharaoh?"

"Without disrespect," Solomon replied forthrightly, "you
were not told precisely because you would have disapproved a
son of the covenant extending friendship to one who is more an
enemy by tradition than by his actions. This pharaoh has done
Israel no harm."

"Solomon should not only have confided in me, but he should
now heed my disapproving voice, which is the disapproving
voice of Yahweh. The crafty Pharaoh, by giving his daughter, has
outmaneuvered our young and inexperienced king. Your affinity
with Pharaoh will corrupt Israel."

"Nathan forgets that the king of the Egyptians is also bound
by his laws and gods not to give his daughters in marriage to
foreigners," Solomon said. "His risk in this wedding is as great
as mine." Solomon could not resist adding, "And no doubt Pharaoh has to contend with his own Nathan."

"There are an abundance of Israeli women who fear and obey
God," Bathsheba argued. "Surely one of our native daughters is
fit to be your queen. Why choose an Egyptian whose loyalty to
our Lord at best will always be suspect, a woman who will cause
consternation and ill-feeling among our people?"

"Why did my mother choose a Hittite? The Hittites have long
lived among us, some embracing Yahweh, others failing to do so.
Was Uriah a servant of Yahweh or was the god of that dedicated
soldier his sword? Did Uriah give greater worship to King David
or Yahweh?"

"Uriah was a believer!" Bathsheba replied instantly.

"Then why did God deal so tragically with him? Was it not to punish him for his sins?"

"You have not yet answered your mother's question, which is also my question," Nathan insisted. "What is the use of a marriage to a foreigner and how will it enhance the glory of God's people?"

The king said, "What was the use of Abraham making affinity with the greedy Ephron? What was the use of Joseph serving Pharaoh? The use of it was survival. And in survival there is glory."

"Solomon speaks as if we were yet nomads and slaves," Nathan responded. "Praise Yahweh, we have survived, multiplied, and flourished in all things. Our enemies tremble before us."

"Benaiah," Solomon ordered, "tell us the facts concerning the Pharaoh's power; tell us how he trembles before Israel."

In a precise monotone, Benaiah recited his assessment of the relative military strength of Israel and Egypt. "In numbers his army is second to ours. But the Pharaoh has iron chariots and tireless horses. He has catapults and new weapons of siege which can easily destroy the strongest of our fortified cities. We have none of these weapons of Pharaoh and we have no bulwark against them. His army is more disciplined and more proficient than ours. Since the lord David put his sword to rest, war has changed. Battles in the future will be fought in a new fashion. If Pharaoh chooses to attack us, I can give no certainty of our victory."

With a wave of his hand Nathan discarded Benaiah's frightening estimate. "The Egyptians would not dare attack Israel."

"Does Nathan speak for Pharaoh or for Nathan?" Solomon asked, impatient of the prophet's lack of understanding military realities. "Nathan too quickly dismisses these fearful weapons and their expert use by the Egyptians which Benaiah has witnessed with his own eyes."

"Nevertheless," Nathan grumbled, "the Pharaoh's daughter will bring a dowry of dissension."

"No, she will bring a magnificent dowry," Solomon said. "She will bring us peace with Egypt. She will bring us Gezer which David, great warrior though he was, never subdued. Only eighteen miles from where we sit the Canaanites mock and defy us from their citadel. They not only threaten an outbreak of insurrection across the empire, but compete with us for an alliance with Pharaoh. If we do not put them down, we raise them up. By inaction we allow more menacing idolators than the Egyptians to assault our God."

"Then," argued Nathan, "why not take Gezer ourselves and be done with it?"

"Its strength is such that with our present equipment it is doubtful we could capture it," Benaiah pointed out. He, too, was growing impatient at Nathan's naivete concerning the battlefield. "So well is Gezer defended and so high its walls, our losses would be such that even a victory would be defeat. Thousands upon thousands of mothers in Israel would wail for a generation for their dead sons."

"Pharaoh will take Gezer for us," Solomon added. "And he will take it without the sacrifice of one precious Hebrew life!"

"Granted that idolatrous Gezer, so close to our gates, is an abomination and dangerous," Nathan said. "But is it not more dangerous for Solomon to permit a foreign army to move across our soil? What if Pharaoh turns his supposedly invincible weapons against Israel?"

"Pharaoh," Solomon said, "is not without trouble in his own realm. The Libyan tribes threaten his western border, growing in strength each day. The king of Egypt saves his weapons to fight his own unruly subjects. He has no wish to fight both the Libyans and Israel. He knows war with us, despite his superiority of arms, would be costly. He will give us Gezer because of his daughter, then he will withdraw his armies. In exchange, we will give him a land route and free access across our roads so he may conduct peaceful trade with us and the Phoenicians, which he is eager to do."

Nathan was still unimpressed. "I do not like the smell of it. Solomon speaks of weapons, trade, and a barter marriage. Where, in all of this, is Yahweh?"

"Yahweh has led me to this alliance and marriage as He led Joseph into an alliance with Pharaoh, and as He led the son of Jacob into marriage with the daughter of an Egyptian priest."

Solomon emptied his wine goblet and rose.

"Benaiah," he said, "see to it that the tidings of my wedding are proclaimed to the people. Station your men strategically throughout the land. If the news is met with opposition or violence, your soldiers are to give battle, but only in defense of their own lives."

Both Nathan and Bathsheba realized further opposition to Solomon's plans would be useless. Still attempting to digest this giant morsel like pieces of meat caught in their throats, they were ill-prepared for his next surprise.

"My caravan leaves for Egypt in two days. Prepare yourselves for the journey and the wedding." Solomon flashed a broad grin. "Be unafraid," said the king of Israel. "Without the cut and slash of a single angry Israeli blade, without one Hebrew casualty, we are about to conquer Egypt, an accomplishment that even Moses would not have considered attainable. No longer must we flee and fear Pharaoh. Now we run carefully toward him."

Solomon's immensely optimistic estimate of the alliance was the most jarring surprise of all for Nathan and Bathsheba. And Benaiah thought his lord's enthusiasm for the pact with Egypt was too sanguine.

"We are at the threshold," Solomon concluded, "of a splendid triumph."

Chapter Ten

Only the harsh, quick sound of a silver trumpet stayed the beginning of what was certain to be a harsh, quick battle, a clash Solomon was about to witness with horrified fascination.

The visit to Thebes, during the past week, had gone extremely well. Pharaoh Siamon, a wiry, wrinkled man in his sixties and a head shorter than Solomon, spared nothing in welcoming his guests from Israel.

There had not been the slightest hint of condescension on the part of the king of the Egyptians toward the king of the Hebrews. Quite the contrary, Siamon seemed overly anxious to please. Nathan, however, was wary and uneasy as a nose-sniffing, skittish lamb who somehow had strayed into a lion's den. The eagerness to make the occasion a memorable one appeared to be an effort by Siamon to resummon what he could of the all but departed glory of Ahmose, Amenhotep, Thutmose, and Rameses. These grandiose, legendary pharaohs had been the country's master builders and conquerors, returning to Thebes from their wars so laden with treasure and trophies of victory that the city had once been the proudest, richest capital in the world.

At its height, the Egyptian colossus extended south and west beyond the far reaches of Nubia. In the north its rule lapped to the shores of the Euphrates. But generations of weak, self-indulgent rulers, and competition among wealthy, ambitious, and powerful families yearning to breed a dynasty by wresting control of the pharaoh's throne had turned the land that was the gift of the Nile to fratricidal strife. While they quarreled among themselves, bold, strong-willed, and purposeful leaders, anxious to unyoke their people from Egyptian slavery, rose among the

107

armor-wielding Hittites, Syrians, and Philistines. Their rebellions were successful. After winning independence, these nations in turn followed the Egyptian example of enslaving the Hebrews until the coming of Saul and David.

Nearly all of Solomon's dominions once belonged to Egypt. What remained of the Egyptian empire was not, for the most part, imposing. It had disintegrated into a group of loosely united small states, having little in common except a necessity to trade among themselves and the shared dread of a new, rampaging enemy—the wild, plundering Libyan legions along the kingdom's western perimeter. Egypt was in much the same position as Israel before David had massed the tribes together through war and Solomon consolidated them with the diplomacy of peace.

Yet Solomon remained convinced that Egypt dare not be dismissed. Although much of its splendor and influence had been eviscerated, it was possible for Egypt to again emerge as a military giant, its power renewed like its most sacred bird, the benu. Larger than an eagle and Scion of the sun, the jagged-beaked creature with reddish-purple feathers had a wingspan longer than a man's body. The benu died every evening, burning itself on its own funeral pyre, only to pulse to life anew each morning. The daily reincarnation—one of the anchors of Egyptian belief—had unfailingly repeated itself since the beginning of time.

As a student of history, Solomon was aware that in stark contrast to the presumed rejuvenation of the benu, the rise and fall of empires was unpredictable. Rarely, if ever, did a doomed, once-aggressive, conquering nation blossom again in full, resurrected glory. Recalling his lessons from David and Nathan as well as his own studies, Solomon offhand could remember no exception to this seemingly intractable truth regarding the cycles of life and death among empires.

But Solomon preferred not to attempt to anticipate history. He could not outguess the future, only prepare for it as best he could. He had to deal with the actualities of power as he found them at the present and as they could expect to remain in the foreseeable future. Egypt might soon follow the example of the benu, renewing itself, or it might one day disappear as a nation of consequence and an enemy to be feared. For now, Siamon was a mountain climber slowly traversing toward the summit, one who had come upon a wide fissure, which could swallow him or which he might safely breast.

Solomon dared to hope he had outflanked and out-thought the Pharaoh. Siamon, by capturing Gezer for him would in effect be fighting his war, yet Solomon could not imagine any combination of circumstances which would draw the host of Israel into battle on behalf of Egypt, a pillar of Solomon's strategy that he had carefully avoided mentioning to Siamon.

Egypt's perilous position might also help explain the pharaoh's overwhelming, wholehearted reception. He was obviously as ardent for the alliance as Solomon. It was less obvious, but still possible, that Siamon was even more desperate for the alliance than Solomon. It served the interests of both Egypt and Israel to have peace with each other. Siamon, in danger from the Libyans, undoubtedly desired a friendly Israel as Solomon, threatened by more than a dozen restive enemies, craved a friendly Egypt.

Up to this moment, Solomon enjoyed the ceremony, pomp, and courtesy of the pharaoh. No detail had been overlooked in seeing to his comfort and that of his companions. Even the hostility of Nathan and Bathsheba had melted to some extent.

Siamon's enthusiasm for his Hebrew guests was contagious. The entire city seemed to be on a continuous holiday in their honor. Everywhere they went they were hailed and accorded spontaneous respect and cheers.

"What", Solomon thought, "would Abraham and Sarah make of it all?"

Siamon's palace was gaudy, reflecting far greater opulence than David's, but it would not compare with the magnificent royal residence Solomon was planning to build for himself. Each meal in Siamon's arena-sized dining hall was a banquet replete with a never-ending parade of entertainment—dancers, singers, magicians, acrobats, and wrestlers. They ate at low tables, refusing knives, forks, and spoons, adhering to Egyptian custom, moving food to their mouths awkwardly with their fingers. Nevertheless, the antelope and gazelle, the honeyed sweetmeats, the sesame-scented bread and cakes were delicious.

Solomon had not yet had a moment alone with Nagsara, Siamon's youngest daughter and his future wife. Their eyes would meet occasionally in mutual curiosity. Then their attention would be diverted by someone engaging them in conversation, by the musicians, conjurers, or endless replenishing of delicacies from heaping platters carried by dark-skinned servants. Nagsara's beauty—she was slim and swan-necked, fragile with an unmistakable suggestion of strength under her tawny, sculpted features—reminded him of the hardy grace of Israel's consumingly lovely desert flower, the rose of Sharon.

With Siamon and Nagsara, Solomon had spent the previous two days touring the temple-strewn Nile aboard the flat-bottomed royal sun boat. He visited the nearby Valley of the Kings where several celebrated pharaohs were buried in eleborate tombs. Their ornate funerary edifices of fine limestone lay at the bottom of a series of sheer cliffs, fronted by a thoroughfare of sphinxes, colossi, and obelisks. But Solomon derived more pleasure and satisfaction from quickly learning how to ride a horse. Siamon had given him a magnificent white stallion as a gift. Horsemanship was almost unknown among the Israelites, and Solomon had plans to introduce the versatile animal at home, making it as common as the mule and the camel. Horses would be especially useful for farmers and the army.

Now, as Solomon waited for the battle to begin, he could see that all the glory of Egypt wasn't buried in the Valley of the Kings.

The opalescent morning sun in the desert outside Thebes had not yet become oppressive. Siamon, still the assiduous host, again had been diligent in detail, so diligent that Solomon was unnerved.

Atop the peak of a shaggy brown sandhill, stamped flat as a blanket, the two kings, surrounded by their subordinates and attendants, were seated in square, deep-cushioned chairs of ebony inlaid with gold. The feet of the kings were protected from the calescent sand by carpets interwoven with intricately designed, gaily colored animals—benus as well as rams, baboons, bulls, cats, crocodiles, and jackals, each of them sacred to one or more of Egypt's bewildering array of deities. They included Horus, the god of heaven; Osiris, ruler of vegetation and the dead; the sun god Re; Shu, sovereign of the air; Nut, whose authority was the sky; and Amon, the master of the wind.

Solomon, aghast though he was at the nature and circumstances of the impending fray, was also hynotically curious as were Benaiah and a dozen of his foremost captains who had made the journey as the king's bodyguard. Less curious, but incapable of ignoring the spectacle, were Nathan, Bathsheba, and Zadok. Solomon had brought his high priest along to officiate at his wedding. Unlike Nathan, Zadok had not protested the arrangement once he had been assured that the Egyptian princess was proselytized. Under Hebrew law, no one, king or cupbearer, could marry a nonbeliever. Zadok had accepted the marriage on the same terms as Solomon, as an expression of Yahweh's pragmatic will which, unquestionably, would benefit Israel. Else why would God have inspired Solomon's startling choice of a bride? Zadok concluded there was holy purpose to what seemed an unholy union. He recalled the precedent of Moses, who had chosen to marry an Ethiopian. Was not the wife of the lawgiver as much a foreigner to the children of Israel as the pharaoh's daughter?

In addition to his marriage to Nagsara, Solomon, during this crucial sojourn, hoped for an opportunity to quietly and unostentatiously inspect the pharaoh's new weapons. He never anticipated he would see the formidable weaponry under actual conditions of conflict. Solomon had vehemently argued against Siamon's outrageous suggestion—staging a demonstration battle to prove the effectiveness of his armaments. When Siamon added that the combat would be kill-or-be killed, that men would die, Solomon was incredulous.

"There is no need for Egyptians to slay Egyptian to provide sport for me," Solomon told the pharaoh.

"The king of the Hebrews misunderstands the willingness and the zeal of my soldiers to show their skill and bravery," Siamon replied enigmatically. "The issue for my warriors is their eternal honor."

When Solomon still demurred, Siamon answered snappishly —his one breach of otherwise exquisite politeness. The pharaoh waspishly told his guest that any further disapproval would be considered a personal insult to him and a national insult to his country. Solomon was quickly convinced that Siamon meant to have his way. Unless he did, the veiled implication was that the entire Hebrew mission to Egypt could crumble in failure.

Thus the battle, momentarily, was to be joined.

From their canopied promonotory, the kings and their courtiers had a sweeping, unobstructed view of miles of mica-flecked desert plain, all of it alive with motion.

Siamon said, "Solomon will see the wonders that have come to Egypt through the blessings of our gods as soon as the silver trumpet sounds. The instrument, incidentally, was apprehended only yesterday and only through the intervention of Amon. The diabolic one who stole the trumpet from the tomb of my ancestor, King Tutankhamon, has had his hands cut off. It has not played a note in more than four hundred years." Siamon continued with a half-smile, "I have heard it said there are those who mock the king of the Hebrews because of his youth. Does Solomon know that Tutankhamon was merely eight years old when he was proclaimed pharaoh?"

"And was he not sixteen years of age when he was deposed by his grandfather?" Solomon replied.

Siamon's hook of a smile vanished. "Yes, his grandfather, who was also his vizier, served the divine child ignobly."

Solomon deflected his stare down the sandhill to his left and saw the gathered infantry.

"Ten companies, two thousand men," said Siamon with satisfaction. "They wear the plume of war, a black ostrich feather, on the back of their heads in tribute to our ancient ritual. The plume is a warrior's sign to his god that he is prepared for conflict. Each company chooses the name of a favorite god. Today the gods are well represented."

Despite his distance from them, Solomon could note the remorseless ferocity of the pharaoh's men. They would give and expect no quarter. Locked in tight formation and arrayed in full battle regalia, they carried shields against their bare chests and were armed with sun-gleaming spears and axes. Their opponents, as Solomon transferred his gaze to his right, were a ragged line of perhaps one hundred chariots, high wheeled and six-spoked, two- and three-horse iron caravans. Each chariot carried a warrior, a driver, and a four-cornered box that held their bows and arrows.

Though the chariot force was outnumbered by better than ten to one, they, too, were men who obviously would give and expect no quarter.

The brutally melodic riff to King Tutankhamon's silver trumpet suddenly cascaded across the desert.

The infantry advanced in a solid mass, their weapons primed for flesh.

The chariots, pulled by snorting, heavy-breathing horses,

rolled forward, increasing speed with every length, swelling quickly into a booming thud of flying hoofs.

At contact the unbroken line of foot soldiers parted like the Red Sea before Moses.

The chariot drivers let their horses run amuck, tying the reins around their bodies to free themselves to fire their arrows in unison with their warrior companions.

One chariot, driving into Re company, overturned, and the high whinny of pain from the horses was excrutiatingly sharp. Axes spared neither man nor beast. The heads of the warrior, the driver, and the animals were scythed away.

But Solomon observed that the one tumbled chariot was the single casualty among the iron caravans.

The horses continued to stampede for nearly an hour amid the ranks of the grounded soldiers, the bowmen in the chariots shooting their adversaries at will, aiming their shafts with almost indecent leisure.

The disrupted desert sand then sent up a great cloud, a swirling curtain through which Solomon could hear the cries of the wounded. When the curtain of sand parted, the chariot force was finishing off the few remaining infantrymen still giving hopeless battle.

Rolling over dead bodies, the pharaoh's chariotry galloped proudly off, leaving behind an abattoir of decimated servants of Re, Horus, and Osiris, Shu, and Amon.

As the no man's land was quickly swept of the dead, the dying, and the dazed, Solomon could not help but admire Siamon's brilliant charioteers. Joshua and David had both defeated armies which used chariotry, but that had been in guerrilla fighting in hill country. In open field warfare, the deadly skill of the chariots was matchless. David had kept only one hundred of the thousand chariots he captured from Hadadezer, the Aramean king, after his victory in the fighting near the Euphrates. The others he burned, hamstringing the horses. His father had never integrated the fiendishly efficient vehicles into his army. He used them only for ceremonial occasions and transportation. That was an error Solomon planned to rectify. Israel's host must have its own chariot armada as a further deterrent to any would-be invader.

Interrupting Solomon's thoughts, Siamon said enthusiastically,

"Never have my charioteers acquitted themselves more valorously and displayed their abilities so magnificently."

Solomon understood the pharaoh's pride, if not the barbarism of the needless bloodshed. A swift, sidelong glance down the sandhill told him that the slaughterground was still stained with bodies and rivulets of blood. The uniformed litter bearers and slaves in breechcloths had not yet removed the last incapacitated combatants. He shuddered when he saw one slave carrying a head under each arm.

"I trust the lesson of the chariots has been of value to the king of the Hebrews," Siamon went on. "We learned the lesson of the caravans of iron when the Hyksos hordes came against us like avenging gods six hundred years ago. Because of their chariots, the Canaanite and Amorite invaders won the Egyptian throne. Your ancestor Joseph rose to be prime minister under a Hyksos Pharaoh. The usurpers were not driven from our beloved Nile until we made the chariots our own weapon."

As casually as he could, Solomon asked, "How many chariots will the pharaoh sell to Israel?"

A peal of laughter broke from the short, irregular waves of Siamon's cockled face. "As I hoped, Solomon *has* been swift to grasp the meaning of what he has seen. Solomon may have as many chariots as he has gold to pay for them."

"And horses?"

"Our finest mounts."

Solomon knew he should avoid asking his next question. But he wanted confirmation direct from the pharaoh's lips of what he already suspected. The question, too, was designed to test Siamon's honesty and forthrightness. "Why does the pharaoh favor us with his generosity, selling us chariots and horses?"

"When Solomon sent his ambassador to offer us friendship, I was doubtful and suspicious." The laughter was gone and Siamon was speaking earnestly. "But Solomon is a great king. Israel is a great nation. Solomon's wisdom has not been exaggerated. The king of Israel by his actions since he came to his throne convinced me that he has no designs against Egypt. I would seal my friendship with Solomon and put my border to rest with my Hebrew neighbor by giving not only my daughter, but giving for a fair price what surplus I have of our invincible chariots. Egypt's attention must focus on the west, for we shall soon be at war with the miserable pretender, Shishak, whose soul is as dark as his skin."

Solomon decided to meet candor with candor. "I have committed myself to peace. Israel will not fight for Egypt."

If the frankness hurt or surprised Siamon, his features did not betray it. "You already fight for Egypt by remaining at peace with us. A tranquil border with Israel frees all my chariots and warriors for the Libyan savage. I wish only that I could sit in such amity with Shishak and also make affinity with him."

"Your war with him is certain?"

"Yes," Siamon answered tightly.

"And how will Egypt fare in such a war?"

"If our gods fail us, disastrously."

"But the pharaoh has said his chariots are invincible."

"Not, I fear, against the barbarians from Libya, whose full strength is a mystery. We know only that they are brutes. They do not declare war openly or with dignity. No trumpet sounds before they give battle. Their warriors are scavengers and cowards who fight from ambush. They are cutthroats who steal upon an enemy at night instead of engaging a foe at the first break of dawn's light. They are hyenas, strangers to the field of honor."

Solomon fell silent for a moment, thinking that Siamon's concern with traditional battle was self-serving. Such warfare was desirable for a nation that had cities and women to protect, an ordered way of life to guard. It was to the clear advantage of civilized countries to have a code of rules in warfare and a defined battlefield outside its gates. War by stealth and ambush, by the quick unexpected stroke, were the unconventional, indispensable weapons of outlaw armies. David could not have won his victories if he had been bound by the limitations advocated by Siamon.

"War," said Solomon, "is by its nature dishonorable. It is also a quandary. The history of Israel seems a continuous battle. Our one God has constantly inspired and led us to war, which meant certain killing. Yet He has, from the time He gave the tablets to Moses, demanded that we shall not kill."

"Solomon's God is wise," Siamon observed. "Had not my ancestors been warlike, I would have no throne and my people would have none of the rewards of peace. There would be no Egypt, no education, progress, culture, refinement. We would know nothing of art and literature, of numbers and the secrets unraveled by our physicians to heal the body of its infirmities. Our learned men would not know why the stars travel their paths in the heavens. Along the Nile there would be turmoil instead of temples. War is the mother of peace, and peace is the brother of civilization. Had your father not been consecrated to war as well as to your God, Solomon would not have a throne, the Hebrews would not have an empire brimming with manifold bounties. Without war there cannot be the blessings that peace affords. When war is holy and just, it has a place in the affairs of men."

"But peace," replied Solomon with conviction, "also has its place among the affairs of men, for surely God loves the peace-maker."

"Peace is a luxury for the comfortable," said Siamon. "The Libyans are not comfortable. They are hungry and aggressive and their aspirations are high. Shishak covets my throne as Absalom hungered for David's place and as Adonijah thirsted for Solomon's royal chair. But Shishak will not have my throne unless he defeats me in battle. I will take Gezer more easily than Shishak will take Thebes."

Solomon was grateful the conversation had turned at last to the subject of the Canaanite stronghold. It was the most delicate and critical part of the alliance, as important to him as marriage to Nagsara.

"The pharaoh has been munificent in offering to deliver Gezer to us," Solomon said. "However, chariots will be no match for its strength."

"The assault on Gezer requires another strategy. It will be taken, without difficulty, by siege."

"But siege is extremely difficult," Solomon said, astonished. "Beleaguerment is long, costly, and requires patience until the defenders are weak from lack of food, water, and fighting spirit. My father was skilled in such tactics. The Ammonite capital of Rebbath and sacred Jerusalem fell to him by blockade. Yet he found Gezer impregnable to siege."

"Thanks to the beneficence of our gods who guided the minds and hands of our weapon-makers, Gezer—or any fortified city— is no longer invincible."

Siamon pointed down the sandhill, Solomon's eyes following the curve of his hand.

In a breath-catching sweep, Solomon saw the renascent weapons of which Benaiah had spoken. The Assyrians, not the Egyptians, had invented the huge siege machines, already sludging like giant crustaceans across the ocean of desert. But it was Egypt that obviously brought the fearsome attack monsters to unrivaled might.

The siege machines were of two types, five of them long, broad platforms, propelled by four wooden wheels. The three others were hand-pushed battering rams.

The eight land whales lumbered unrelentingly toward a high stone and earth fort about a hundred yards away, similar to dozens that Solomon had toured on the outskirts of Thebes. The parapets were the city's first line of defense. Solomon could see the lone bulwark was densely protected, the plumes of war arching above the heads of the defenders.

Crouched behind mantalets on each of the platformed machines were several dozen archers. As they came within range of the fort, the bowmen sent up a heavy barrage of arrows to divert the besieged soldiers inside the redoubt from concentrating too much of their return fire on the hundreds of shield and spear-carrying infantrymen who were advancing ahead and abreast of the siege engines.

With nothing to bar their path, the battering rams soon smashed gaping holes in the walls of the fort. Then scaling ladders from the siege machines were thrown up, dozens of warriors scrambling toward the top. The first wave was met by the last resource of the defenders—upended vats of boiling oil.

The scene was carnage. The attacking soldiers writhed, wailed, roared, and shrieked, as they fell in deadly paroxysms after being doused with the fiery liquid.

But after the supply of oil was expended, the fort was doomed as waves of infantrymen climbed the scaling ladders. Other warriors poured through the apertures carved by the battering rams.

Everything but the customary slaughter of the last defender was over when Solomon thankfully heard the merciful hurl of the trumpet calling retreat. He closed his eyes in relief.

The clang of battle became a hush except for the spasmodic ululations of the wounded. He knew that the howling of the gashed, torn, lacerated, stabbed, bruised, and burned men would never leave him. The waterfall of woe would be with him to his last days.

"So will Gezer fall," the pharaoh said matter-of-factly.

Solomon looked directly at Siamon and saw that he was un-moved by the tragedy of the hundreds of men who had died. It was still beyond Solomon's understanding how Siamon could find nothing unremarkable about the two holocausts he had com-manded to be fought.

As for himself, Solomon had seen too much death, and in him coursed a renewed pledge to devote his life to the line-and-plummet.

"So will Gezer fall," Siamon repeated. One of the pharaoh's aides approached and gave him a convex of metal, which Siamon then pressed into Solomon's hands.

"Between Hebrew and Egyptian," the pharaoh said, "may this silver trumpet remain silent for another four hundred years."

Siamon walked off, Solomon lingering, his eyes battened for several long moments to the battleground below.

Chapter Eleven

In deciding to seek a private meeting with Nagsara so soon before their wedding, Solomon knew he was shattering the unwritten Hebrew tradition that forbade a betrothed couple from seeing one another except in the company of others. This may also have Egyptian custom, since he and Nagsara had been allowed to come together only in public. No one in the Egyptian court had bothered to explain whether or not this was so. But within Solomon there was an urge to speak intimately with Nagsara. The urge had become irresistible.

Though he had known much of Egypt before setting foot in Thebes and had learned much more during his visit, many of the nuances concerning the beliefs and attitudes of his new ally escaped and confounded him. Coupled with his driving desire for at least one candid, uninterrupted conversation with Nagsara, he particularly longed to understand the reason for the unnecessary human sacrifices at Siamon's battle exercises. That had not been explained either.

Solomon shouldered the irony of his position uneasily. All he had sought in Egypt had been gained. He was to have Gezer and Nagsara, horses and chariots, and in a brief ceremony the previous evening he and Pharaoh signed a treaty satisfactory to both. It pledged Israel and Egypt to mutual peace and free-flowing trade. Still, Solomon was disappointed and frustrated. Since his arrival both Siamon and Nagsara had been polite yet distant. He felt isolated from both of them. Despite Siamon's proper surface affability, there was about him an impenetrable aloofness, a regal inscrutability. Pharaoh had not permitted him the extra dimension of personal friendship he desired in their relationship.

Perhaps Nagsara would speak to him as a friend.

After a discreet inquiry of a passing servant outside his palace apartment door as to the whereabouts of the princess, he was directed to the opposite end of the causeway-long king's residence. He threaded his way through a maze of warrens and corridors until he found himself standing at the entrance of a sun-drenched atrium, part of which was shaded by a portico supported by four thick, tapered, elaborately carved stone columns.

The scene was pleasant chaos. Solomon drank it in with delight. His tenseness vanished as he remained in the doorway, unnoticed, his eyes drawn first to the large rectangular pool, its gently bobbing surface supporting a raft of rose-purple lotus blossoms.

In elegant repose, Nagsara floated on the liquid greensward.

Children were everywhere. Solomon surmised they belonged to the pharaoh and his wives and concubines. Half-a-dozen naked young boys, their heads shaved save for long braided locks that trailed back to their collar bones, scampered and chased each other. As many pubescent girls, decorously dressed in knee-length cloaks, upper arms encircled with jeweled bracelets, their hair in pigtails, played with wooden dolls that had movable arms and legs.

Animals were also everywhere. A brown-backed yellow-necked goose, sacred to the god Amon nested undisturbed on the grass-colored water of the pool. Screeching monkeys danced in and out of the neatly trimmed foilage and leaped up and down the columns. Curly tailed black salukis and long-eared basset hounds sent up an occasional muted bark. Several sand-colored tiger cats, their eyes whirls of orange, hunched and ambled along the stone decking of the atrium.

An ancient woman, her face attractively seamed, occupied herself with weaving a headband from white cotton thread, which she twisted dexterously around a small spindle.

A knot of servants appeared suddenly from another doorway, clapped their hands, and the children quickly disappeared. Two of the monkeys sprinted after them.

A moment later a slightly stooped figure appeared, materializing from nowhere. He went to a backless chair in front of which stood a harp. The musician tripped the strings and began a melodic serenade to Nagsara.

Her hair is blacker than night, blacker than sloes.
Red is her mouth, redder than jasper.
Were I her Negress that is her handmaid,
Then would I behold the color of all her limbs.

All at once Nagsara caught sight of Solomon. She flew to the rim of the pool in four swift butterfly strokes, refusing, after emerging from the water, a benu-decorated towel proffered by a giant, muscled manservant.

Walking toward her, Solomon chained his eyes to Nagsara's flawless, smooth-textured skin and the angular lines of her figure, alluringly emphasized by her clinging wet garment, a bosom to calf hem-embroidered, flame-red cloak. One shoulder strap had fallen, and she made no move to adjust it. He checked his excitement and was embarrassed by his next thoughts. He had brought none of his concubines with him to Egypt, anticipating such companionship might needlessly antagonize Pharaoh and Nagsara. He had sought Nagsara out as a friend, but now he desired her as it was natural for a man to desire a woman.

The atrium faced the north, to catch the least shuffle of cooling wind, and as Solomon sat next to Nagsara in a plaited-leather chair, a breeze caught and held.

The setting was idyllic, the song of the harpist still caressing the air.

Red is her mouth, redder than jasper . . .

The manservant, wearing a long, belted loin-cloth, brought silver bowls filled with sycamore figs and slices of green-striped melon. He poured a black wine into heavy gold goblets.

The face of the Egyptian princess held no hint of reciprocal desire. It mirrored neither pleasure nor disappointment at Solomon's unannounced arrival.

"The King of Israel," she said, the tone feminine yet firm, "flouts Hebrew convention by this tryst with his intended bride. It is especially tasteless since in less than a day his priest will perform our wedding ceremony."

"You speak knowledgably of our customs. I wish I could speak as knowingly of yours."

"I have accepted your God and your ways. Therefore, the burdens of adjustment and learning the traditions of my new country are mine. Solomon need not trouble himself to understand me or our beliefs."

Her directness caught Solomon off-guard. Except for Bath-sheba, no women had ever expressed herself to him in such straightforward terms, whether from fear of his position or because women in Israel were expected to show respectful subservience to men. He lifted his goblet and found the bouquet of the wine sensual, the taste more sweet than dry.

"Nagsara races to a harsh judgment. There is much I long to understand of Egypt and the pharaoh's household."

"It is best that Solomon does not attempt to understand us, for he will find our beliefs a source of confusion."

"I confess confusion as to why your father has not permitted us to be alone."

"For what purpose? My father and Solomon plot for empire, giving no thought to our marriage other than how it will enhance the thrones of Egypt and Israel." A cat bounded into her lap and Nagsara's slender hand automatically began to stroke it affectionately. "Your need is for Gezer, not the daughter of Pharaoh."

"Yes, I am anxious for Gezer. But is it not conceivable for me to also long for Nagsara?"

"The king who already scandalizes the world with the number of his concubines may at best have a passing passion for an Egyptian princess. Such is lust, absent of affection and esteem. Absent, too, of love."

"You are to be my first wife and I will take other wives as is a king's privilege and obligation. But you will be my principal wife."

"The principal wife of Solomon is yet a concubine. In time she will be invisible among his herd of women."

"Then our marriage gives you no gratification?"

"I am resigned. I could have refused this loveless union. Egyptian women may not obey the wishes of their fathers in choosing a husband. I marry Solomon to serve Egypt as Solomon marries me to serve Israel."

He was appalled that this bold, fiery girl found his motives so transparently pragmatic, and had the courage to tell him so. A stray thought came to mind—he wished somehow that Bathsheba understood more and Nagsara less of the wild inconsistencies that statesmanship and peacemaking necessitated. Now he discovered a wild inconsistency in himself. Instead of taking offense, he found Nagsara's honesty and spirit as appealing as the lissome curves under her vivid cloak.

"When we return to Jerusalem," Solomon offered, "there will be much opportunity for our relationship to deepen."

"Will I reign beside Solomon, becoming a true queen as was Nefertiti, who ruled equally with her husband, Pharoah Akenaton?"

"No!" he answered forthrightly. "But Nagsara can serve Israel with dignity and purpose. There have been heroic women in our history. We venerate Sarah as the mother of Israel and all nations. Miriam, the sister of Moses and Aaron, was brilliant and courageous. 'Sing unto the Lord,' she cried and thereby helped inspire the children of Israel to throw off four centuries of bondage inflicted by your ancestors. And Deborah, tall and handsome, lived only for God. A prophetess, and some say the equal of Gideon as a judge."

The recitation of Israel's noblest women did not pacify Nagsara. "If Solomon should die before me"—her question was a whip seeking a welt—"will I reign in his stead?"

The mere suggestion dismayed Solomon. His own struggle for the throne had been ugly and deadly, even with the blessings of God and his father. The crown of Israel could not be passed to a woman as a suitor handed his beloved a gemstone.

"An Egyptian queen on the throne of Israel! It would not be possible," he said, "and were it possible, it would not be tolerated."

"A woman once ruled Egypt as pharaoh after the death of her husband," Nagsara replied truculently and with an air of superiority. "The position of female nobility in Egypt is greatly different than that of high-ranked women in Israel. In the Egyptian royal family, it is the women who inherit the land. It descends from mother to daughter, but then, alas, it passes to the pharaoh as a condition of the marriage contract. It is this land as well as our gods which give our monarchs their power."

Nagsara paused, enjoying Solomon's unmistakable perplexity.

"I will now add shock to Solomon's confusion," she continued. "Tell me, is it true that death is demanded in Israel for both sexes when incest occurs?"

"Yes," he said, astonished at the oblique turn in the discussion, which was not proceeding as he had hoped. It was clear by now that in coming to Nagsara as a friend he had instead found an adversary.

"If incest had not been practiced in Egypt, our history would be very different. Since the land is inherited by the women, when the queen dies, the ruling pharaoh, to protect his throne, marries all the surviving females in his household, his mother, grandmother, young daughters, even newborn infants. And there have been instances when a Pharaoh has found his own mother and daughter attractive enough to summon them to his couch. Does Solomon find us barbaric?"

"Solomon finds such customs unique," he replied. He found himself wondering if Nagsara was married to Siamon, whose wife, he recalled now, had died several years before. He dared not inquire of this blunt princess if it were true, apprehensive of what her answer might be. "Tell me something of the woman who was Pharaoh," he said, purposely redirecting conversation.

"Wearing the headdress of a vulture," Nagsara recounted, "Queen Hatshepsut presided over war and peace. The obelisks that Solomon has seen on the west bank of the Thebes, those great carved stones adorned with silver and gold, were built by Hatshepsut. So was our finest temple. As Pharaoh, Hatshepsut sent Egyptian ships on the endless voyage to the land of Punt to bring back incense and myrrh for offerings to our gods."

"A wise ruler," Solomon said with sincerity, ever the admirer of a sovereign interested in trade.

"Wise and divine, for she was the direct child of divinity. Her father was the god Amon."

Solomon's face reshuffled itself into a question mark, Nagsara easily reading his skepticism.

"The king of the Hebrews," she went on, "should not doubt the supernatural birth of Hatshepsut. Was not Sarah, of whom you spoke a moment ago, divinely mated with the God of the Hebrews? It was the same with Hatshepsut's mother, Queen Ahmose. The story is told that Amon found Ahmose resting amid the splendor of the palace. When he appeared before her in human form, his fragrance awoke her. She smiled at his majestic handsomeness. Then, filled with passion for her beauty, he went into her. From this union came Hatshepsut, born in Amon's godly image, his living statue on earth."

Putting aside his doubts, Solomon asked, "Was it Hatshepsut's divine birth which ushered in a glorious epoch for Egypt?"

"Glorious and inglorious. She had a long reign, successful despite its turbulence. She was deeply resented by our male nobility, who contended ceaselessly with one another for her throne. It ended in despair because Hatshepsut, a tender woman, could not personally lead the Egyptian army in battle. She died in disgrace, her name afterwards all but stricken from our chronicles, though she served Egypt magnificently."

"War is not woman's work, or, rightfully, man's work, either." Remembering now: "I am gratified that you spared yourself the sight of the violence and suffering when your father exceeded all my expectations of hospitality by showing me the might of his army and chariots."

"I did not come to the place of battle to spare myself from what Solomon calls violence and suffering. I was absent only to make preparations for our marriage ceremony."

"Yet it was well that you were not in attendance. The casualties were high."

"What of it?"

"I make much of loss of life."

"Solomon is mistaken. There was no loss of life on the battlefield. There was *maat*, which is the truth as we conceive it. The men who fell in battle were fulfilling their proper function in the service of our gods."

"But the proper function of life assuredly is to preserve it and serve God on earth."

"Life to the warrior and to all Egyptians does not end with death. That is why our people spend half their lives preparing for death; that is why our pharaohs build their unparalled pyramids and have their queens, servants, pets, and all the treasures of their palaces buried with them, so everything they hold valuable may be enjoyed in the afterlife. This pleasure will be denied me since I forsake our gods and will not so much as share a tomb with Solomon, my husband." Nagsara raised her hand, palm outward, a barrier against Solomon's reply until she could make her most important point. "The warriors who died before Solomon's eyes died joyfully, knowing they would pass on to the afterlife."

"And what is the nature of this afterlife?"

"It is exactly as Egypt was the height of her glory. There is no hunger or suffering. There is companionship with the gods. The warriors who fell are already enjoying the company of Horus, Re, and Amon."

"I can understand men dying for the sake of God. Among us, this has happened often. I would give my own life for Yahweh. But we do not speculate upon the next life, leaving our eternal fate to Him."

"How barren then is the life of the Hebrews. I am filled with sadness and pity for the king of Israel and his countrymen. I am filled, too, with sadness and pity for myself. By our marriage, by embracing Yahweh, I relinquish my opportunity to live forever with the gods of Egypt. I pay the price of immortality for my wedding to Solomon."

"Our scrolls record that a Messiah will make this life as glorious as the future you describe for those who worship the Egyptian gods. Perhaps He will also enlighten us about the afterlife."

"When will your Messiah come?"

"I do not know, but His coming is a certainty."

"The people of Egypt already have their messiahs. They enjoy the supreme gift which the Hebrews are denied, which they must wait for with long-suffering, and the patience of our Sphinx. Were you to take Egypt's gods rather than my taking your God, Solomon would never die."

"I assumed it was Nagsara who was proselytized. Is Nagsara attempting to wean me from my God?"

"A concubine does not convert a king." she said sullenly. "I will make Solomon a dutiful and obedient wife, for such is my father's wish. But I cannot forget all that has been taught to me of our gods. Though I forsake them, perhaps they will nevertheless treat me with kindness."

As Nagsara rose, the cat spilling from her lap, she adjusted her shoulder strap. "Solomon knows now," she said, "why there can be no deep relationship between us. Siamon and Solomon can make affinity with each other. But there will never be affinity between our gods and Yahweh or between Nagsara and Solomon."

She slithered off, her strides more nimble than the cat that trailed her steps.

Nagsara's parting words were a lesion pricking his heart. He still wanted more of her than she was willing to give. Unhappily, he realized his marriage was to be inescapably political. He would not, however, judge it as cynical since he had made it clear to Nagsara that he was offering his love . . . and she had rebuked him.

Nagsara was correct. It was not likely that their relationship would deepen.

The gap between them appeared unbridgeable.

* * *

Siamon's sun-dried brick-and-cedar beamed palace was ablaze inside and out with regal radiance, and luster mated to luxury for the wedding of Nagsara and Solomon.

Within the Great House, where the feast would be held following the ceremony, the light and airy rooms bulged with three thousand years of Egyptian craftsmanship and booty.

Finely wrought tapestries flared against the walls and the heavy, skittering rugs seemed alive—so deft were the representations of yet more sacred animals—hawks, falcons, and crocodiles. There were also the ubiquitious benus as well as fire-eyed cats.

Chests and tables brimmed with crystal goblets and gray porcelain drinking vessels. Glass vases overflowed with bunches of long-stemmed, narrow-petaled blue and rose lotuses, Egypt's royal flower. In small, dainty, scarab-decorated bowls swam miniature gardens of white daisies with yellow centers, red poppies, slim-stalked rushes, and blue cornflowers.

The chairs and other furniture were crafted of gold, silver, copper, ivory, and ebony.

The banquet tables staggered with ten different kinds of meat, five varieties of poultry, sixteen choices of bread and cakes, six selections of wine, four types of beer, and a profusion of rare fruits and sweets.

Outside, the double gates—symbolizing the supposed unity of the two ancient kindgoms of Upper and Lower Egypt—had been unlocked, and the huge courtyard of the pharaoh's residence was aflood with people, lesser courtiers mixing with farmers, copper mine and stone quarry workers, merchants, slaves, women, and children. The flood ran down to the silvery lake, about a mile long and more than a thousand feet wide. The lake was normally shallow, but the sluices had been opened and the Nile fed in a crammed navy of boats, bodies, and color.

As in the military maneuvers outside Thebes, Siamon's touch for the dramatic had not deserted him. He wanted his iaughter and Solomon to be married in as public a ceremony as possible and had chosen the wide, column-buttressed balcony of the palace. Reposed in a carpet of cushions, the royal couple could be seen from every vantage point.

In contrast to Siamon's resplendently jeweled, saffron robe, Solomon wore a simple violet-purple cloak, his only ornament a seal ring, which he had ordered designed especially for the ceremony. It was engraved with a single word, *Lmlk*—belonging to the king.

On Nagsara's head was a tiara of forget-me-nots and she held a nosegay of buttercups. Her ankle-length gown was also purple, and cut in a V at the neck, with cape sleeves. A loosely tied sash embraced her waist, giving emphasis to the suppleness of her body. Her eyelids were painted green, her hands and nails stained with henna. Red ochre lipstick charged around her mouth.

Solomon reflected that Nagsara's beauty at this moment would have shamed Nefertiti.

Sporting no armor, Benaiah was in a pleated military mauve tunic, a running leopard emblazoned across the chest of his garment.

Their backs to the lake, both Zadok and Nathan, separated from Solomon and Nagsara by a portable altar, wore sacred ephods, breastplates of finely twined linen in gold, blue, purple, and scarlet. Chains of pure gold streamed down their vestments, and the glitter of twelve precious stones on each ephod blinded the eye. Beneath the ephods were sky-blue robes.

As Zadok intoned the vow—"This is now bone of my bones, and flesh of my flesh. Therefore shall a man cleave to his wife: and they shall be one flesh—"Solomon wondered if Yahweh was truly rejoicing at his union with a princess who was not an idolatress but who was yet a prisoner of the idolatry she had been taught from childhood.

Late the previous evening he had composed a prayer and asked Bathsheba to read it aloud following the conclusion of the ceremony. He hoped it would please Yahweh, that it would be a counterpoint to the pragmatism of his marriage.

After Zadok joined them in the sight of the Lord as man and wife, Solomon took Nagsara's hand and slipped on her finger a matching seal ring. It, too, was engraved *Lmlk*, for Nagsara now belonged to the king.

Bathsheba, in a flowing white silk cloak and a silver necklace, chanted the prayer, the words a plea to Yahweh, to Nagsara, and another pledge from Solomon that Israel's welfare stood above all else.

"What, my son? And what, the son of my womb? And what, the son of my vows?" Bathsheba's voice pitched forward in a slowly rising crescendo.

"Give not your strength to women, nor your ways to that which destroyeth kings. Open your mouth for the dumb in the cause of all such as are appointed to destruction. Open your mouth, judge righteously, and plead the cause of the poor and needy. Who can find a virtuous woman? For her price is far above rubies. She will do him good and not evil all the days of her life. Strength and honor are her clothing; and she shall rejoice in time to come. Favor is deceitful, and beauty is vain: but a woman that feareth the Lord, she shall be praised."

There were several moments of stillness when Bathsheba finished. Solomon, looking at Nagsara, was delighted to find that her face was a wreath of pleasure. He could not imagine why.

Now the balcony was turned into a proscenium of celebration as the people shouted their approval of the royal marriage. Siamon and his court officials congratulated them.

Chapter Twelve

"The pharaoh moves against Gezer!"

So animated was Benaiah as he relayed the news of the midnight attack against the Caananite citadel that he had forgotten to knock before entering Solomon's chamber. He also had neglected to bow to the king.

Taking scant notice of the breach of respect, which he realized was unintentional, Solomon immediately eased himself from his writing table and stood, his excitement equaling that of his general. "Praise Yahweh!" he said fervently. "Siamon makes good his pledge of the dowry."

Solomon had received a secret courier from the pharaoh several days before with a message that the assault on Gezer would soon be mounted. With that assurance, he had gladly left the military details to Siamon, instructing Benaiah only to keep observers close to the city and report to him when the pharaoh's offensive was launched.

"How fares the battle?" Solomon asked.

"My captains declare that for Siamon's weapons, the city is as clay in the hands of a potter."

Again Solomon gave thanks to the Most High that not one Hebrew life was endangered by this clash of arms and men.

"Send a servant for Nagsara and have the royal chariot prepared," Solomon ordered. "We leave for Gezer at once."

"My lord," protested Benaiah, "I well remember Solomon's bitter distaste for the maneuvers he witnessed in Egypt. Why smell more blood? Let the pharaoh's men gather their sheaves of scarlet while the king sleeps."

Solomon would not be dissuaded. "You will drive the chariot

131

as far as the watchtower on the city's outskirts. Then I will have a further task for you."

Solomon's was the voice of command. It was useless to argue. "As the king wills," Benaish said without further debate.

Twenty minutes later, Solomon, Nagsara, and Benaiah were rumbling down the inner edge of the coastal plain toward Gezer. The chariot licked the mountainous road greedily under a sky flash-flooded by a full moon. Despite sharp curves, the horses charged forward without hesitation, the purple plumage bolted to their harnesses bent nearly double by the night wind.

It was the same chariot in which Solomon had returned to Jerusalem a little more than a year before with Nagsara. Beyond his fondest expectations, Israel had accepted his Egyptian bride. There had been no public protests or disturbances, no outcries accusing him of breaking faith with Yahweh. Hence there had been no need for Benaiah's troops to use any force whatever. The prevailing attitude among Solomon's brethren was that the king, guided by Yahweh, had acted with wisdom, wisdom that Israel already accepted as proverbial. The alliance with the throne of the Nile, though it had produced an Egyptian wife, had brought first and foremost friendship and peace with an obstreperous, potentially carnivorous neighbor. Even Nathan and others who shared his absolute purity of belief that Hebrew and foreign blood should not be mixed, couldn't convincingly object to Nagsara's conduct since she had come among them. If she was not seen at the tabernacle celebrating Yahweh, neither was she observed paying homage to Egypt's pagan gods. There had not been so much as a hint that Nagsara was practicing idolatry.

As the chariot lurchingly navigated a wide bend, Nagsara's body buffeted against Solomon. She manacled her arms around his waist. The quick current of air churned by the chariot did not drown out whiffs of her alluring powder and perfume.

They hadn't been this close physically since the day of their marriage, when Solomon was overcome by passion. He had carefully avoided sharing his couch again with Nagsara, an arrangement with which she had concurred.

He still found her attractive and desirable, but had held himself back out of fear that intimacy might produce a child. With terror Solomon apprehended that if their union yielded a son, he would be the firstborn and thus have a strong, plausible claim to succeed him. Though the days of Egyptian bondage were far removed, the wounds and mortifications suffered by Hebrews at the hand of the pharaohs were indelibly etched in Israel's memory. An Egyptian bride was acceptable for practical reasons; a king descended from an Egyptian pharaoh—never.

Nagsara had yet to set a foot in the throne room; nor would she. To completely avoid criticism of being influenced by his Egyptian wife, Solomon had gone so far as to provide her separate quarters far removed from the palace, where Nagsara lived a near-reclusive life.

Benaiah jerked the snorting horses to a halt at the crumbled, smoldering shaft of what once had been the strategically placed watchtower. This had given the Gezerites an unobstructed view of the road to Egypt and the high ground eastward toward Jerusalem.

The night was bright as morning as they rode into a clearly discernible conflagration, the heavens lighted by yellow, orange, and red flames. The earth thumped and thundered. From Gezer came a massive temblor pierced by reverberating, agonizing screams.

Solomon did not smell blood. He could taste it. Outlined in the reflected light of its own pyre was what remained of Gezer. It was almost totally decimated. The city's three defensive walls of hard-packed earth, brick, and stone had been no match for the Egyptian battering rams, siege engines, and infantry.

"Benaiah," Solomon said, "seek out the pharaoh's commander and have him spare as many Gezerites as are still alive."

Nagsara, her temper unbridled, cried out, "Solomon punishes and disgraces my father in the eyes of his gods, who demand the lives of his enemies. If he is interfered with and the wrath of his gods is not vented by killing all Canaanites, my father will lose divine favor."

"The mercy of *our* Lord is from everlasting to everlasting," replied Solomon.

"The king speaks glibly and hypocritically of mercy," Nagsara said angrily. "Solomon craved Gezer, and now that his craving is satisfied he becomes a coward. He does not respect my father's gods, and so breaks his bond with Egypt."

"If mercy is cowardice, I am guilty," Solomon said. "But the alliance is not broken. The gods of the pharaoh by now have been more than placated. There is no profit for God or man in the victor's custom of slaughtering the last life. There is no profit in slaying Canaanite men who will be more valuable to Yahweh if they are permitted to live. As captives, they will serve Him by helping to build the temple."

"If Gezer had surrendered," Nagsara persisted, "only a few hostages would have been taken to ensure the payment of tribute and the happiness of the Egyptian deities. The Canaanites die because of their own foolishness."

"Foolish or not, the Canaanites have suffered enough," Solomon said with finality. "They are defeated. I desire no further death and cruelty for the sake of death and cruelty and for the sake of gods which I do not worship."

Solomon repeated his order to Benaiah.

The brawny general sped toward the embers of Gezer in the chariot, its iron wheels grinding a shower of darting sparks.

Standing in the glow of the flame-flowered firmament, Solomon and Nagsara watched Benaiah's departure.

"Now Solomon has Gezer," Nagsara said with a petulant toss of her head, "but I have nothing. My life is empty of purpose and pleasure. I long to return to Thebes. Solomon has no further use for me."

"You are free to go back to Egypt. However, I ask you to consider remaining in Israel."

"For what reason?"

"To serve Yahweh."

Suspicion clouded her face. "How?"

"Gezer," Solomon said, "must be rebuilt, stronger than before. A new aqueduct, walls, and homes are needed. The people must be fed and clothed. Most of all leadership is required—your leadership! I will have Benaiah arrange for the city to be garrisoned for your protection and to prevent new mischief among the Cannanites. Otherwise, Gezer will be yours in all ways. It is not the throne in Jerusalem, but in Gezer you will truly be a queen."

Nagsara's features relaxed. She understood that Solomon was offering as much as it was possible for him to offer her.

"My father has given Solomon Gezer, and now Solomon returns it to me?"

"Yes!" he answered forcefully, convincingly. "Let Nagsara make Gezer rise again like the benu."

Excitement in her voice, Nagsara said, "Done. I will serve Yahweh as Queen of Gezer."

In the firelight Solomon could see her head tilt proudly. Sullenness and resentment had fled from her face. They had made affinity at last.

Solomon summed up the advantages of placing Gezer under Nagsara's sovereignship. By taking the step, he gained much—a new and friendly fortified city, an end to the increasingly embarrassing problem Nagsara had become since her failure to publicly embrace Yahweh, and he had given her a task to fill the void in her life, thus warding off the machinations that an idle and strong-willed woman such as Nagsara might cause. Siamon would be pleased and their friendship further strengthened. As a vassal, queen Nagsara would rule the outpost efficiently. She was intelligent and trained for high position. Solomon was also certain of her loyalty. Nagsara knew without being told that the presence of the Hebrew garrison, hovering unobtrusively but ubiquitiously in the background, could wrest the city from her at the first sign of disloyalty. But she would have nothing to gain by scheming against him or causing difficulties. Nagsara's stewardship over Gezer guaranteed its pacification. Gezer would be her pyramid; it would become as sacred to her as the tombs of the pharaohs in the Valley of the Kings.

Already Nagsara—as they waited near the gutted watchtower for Benaiah—was talking loquaciously of the city's future. "Gezer," she concluded, "will be the friend of Israel and Egypt."

He could not ask for more. In all, Solomon concluded, the move was wise, one that solved a great many problems. Now that the backbone of the city's long resistance had been crushed and Canaanite power pulverized, Solomon was certain he would have no further trouble from Gezer, a particular blessing since his energy was needed elsewhere.

Benaiah returned in a roaring, russet cascade of iron scraping sand.

"The pharaoh's commander," he reported, the geometry of his visage a sphere of satisfaction, "reluctantly honors the request of my lord. The Egyptians will withdraw tomorrow. Thousands of Canaanites will live."

To force the decision from Siamon's commander, Solomon guessed that Benaiah had threatened reprisals or had bribed him. Or perhaps the general from the Nile did not share Siamon's fanaticism, feeling that he could explain to the pharaoh that the vetting of Gezer was sufficient to please their gods. No matter.

"Send captains to King Achish of Gath, and to Shobi, king of the Ammonites. Send captains to all the kings within the empire," Solomon declared. "Let them hear of Gezer's fate, let them hear the woe of those who threaten the Hebrew throne." He briefed Benaiah on his plans to renew Gezer with the aid of Nagsara. "Tell the kings also of the rewards of friendship with the throne of Israel."

On the ride back to Jerusalem, Solomon reflected on the importance of the conquest of Gezer: for the first time since Abraham's convenant, Israel was realistically at peace. No enemy remained that was strong enough to seriously threaten her. Unopposed, he now reigned over all the land from the river Euphrates to the lands of the Philistines and Canaanites and to the frontier of Egypt. Now he was free to give his attention to the sacred charge of building the temple; the golden dawn of his reign could now burst into golden daylight.

* * *

The next day, while Gezer yet smoked, Solomon prepared a message to Hiram, the king of Tyre.

"You know," wrote Solomon, "that David my father could not build a house for the name of the Lord his God because of the warfare with which his enemies surrounded him, until the Lord put them under the soles of his feet.

"But now the Lord my God has given me rest on every side. There is neither adversary nor misfortune. And so I propose to build a house for the name of the Lord my God, as the Lord said to David my father, 'Your son, whom I will set upon your throne in your place, shall build the house for my name.' "

"Now, I pray, command that cedars of Lebanon be cut for me; and my servants will join your servants, and I will pay you for your servants such wages as you set. For you know that there is no one among us who knows how to cut timber like the Phoenicians."

The papyrus was carried north by a horseman to Tyre, the powerful merchant city and port from which stout, intrepid ships traversed the known world. For the building of David's palace, the Phoenician monarch had sent his most gifted architects and craftsmen as well as the precious, almost priceless, cedars of Lebanon—hard, reddish, close-grained wood, resistant to dry rot and insects.

Hiram had been David's friend and he would also, Solomon was certain, extend friendship to him. They were kindred spirits and natural allies, both possessed by peaceful pursuits of building and trade. Hiram, upon taking his throne, had completely rebuilt Tyre, including the harbor. He had also erected for himself a sumptuous palace.

In less than a month Hiram's reply came and Solomon was not disappointed.

"Blessed be the Lord of the Hebrews this day, who has given to David a wise son to be over this great people." Hiram wrote. "I am willing to grant your every wish."

There were demanding stipulations to Hiram's agreement, which Solomon agreed to readily. He was exuberant with joy and anticipation now that the totality of Israel's energy would be committed to the unrivaled structure he planned for the Lord. To complete the raising of the temple, no sacrifice, even those which Hiram's conditions entailed, would be too great.

And it came to pass in the four hundred and eightieth year after the children of Israel were come out of the land of Egypt, in the fourth year of Solomon's reign over Israel, in the month Zif, which is the second month, he began to build the house of the Lord.

Chapter Thirteen

Beneath an umbrella of dark, fast-gathering rain clouds, Solomon stood with Nathan on a rocky incline near the summit of Mount Moriah.

The king had summoned his prophet and driven with him in his chariot to the temple site in order to share the vaulting news from Tyre.

Solomon was oblivious to the menacing weather. "Hiram," he said, excitement kindling his voice, "pledges friendship, cooperation, the cedars of Lebanon, and his most skilled artisans to raise the temple as he raised my father's palace."

"There is a shadow-and-substance difference between a temple and a palace," Nathan snorted.

"Surely Nathan favors the building of the abode of the Lord."

"I am of two minds regarding the temple," the prophet declared. Ordinarily a pillar of absolutes, Nathan was reacting with uncharacteristic indecision. "I see the good of it, and I see in it potential for evil."

Solomon was shocked that Nathan expressed the slightest doubt concerning the desirability of the temple. It had never occurred to him that his plan for the house of the Lord would be met with anything except enthusiastic approval from the prophet who spoke for God. Nathan had rightfully opposed David's building of the temple because he was a warrior. But on what grounds could Nathan criticize him for proceeding with the grandiose structure where the Lord would manifest His presence and abiding virtue, where men could meet Him in adoration?

"Speak freely, as you always have," Solomon urged as he inspected Nathan closely. The prophet was aging fast. He had a haggard, troubled look. His back was bent and his bony shoulders sagged. "Tell me your objections to the temple."

Nathan's answer was a hiss of rage and pent-up frustration. "First, an alliance with the Egyptians and their pagan gods—as many gods as there are blood-sucking bats in the caves of Judah. Now Solomon allies himself with Hiram, also a pagan who worships Baal, the false god who was denounced by Moses and our prophets because of the licentious rites he demanded. Baal, the cruel god for whom fornication is a joy, the savage deity for whom torture and human sacrifice are necessary."

"Still it is true that in building the temple Hiram will serve Yahweh, not Baal."

"I wonder. The worship of Baal is not dead in Israel. Why has not Solomon busied himself rooting out this blasphemy? Solomon's intimate league with another king who bows to an idol gives succor to those among us who cleave to a god who holds in his hands a thunderbolt, a spear, and a mace."

"We have no other recourse. Without the proficient architects of Hiram we cannot build the temple."

There was a sudden, rapacious mid-air bleating of wings and a strangled caw as a falcon dug his talons into a hapless crow.

"I ask my lord Solomon, will the architects of Tyre fashion a bulwark to Baal or Yahweh? How can those who supplicate themselves before Baal build for Yahweh?"

As they watched the predator follow its prey down the mountain shaft, Nathan said, "In this union with Hiram, is Solomon the falcon or the crow?"

"Nathan views the world with unrealistic eyes. We have no artisans in Israel who can craft the temple. Is it not preferable, therefore, that we use the talents of the Phoenicians?"

"Has Solomon never considered why we have no architects, why no Hebrew has painted a picture or carved a statue?" The prophet straightened his shoulders and ran a gnarled hand down the length of his beard. "Our supreme gift to the world is knowledge of the one true God, worship at its noblest and purest. We have given the world our great scrolls which sing our history in inspired verse, poems, psalms, and proverbs. To the world we have given music and efficient agriculture. David taught the nations the mixed blessing of expert warfare. And now, because of Solomon, we also teach the world how a small nation can excel in trade and peace. We have done much, but we have never made an image of anything because Yahweh forbids the making of a likeness of anything that is on, above, or under the earth. Such is idolatry. Yahweh has forbidden it to us because if we accustom ourselves to images we, too, would come to grovel before them as do all other nations. The temple will introduce cherubim, images dedicated to Yahweh, but images nevertheless. And will not the temple itself be an image? Will Israel come to worship the grandeur of the temple instead of the grandeur of Yahweh?"

"Would Nathan prefer that the temple not be built?"

"The people sacrifice at the high places. We have the tabernacle and shrines and altars in abundance. We are not without recourse to worship."

"But the charge for the temple is a command to me from the Lord and an inheritance from my father. Here on Moriah the Lord spared Isaac from Abraham's blade and made this mountain a holy place, befitting a temple. And here David chose Ornan's threshing floor to hew the Lord's house."

"That is the good of it. Solomon's charge *is* well-established and sacred. I fear, however, that in building the temple Solomon also expresses unhealthy ambition and a desire for his own glorification."

"By creating His abode, as Nathan should know well, I strive only to serve Yahweh."

"If that is Solomon's true motive, then I say the king pursues a worthy purpose. But is Solomon certain within himself that he builds the temple for the Lord and not for Solomon?"

"Let Yahweh examine and judge my intentions. In my heart, He will find that the temple is tribute for all He has bestowed on me."

The sky was turning moody black and Solomon, anticipating rain at any moment, was about to suggest they return to the palace.

But Nathan was heedless of the mustering shower. Thoughtfully he said, "Would Yahweh not be as grateful for an edifice that is less ostentatious and costly?"

"Considering what the temple will accomplish, cost is of no consequence. The house of the Lord will unite us as never before, bring us together in spirit as well as in body. Without the temple, the security of Israel is precarious, if not hopeless."

"And with the temple will our security be assured from everlasting to everlasting? Can one structure so reward us? Can even a temple of the finest cedar, gold, and jewels guarantee we will be sustained forever?"

"I do not know. I can only prepare for the future, not speak for it. Such questions can best be answered by men who will be alive a thousand, five thousand years from now."

"The life of a building, no matter how sturdy, flickers briefly in comparison to the infinity of time. As I am the prophet of the Lord, I can assure Solomon that if his acts are wise, just, and reverent, his name and wisdom will stand long after the temple is no more."

"But the Lord has filled me with an unquenchable obsession to build His house as a marvel before Israel and the world."

"Solomon has neglected to mention the conditions that come with Hiram's aid. Surely the Tyrean monarch who besports himself before Baal does not build the temple as a free-will offering to Yahweh."

"Hiram asks two hundred and twenty thousand bushels of wheat a year and one hundred and eighty thousand gallons of our finest olive oil for his household and workmen."

"It is too much."

"For the Lord, the price is small."

"What will be the price in labor for our Hebrew brothers?"

"Thirty thousand men of Israel will help Hiram's servants fell and square the trees of cedar and cyprus."

"Will they serve voluntarily?"

"I shall demand their labor."

"Solomon will impress thirty thousand of Yahweh's blessed into slavery?"

"They will work for the Lord's temple only one month in three. While ten thousand are in Lebanon, twenty thousand will remain in Israel to till their soil and freely attend to their own affairs. That is not slavery."

"Neither is it freedom when so many are forced into hard labor at the pleasure of their king."

"I do not send my brethren to war or to their deaths. I send them to tithe their labor for God. Some among us will find the task disagreeable. But it is the duty of a king to thrust nobility on those of his subjects who are unwilling to serve Yahweh as they should."

"They will serve no doubt under the whip of Adoniram, that merciless son of Abda, whose brutality reminds me of Joab."

"Adoniram will see to it that each man performs his labor as ordered. He is harsh, but fair."

"He is a man who bears Cain's mark, and such men come to violent ends. He will not die peacefully on his couch with his loved ones surrounding him."

Solomon stepped to the brink of the incline, extending his arms as if to embrace the alabaster city.

"Nathan," he declared, "within me there is a great vision for Jerusalem, Israel, and the empire. Do not concern yourself with the few reluctant Hebrews who will be compelled to aid in the building of Yahweh's temple. Their service is holy. Do not concern yourself with the one hundred and fifty thousand Canaanites and Philistines who will aid in the construction of the Lord's abode. Though they be unholy, their service is also holy. My vision extends beyond the temple. When it is finished, I must build a palace of wonder, a palace the like of which no man has seen. Then our cities and the walls of Jerusalem must be fortified for our protection. My vision does not exclude the building of an entirely new city so that our ships, like those of the Phoenicians, may span the waters of the earth. The construction of great works requires immense offerings in labor and treasure. But build we must, for if we do not build, we shall fall into decline."

Solomon turned his back on Jerusalem and for a moment debated whether or not to tell Nathan how far he was willing to go to achieve his plans. He decided to plunge on.

"To accomplish all that I wish, Hiram, who I acknowledge serves an idolatrous god, is indispensable to me as an ally and friend. If necessary, I will borrow gold from him, give him parcels of our sacred soil, marry one of his daughters. All this I will do in the name of keeping us safe; all this I will do in the name of peace."

"To achieve Solomon's peace, the burdens will be heavy. Grinding the nation into debt, shedding even an inch of the Promised Land and taking another foreign wife will not find the king favor with Yahweh." Nathan had reached the outer limit of his frustration. "Perhaps Adonijah would have made a better and wiser sovereign, and led us down a path to peace that was less costly, less fraught with danger."

The reference to Adonijah grieved Solomon, but he chose to

overlook it, saying, "Yahweh has kept His oath to make us great. As king of Israel I must decide what is required to protect and expand our greatness and honor our God."

Harking back to what he considered the most perilous part of Solomon's diagram to avoid decline, Nathan asserted, "Foreign laborers among us and foreign wives in the palace will spread more idolatry."

"The idolatry will not be mine. Nagsara did not win me to her gods. I remain steadfast to Yahweh, and will always be loyal to Him. Can the lure of idols challenge any true Hebrew believer? If so, his faith is a mockery. I am saddened that the teacher of my youth, he who pressed me to become king, does not share my vision nor my fervor for God."

"Idolatry, borrowing gold, and forcing labor of men breed a strange vision and a strange ardor for the Lord. If Solomon continues this course, his last days will be troubled and empty. And Yahweh will punish us all for the sins of the king."

Solomon looked at the sky, and saw it was ready to explode.

"Dear, quarrelsome friend and prophet," he said, "is not the purpose of man during the shortness of his days to serve God?"

"That is truly the purpose of man," Nathan replied. "But I still question whether Solomon serves God or his own glory."

The windows of heaven opened, and the downpour drenched them to the skin.

Through the curtain of rain Solomon looked again at Jerusalem.

The king of the Hebrews, straddling Moriah, was not completely certain now whether he was the falcon or the crow.

Chapter Fourteen

Solomon had almost reached the conclusion that he was more crow than falcon when he received word that the first three shipments of cedars earmarked for the temple had been lost in transit while moving southward on rafts down the bobbing, zig-zag coast of The Great Sea to Israel's tiny port of Joppa.

Since his disturbing conversation with Nathan six weeks before, Solomon had felt a growing sense of uneasiness concerning building of the house of the Lord. Nathan's arguments lingered, though they had not stayed him from proceeding with construction. He badgered and searched his soul, wondering if indeed the ambitious sanctuary would please Yahweh.

Was the temple, after all, as Nathan suggested, a monument to his own pride? He freely admitted to himself, particularly since his visit to Egypt, that he had acquired a love of pomp. This seemed to superimpose itself on his taste for architectural vastness and his omniverous hunger to build. Could it be true that the erection of the temple was imposing unnecessary and unfair hardships on his people and that it was desecrating rather than elevating Yahweh's name?

He saw with fresh clarity that the Lord's dwelling place would not only be forged by heathen craftsmen, but would bear more than passing resemblance to a gigantic, elaborate tomb exalting Amon and Re that he had visited in the Valley of the Kings. Was he creating a replica of a foreign monument to gods he despised, or a singular temple to the God he venerated?

Solomon stood on the balcony of the palace quaffing the nectar of which he never had his fill—the white wine that was Jerusalem. Seeking reassurance, he intoned his purpose aloud to God:

"I build a house to the name of the Lord my God, to dedicate it to Him, and to burn before Him sweet incense, and for the continual offering of the showbread, and for the burnt offerings morning and evening, on the sabbaths, and on the new moons, and the solemn feasts of the Lord our God."

His confidence soared: "This is an ordinance for ever to Israel. And the house which I build is great: for great is our God above all gods."

Confidence ebbed: "But who is able to build Him a house, seeing the heaven and heaven of heavens cannot contain Him?"

Doubt and faith mingled: "Who am I then, that I should build Him a house, save only to burn sacrifice before Him?"

But the last of his intonation was reclaimed certitude: "The house which I am about to build shall be wonderfully great."

Solomon longed for divine affirmation, for the return of the soothing, tranquilizing voice of the Most High, to again hear Him as he had so rhapsodically at Gibeon.

But God would not grant the king of the Hebrews an audience. Not for a year did Solomon receive any indication that seemed to manifest His will. And when the sign came, it was gravely negative.

Early that morning, a servant awoke him, announcing that the prophet Nathan was stricken with illness.

Solomon slipped hastily into a cloak after ordering the shaken servant to immediately summon the physicians. In long strides, leonine head cowed, his body quivering, Solomon raced to visit Nathan, filled with regret that he had not heeded his prophet's advice. Despite massive problems, work on the temple had progressed without significant interruption. Two of the most difficult tasks had been completed—the raising of the ground to a level with the threshing floor, and the laying of the foundation platform of costly stones. All were heavy, hewed, squared, quarried blocks sixteen and twenty feet in length. And only yesterday, on the latest of his almost daily trips to Moriah, he saw the men of Hiram casting and measuring the walls and porch.

Solomon entered Nathan's apartment and hurried to the prophet's side. The king went to his knees and cupped Nathan's slim, yielding hand in his own.

"I cannot lift myself from my couch," the prophet said.

"I beg forgiveness, dear friend," Solomon pleaded. "God has

chosen to manifest His wrath against me by afflicting you. I will order construction of the temple halted at once."

"My travail," Nathan said huskily, "has no connection with the house of the Lord."

"How else am I to interpret this onslaught against you?" Solomon was close to tears. "It is I who should have been visited with the vengeance of the Lord, for the temple is my sin."

With a shudder of a painful memory returning, Solomon saw that Nathan looked unbelievably achromatic. He was almost as colorless and inert as David in his final days. Solomon drowned an impulse to lift the frail body in his arms and carry Nathan to Moriah to beg healing for him from Yahweh.

"The king errs in presuming God has brought illness to me as vengeance against Solomon," Nathan said.

"Then why do you suffer?"

"Only because I am as rich with age as the Lord is rich with perfection."

"Yet I cannot escape the feeling that your affliction is a sign of Yahweh's displeasure with me."

"No!" Nathan's denial was emphatic and final. "The sign of rightness or wrongness of raising the temple will surely be given to Solomon before it is completed. God will signify His approval or disapproval."

However brittle his body and bones, Solomon was cheered that Nathan's animation for God had not failed him. Though he could not bestir himself from a supine position, the prophet's eyes crinkled with life, his tongue had not lost its fluency and his mind was not devoid of prophetic utterance and spirit.

"Does Solomon forget the awesome signs given to Moses when he received the laws?" Nathan quoted the grandiloquent words from the scrolls, and Solomon instinctively closed his eyes. The prophet's tone was dulcet and ardent, uncanny in its similarity to David's. Listening to Nathan, Solomon could visualize every detail of Moses at the threshold of a seminal sunburst in Hebrew history:

"And it came to pass on the third day in the morning . . ." Solomon could feel and was reliving the drama of that unsurpassed moment of the exodus . . . "that there were thunders and lightnings, and a thick cloud upon the mount, and the voice of the trumpet exceeding loud; so that all the people that were in the camp trembled. And Moses brought forth the people out of the camp to meet with God; and they stood at the nether part of the mount. And mount Sinai was altogether on a smoke, because the Lord descended upon it in fire: and the smoke thereof ascended as the smoke of a furnace, and the whole mount quaked greatly."

"Shall Moriah quake for me as Sinai did for Moses." Solomon asked imploringly.

"I know only that God will not ignore the house Solomon builds in His name," Nathan said, fatigue now evident in his voice. But he found the strength to add: "Meanwhile, since you have set your course, continue the temple. Do not, on my account, let the rhythm of construction be broken. There are worse things under the sun than a house of God built by a king who may or may not be seeking his own glorification. In the end, God will retain all the glory, whether or not the temple is completed."

The physicians arrived, bowed to Solomon, and began their examination.

* * *

Pacing the throne room, Solomon awaited the diagnosis, praying that Nathan's malady was not serious. Finally the chief physician, a rotund, veiny man smelling of herbs, came to him and reported: "The prophet's bones wither and he coughs black bile. His heart beats slowly."

"Will he—" Solomon could not complete the question, afraid that he already knew the answer.

"I have seen some in similar condition live on for years, and others have succumbed into final sleep of day or two after they were taken ill. The fate of the prophet is with Yahweh."

As with his father, Solomon had the sinking dread of another deathwatch. As with his father, the physicians could do little, and he raged inwardly at his own helplessness.

Over the next few months, Solomon visited Nathan each day to report on the progress of the Lord's abode. The prophet's condition was neither improving nor worsening.

Because Nathan continued to give him some reassurance that God might bless the temple, Solomon continued with the monumental task of hastening it to completion. Each day Solomon fanatically whipped his chariot to Moriah to measure the pace of construction. Always, he half expected or hoped that the mountain would quake.

Except for his zeal the great project would have crumbled. He also managed to keep his enthusiasm at fever pitch because at the core of his being he felt the Lord wanted—yes, needed—the temple. And if Israel did not thus magnify God, then Israel did not deserve to survive. Solomon also felt that the prodigious parade of Hebrew heroes, from Abraham onward, were somehow from their graves giving assent to the edifice of the Lord. Also, Solomon never forgot the charge of his father. "I have set my affection to the house of my God," David had said. "I have prepared with all my might for the house of my God."

Solomon was contending, meanwhile, with the stupendous problems deluging him from every quarter of the staggeringly complex supply network he had created, all the ventricles meeting on the temple site.

In the high mountain quarries on the outskirts of Jerusalem, hardly a day passed without several men falling to their deaths. Was the temple worth the lives of these mortally wounded Philistines and Canaanites? Yes! Though he valued the life of each man over whom he held sway, slaves not excluded, he yet could discern no more exalted purpose for which they could give their lives.

Adoniram sent word that many in the labor crews at Lebanon complained of the rigorous work. Some were close to rebellion. Solomon responded by commanding Adoniram to redouble his discipline. If necessary, Solomon said in a courier-carried dispatch, he was prepared to visit the Lebanese forests to personally oversee the felling of the cedars. He would, in face-to-face confrontation, dare the lazy and uncommitted to defy him in his holy mission.

Because of poor navigation, overloading, or storms, raft after raft went to the bottom of the Great Sea, causing the loss of a considerable number of other lives as well as the precious cedar. Solomon always sent word to Adoniram to replace the timber at once.

Joppa, thirty-five miles from Jerusalem and its closest port, was never meant to handle the huge traffic flowing in from throughout the world. The harbor was treacherous and shallow, no more than a small natural breakwater. Solomon diverted several thousand laborers to the task of widening the breakwater.

He also widened the narrow Joppa-Jerusalem highway to keep his valuable cargoes moving overland. Roaming crews of officer-overseers swept the road of animals who fell dead under their burdens.

The wood was brought from accessible Lebanon, and the smooth-surfaced limestone was gouged from the quarries near Hebron, south of Jerusalem. But the gold, silver, ivory, and bronze had to be imported from Ophir and other far-off lands aboard Phoenician ships. The cost was high, and the treasure that David had set aside for the temple was exhausted. And Hebrew produce was not enough to pay Hiram for all the needed materials. To make payment, Solomon began a vast program of buying horses and chariots from his father-in-law.

Fortunately, Siamon charged him a modest price and Solomon found he could trade these prize commodities or resell them at a profit. Thus through barter and gold and silver earned from the horse and chariot sales he obtained the aggregate of expensive essentials he needed. Nothing less than the finest was due the Lord's house.

Despite all obstacles, man-made or perhaps engendered by a displeased deity, the work on the house of the Lord continued.

Besides the temple itself, one important dividend accrued to the nation, little noticed by anyone except Solomon. For the first time in the long saga of the Hebrews, men of Israel were learning new occupations, becoming stonecutters, carpenters, and metal workers. Hebrews labored side by side with the Phoenicians, absorbing their skills and craftsmanship. Solomon was especially gratified that Hebrew workers had aided in setting each of the temple's foundation stones, which had been squared and shaped at the quarries, then fitted together before the Lord's abode without sealing.

The Phoenician masters were so adroit that no sound of hammer, axe, or any tool of iron was heard as the house proceeded. This pleased Solomon greatly. God's work was being done with as much care as possible and with as little noise as possible. Already the atmosphere of a quiet, muted, meditative sanctuary where the Spirit of God could emerge was a palpable reality on the sacred sierra.

Facing the sunrise, the resplendent house—ninety feet long and thirty feet wide—began to loft itself to the sky. Its height was forty-five feet, an impressive three stories tall. The temple somehow generated the illusion that it stood even higher and wider. The walls, more than twelve feet thick, were the strongest in

Israel. The porch before the nave of the house added another thirty feet to the length. Its inner chambers were connected by a graceful, curving stairway under a cedar-beamed ceiling. Against the walls of the structure ninety rooms for the priests were built, also of cedar planking.

And yet it was not done.

In the third year of construction, Nathan, hovering still between life and death, called for Solomon.

"I have," he said tersely, "heard from the Lord regarding the temple."

The prophet brought the long-awaited decision to Solomon without any hint in voice or expression as to Yahweh's reaction. Solomon feared the worst. Nathan's face was more pallid and cadaverous than heretofore, possibly due to the lingering strain of his illness, but possibly because the judgment from the Most High was negative. The king held himself rigid, feeling he might swoon at any moment. He was terrified, yet he girded himself, vowing that if he must he would destroy the half-built temple as effectively as Samson tumbled the pillars of the temple of Dagon.

Now Nathan said that which the Lord had given him to say:

"Concerning this house which you are building, if you will walk in My statutes, and execute My judgments, and keep all My commandmants to walk in them; then will I perform My word with you, which I spoke to David your father . . ."

Nathan's face sought and found a smile as he concluded:

"And I will dwell among the children of Israel, and will not forsake My people Israel."

At last!

The verdict had come gently through the vessel of his ailing prophet. There had been no quaking of a mountain. Yet there was encapsulated vibration within the king of the Hebrews. Solomon's frame quaked as he gave praise and thanksgiving to the Almighty.

Chapter Fifteen

Renewed and fortified by the encouragement he had received from the Lord, Solomon lashed himself to the further work of the temple.

"Concerning this house which you are building . . ." so had the Lord's blessing begun. Solomon read far more into the words than approval for the masterwork taking shape. He interpreted the Lord's response as approbation for all he had done thus far during his reign. Surely God would not have given His confirmation to carry on with the temple if he had dishonored Him by those wrenching decisions for which he had been most severely criticized—aligning himself with the idolatrous rulers of Egypt and Tyre, his marriage to Nagsara, the levy of laborers, and the necessity to increase taxes.

True, God had not specifically sanctioned these controversial policies, but neither had there been rebuke or punishment.

At his chamber desk the following day, Solomon, after much contemplation, wrote a proverb that was torn from his innermost being: "The Lord gives wisdom: out of His mouth comes knowledge and understanding."

The proverb, as he reread it, was somehow inadequate. It implied much more than it said. Who except God knew whether the abstractions of wisdom, knowledge, and understanding, when transferred into decisive action, especially by a king, produced good or evil?

Solomon's elation was now, unexplainably, flecked with brooding introspection as he considered the nature of kingship.

There was a divine sacredness—to what extent he was certain —in being a ruler. There was also a devilish propensity in mortal power. Kingship, too, was impossible.

And lonely. Despite the servility and awe accorded him and despite his crowded harem, the throne could be as unsatisfying as an empty bowl to a famished beggar.

Yet men the world over, given the opportunity, contended to reach the king's chair and maintain themselves in it—at the cost of their lives if necessary.

Why?

For power, wealth, and women. To accomplish deeds so vast their names would be forever written in the chronicles of time.

But even these rewards were not sufficient.

For Solomon, looking through a glass darkly, the penalties of the throne often seemed to exceed the compensations.

The throne was a cargo of pressure; power an almost unendurable weight. Was there not such a thing as too much power, too much responsibility for one man? And even with wealth, a man could starve to death. Gold and silver could not by themselves purchase a moment's spiritual contentment. The harem he dismissed contemptuously, his concubines no more than a pack of frivolous, contending she-wolves, none of whom could bring solace to his soul. His marriage to Nagsara had brought Israel Gezer, a calm frontier, and fruitful commerce with Egypt. But on a personal basis the relationship had been a failure. And though he had an earnest respect for history, Solomon cared not, at this particular time at least, how the ages would judge him as a ruler. He was more concerned with himself as a human being, selfishly instead of selflessly considering the fabric of his life.

It was perplexing that for all the power of a king, no sovereign could decree happiness for himself.

He was Israel's third king, and he recalled grimly that the throne had not bestowed a harvest of happiness on his predecessors. The throne had not kept Saul from melancholia and suicide. It had not kept his father from frequent waves of despair or the sins of adultery and murder.

Never before had he asked himself if his father had lived and died a happy man. Reviewing David's life, he doubted it, and wondered if any king lived and died happily. The best that could be hoped for were passing tides of contentment and fulfillment. Was this an ample return for all that a king must do?

Every decision a sovereign made won him a new crop of enemies. And every decision bred further decisions and difficulties stemming from earlier decree. It was a thankless, frustrating process, endlessly piling up fresh enemies and problems. How many enemies could a king afford? How many problems could he deal with, much less solve?

And kingship, inevitably, brought compromise and temporizing. The chair of a king could not be occupied by an idealist.

The view from the throne was vastly different than the perspective of Nathan, Bathsheba, Benaiah, Zadok, the court officials, Israel's elders, and the mighty men.

For a king, there could be purity of purpose, but rarely, if ever, pure execution of his purpose. Without his league with Siamon, that anomalous and sanguine pharaoh, Israel would yet have within its boundaries the volatile threat of Gezer. Without Hiram's cooperation, the temple would have been a fallow dream.

It was ironic that he had become the ally of kings who prostrated themselves before horrific gods so he could accomplish the work of Yahweh. God found a way of using every man, even those who were His sworn, idolatrous enemies, in order to achieve His divine will.

He also found irony in the knowledge that as king of Israel and through personal choice and persuasion he was anything but an enemy of the Most High. He was Yahweh's champion. To the best of his ability, he had walked in His statutes and commandments, but God nevertheless had left him profoundly unfulfilled as a man. Where was the sense, the logic in his predicament?

Again he thought of giving up the throne, abdicating all his oppressive and onerous responsibilities. He would do so for the most fundamental of reasons: to pursue happiness, which he was certain would never be his while he remained king. Then he excised the notion of abdication, realizing there was no guarantee his search would end if he were not king.

He was trapped, and his spirit languished at the nadir of his despairing mood.

Suddenly he felt the need for physical movement. Unconvinced that his tomorrows held hope and promise, he scrambled from his chamber to the courtyard, leaped into his chariot, and with unaccustomed ferocity flagellated the horses at full speed to Moriah.

The sight of the uncompleted temple briefly lifted his spirit.

"I will dwell among the children of Israel," recalled Solomon, "and will not forsake my people Israel."

Solomon, king over Israel and beyond, Israel's tower of wisdom, prayed humbly: "Lord, do not forsake your servant, Solomon."

* * *

"My son lavishes too much attention on the temple," Bathsheba told Solomon that evening as they dined together. Her voice was tart, annoyed.

"God's house deserves my full attention."

"Not to the exclusion of other important matters."

"Nothing competes in importance to the temple." He repeated the argument he had used with Nathan. "Once the house of God is completed, our future will be secure."

"By no means will our future then be secure." Bathsheba pointed her golden fork at her son like a small obelisk. "How can my son claim Israel's future is safe when the king does not have an heir? My son has no manchild of his own to give him comfort and pleasure, a son who will succeed to the throne and carry forth Solomon's work."

A son? He had come to the royal chair himself, or so it seemed, only yesterday. Still not thirty, was it already time to consider a successor? Did life pass that swiftly, earthly existence only a chain of running moments?

"My mother is quite correct," Solomon said quickly. "I will have a son."

Bathsheba was more dismayed than pleased. Solomon had made the decision too casually, almost cold-bloodedly, in a compact monotone, with indecent haste. There was no joyous anticipation of parenthood, tenderness, or sensitivity. It seemed to Bathsheba Solomon's decision to have an heir was no more than a matter of state policy.

"And who will bear Solomon's son?" Bathsheba pressed, refraining with difficulty from commenting on Solomon's headlong declaration of becoming a father. "Certainly, it will not be his Egyptian wife."

Bathsheba's attitude toward Nagsara was ambiguous. The pharaoh's daughter caused no major problems and seemed content to oversee her small kingdom. And Nagsara had shown no inclination to displace her at Solomon's right hand. But Solomon's Egyptian spouse was inexcusably remote and far too independent. They had not developed a rapport as women. During their infrequent meetings nothing passed between them except perfunctory courtesies. The queen mother thought Solomon too permissive in allowing Nagsara to rule Gezer. Moreover, Nagsara was still not of Yahweh. Bathsheba accepted her daughter-in-law as the nation accepted her—as a necessary political evil—and shuddered at the possibility of Egyptian blood being introduced into the royal line of Israel. Bathsheba, therefore, emitted a gasp of undisguised relief when Solomon said, "Nagsara would be unsuitable."

"Then who will be favored? From which Israeli womb will come the next king of Israel?"

Solomon had no reply that would please his mother. Contrary to widespread opinion, he rarely indulged in sex. He still considered the act, if it was devoid of love, unrewarding save for a brief, quickly forgotten burst of relief from tension and natural physical hunger. Despite his many women, the world would be astonished at the depth of his loneliness, a condition he was beginning to accept as inevitable but which remained the major disappointment of his life. He would gladly trade all his gold for one wife he could adore as Abraham had adored Sarah. He envied their beautiful, enduring relationship that had overcome all obstacles. He feared that such a relationship would elude him all his days. The world counted the number of his women and imagined him a sex-sodden orgiast. From outward appearances, he could understand such an assessment. He had the largest harem on earth and so it followed that he must have an unappeasable sexual appetite. The travesty of his situation was that there was not one woman he knew who could arouse in him the passion David had felt at the sight of Bathsheba. Not one woman to whom he could pour out his soul and share a total intimacy of body, mind, and spirit; not one who could offer him complete companionship.

Solomon was baffled. Why had Yahweh given wisdom and yet denied him a loving wife? Was his only real marriage destined to be the cold wedlock of the throne? Why was it that humble fishermen could find love and he could not, he who was soverign of an empire and had his choice of women? Perhaps as king he had too much choice. How could he discern which lily of the field was the most desirable and most fitting to be his queen? For all his wisdom, Solomon could find no explanation as to why the love of a single, righteous woman had thus far been denied him.

The prospect of becoming a parent actually thrilled him. He

would be a kind, yet stern father, indulging himself in the secret glee and pride of watching a son thread his way from infancy to manhood. He would want to be as close to his manchild as Abraham was to Isaac. He had not idly agreed with Bathsheba— it was necessary for him to have a son to carry forward his work as he had advanced the labors of David. It would take scores of generations of sons to keep intact his dearest wish for Israel— 5,000 years of peace ... and then 5,000 more.

"It is enough for now," Solomon finally said, "that I have decided to have a son."

Because he did not know and refused to speculate, Solomon did not say who the mother would be.

He was also unaware that his plight would soon resolve itself from an unexpected, quarter ... the mother of his heir would come as a lily of the field spewed from the flame-pitted maw of the cruelest god in the empire.

Chapter Sixteen

Solomon had seen an unending parade of visitors, all of whom brought disquieting news. And adding to Solomon's discomfort was a dry, parched sirocco, trundled in from the desert and suspended over the city. Except for his busy schedule, Solomon would have sought the shade of the mulberry grove near Gihon where he and Nathan, whose afflictions still confined him to his couch, had spent so many pleasurable hours.

In separate meetings, four of his governors from the northern provinces had given him virtually identical reports. The leaders of Dan, Manasseh, Naphtali, and Ephraim said their people were complaining with mounting intensity about payment of taxes. Much talk of rebellion churned through the cities and villages because of what was considered an oppressive levy. Solomon had not hesitated in making his decision clear to each of his governors. He ordered the taxes to be paid in spite of the possible consequences. Loose talk of rebellion did not cow or worry him. Rebellion, particularly on the issue of taxes, would, if necessary, be met with total resistance from the army. He still viewed taxes as an uncompromisable, rightful tithe to God. Payment of the levy, he felt, should not be a forced obligation emanating from the throne, but a matter of honor, a privilege for each Israeli to give a share of his bounty to the Lord. The people were prospering as never before, yet grumbling at the small tax, displaying ingratitude to Yahweh as well as the crown.

Zadok had told him with horror that a growing number of sodomites, the unspeakable male prostitutes who practiced their perversity as worship to the old Canaanite deities, were flooding Israel and the empire. Solomon promised his high priest he would seek divine guidance as to how he might best root out and punish the idolaters.

Bathsheba had relayed requests from a dozen of his Hittite, Midianite, and Edomite concubines, all seeking permission to build shrines to their gods. Sternly he had refused.

Solomon looked hopefully at Benaiah as he entered the throne room. "My heart would be gladdened by good tidings," he sighed. "The climate and the empire conspire maliciously against me today."

Benaiah wasn't certain he could oblige his king. A hint of trouble swirled in the cups of his eyes as he said, "Shobi, king of the Ammonites, speeds to visit my lord."

"Then the tidings *are* good," Solomon replied with a soft smile that relaxed his face. He had fond feelings for the Ammonite ruler. Though Shobi was a vassal king, Solomon considered him a friend and ally. And Israel owed him a great debt. In a dark period during the revolt of Absalom, it had been Shobi who generously supplied David and his exhausted men with food and equipment at Mahanaim, thereby making a substantial, timely contribution to his father's ultimate victory. Afterwards, Shobi remained loyal to Israel. Solomon was delighted at the unexpected opportunity for a first meeting.

"For what purpose does Shobi come?" he inquired idly.

"I am not altogether certain," Benaiah said. "It is unfortunate that we do not maintain a garrison in Ammon."

"There has been no need. Shobi has proved himself trustworthy."

"Yet it would do no harm if we had Hebrew ears in Rabbath. If we did, I could better protect my lord's interests. As it is, I have only recently heard rumors of serious quarrels in the Ammonite palace."

"Why was I not informed?"

"I had no wish to add to the king's vexations or divert his attention from the consuming task of building the temple unless I was certain the rumors had substance and required action from my lord."

Solomon could not fault Benaiah. He suddenly realized that his preoccupation with the house of the Lord, now in its fourth year of construction, had discouraged his intimates from coming to him with anything other than the most urgent matters. But Solomon recognized the peril in not keeping himself informed of all that occurred in the empire, minor as well as major problems. He resolved to insist to his chief aides that henceforth the practice of withholding unpleasant or seemingly unimportant information be abandoned. He must not fall into the same dangerous trap—contempt of detail—that brought unnecessary grief to his father. He must somehow find time to tamp out small fires while they flickered low.

"What then are the rumors from Rabbath?" Solomon asked.

"That Shobi and his irksome brother Hanan contend with one another for the throne. Hanan has resented Israel since the lord David took the crown from him and gave it to Shobi. Hanan despises his brother and is not Solomon's fiercest admirer."

"Hanan is a traitor and malediction to Yahweh and Israel," Solomon flared. "Have you heard anything more?"

"No, my lord."

"Then we shall hear the worst or best of it from Shobi. How soon does he arrive?"

"One of my captains sighted him at the border and rode ahead to inform me. Shobi should be here within the hour. My men are escorting him." Benaiah paused before adding, "Shobi's visit should have one compensation. He is accompanied by his daughter, Naamah. My captain declares her the most perfect and beautiful maiden he has ever seen."

The last observation did not arouse Solomon's interest. What concerned him was the reason for Shobi's visit. His initial reaction of delight turned to apprehension. Such a quick, unannounced journey from one king to another without the formality of an invitation and time to prepare hospitality indicated an emergency. He had long planned a meeting with Shobi to express his gratitude to his father's benefactor and to solidify the alliance with the Ammonite ruler who was aiding his plans immeasurably. Ammon, however, regularly paid its tribute and supplied its quota of laborers. Thus there had been no pressing need for a face-to-face encounter.

While he waited, Solomon thought that except for Shobi and his allegiance to Israel there was little to recommend the Ammonites. He considered the dreadful, furious legacy the kingdom southeast of Jerusalem had given the world.

Lot, Abraham's nephew, had seeded Ammon, a ghastly birth stemming from a friendship that had turned to strife. During their first wanderings in the Promised Land, Lot had helped

Abraham build altars to Yahweh at Shechem and Bethel. They became close enough for Abraham to call Lot his brother.

Later, when both came to prosperity, each owning vast herds of goats, sheep, and cattle, their herdsmen quarreled over water and pasturage. It soon became apparent that the land could not support Abraham and Lot dwelling side by side.

Lot chose to settle in the lush valley next to Sodom. So licentious was Sodom and its sister city of the plain, Gomorrah, that the Lord decided to destroy them, but not before sending two angels with a warning to Lot, who was deemed worthy of a special deliverance because he had been so close to Abraham.

"Arise, take your wife and two daughters, lest you be consumed in the iniquity of the city," the angels said. "Look not behind, escape to the mountain lest you be consumed."

Lot conveyed the message to his family and they fled as the Lord rained fire and brimstone out of heaven on Sodom and Gomorrah, overthrowing the cities, the inhabitants, and all which grew on the ground.

While the two pustules near the Dead Sea were still burning, the family reached the safety of high ground. As they paused for breath, Lot's wife, neglecting the warning from the angels and feeling a pang of remorse—she had been reluctant to leave Sodom despite its sinfulness—looked back. Her disobedience cost her life as she was turned into a pillar of salt.

Shocked and numb, Lot was pushed onward by his daughters. They found shelter in a cave, the smoke of the furance of the two smitten cities still stinging their nostrils.

Lot and his children did not give thanks to the Lord for sparing them. Consumed by grief at the loss of his wife and possessions, Lot became addicted to strong drink. His daughters, more terribly, were consumed by the incestuous customs of their lost home.

"Our father is old, and there is not a man on earth to come into us after the manner of all the earth," said the firstborn to her sister one night shortly after their arrival in the cave. "Come, let us make our father drink wine and we will lie with him, that we may preserve the seed of our father."

Instead of seeking out Abraham and his followers for help, the daughters justified the outrageous acts in the name of perpetuating the race.

That evening they made Lot drink a copious amount of wine,

and the oldest daughter lay with her father. The following morning the daughters again fed Lot wine in abundance, and the youngest proceeded to have intercourse with him. Lot again was too drunk to understand the wretched, forbidden way in which he was being used.

Both daughters became large with child. The firstborn gave birth to a son, Moab, who became the father of the pagan Moabites. Her sister also had a son, naming him Ben-ammi, who founded the people of Ammon, worshippers of Moloch, the fire god who demanded human sacrifice.

God was not pleased, and the Moabites and Ammonites earned His enmity because they were conceived through forbidden mingling and had enslaved themselves to cruel gods loathed by the Most High. Generations later Moses and his followers met bitter opposition from the Moabites and Ammonites as they moved toward the Promised Land from Egypt.

The high point of Ammonite power was reached under King Nahash, who led his army unopposed as far north as the town of Jabesh-gilead, a fertile farming center south of the Sea of Galilee. To retake it, Saul the Benjaminite raised a force of picked men. His victory there preceded his crowning as king of Israel.

With the rise of David and his unconquerable legions, Nahash maintained peace with Israel. When Nahash died, David sent a delegation to Hanan, the new king, to express his condolences. But the warhawks around Hanan accused the Hebrew emissaries of spying. The Ammonites committed the unpardonable insult of shaving off half the beards of David's representatives. This, along with plundering Ammonite sorties against Israeli settlers, caused David to wage war against the descendants of Lot. Joab was unleashed and he ravaged the countryside, then successfully besieged the fortress Rabbath, finally inflicting a terminal defeat on the Ammonites.

David replaced the contentious Hanan with his brother, Shobi. Since that time peace had reigned between Israel and Ammon.

Shobi had not objected to being a subservient king. His nation was enjoying relative prosperity, in spite of its heavy export of treasure and laborers to Israel. Ammon, under Shobi, was the first of the conquered peoples to take advantage of Solomon's policy of liberality in exchange for loyalty. Solomon allowed the

Ammonites to exact heavy tolls from the camel caravans moving across their land on the rich north-south routes from Phoenicia and Damascus to Moab, Edom, and the cities of the Red Sea area. The Ammonites also conducted a brisk trade of their own with other desert peoples, bartering or selling crops, iron, limestone, and pottery for gold and silver.

During David's reign, Israel and Ammon became close allies through inter-marriage. Thousands of Israeli men took Ammonite wives and Hebrew women took Ammonite husbands, and, to Solomon's consternation, often gave up worship of Yahweh in favor of Moloch. They did so because wives were expected to follow the faith of their husbands. But in many cases, the process was reversed, Ammonite men embracing Yahweh. So long as the borders between Israel and Ammon remained open, Solomon could not easily prevent the mixing process. Too, there was a natural attraction and a kinship between Ammonite and Hebrew. Although their seed was incestuous, the Ammonites were of Hebrew stock. Israel, in any case, was becoming too sophisticated for the priests who demanded total purity of Yahwehite marrying only Yahwehite.

*　*　*

Shobi swept into the throne room, a gaunt man of some fifty-odd years, an aureole of white hair surmounting a crinkled forehead and busy brown eyes. A respectful pace behind him, his daughter came to a graceful, sandal-silent halt. Solomon could not help but agree with the assessment of Benaiah's captain. If anything, Naamah's beauty had been understated. She was lovelier by far than Abishag when she had come to David as the primal beauty of the kingdom.

After polite greetings and introductions were exchanged and Solomon expressed his long-delayed gratitude to the Ammonite ruler for his kindness during David's adversity, Shobi, disturbed and excited, explained the reason for his hurried visit.

"We have been forced to flee Rabbath! My brother has gathered his hotheads around him again, and they threaten Naamah's assassination and my own." Solomon frowned as Shobi continued passionately and with bluntness, "They charge I am as much a slave to Solomon as our Ammonite countrymen who toil for the king of the Hebrews. I weep for my subjects who labor so mightily for Israel. Yet we are a defeated people, and must accept defeat. Solomon has been a kind and generous emperor. There are many among us, and I am one, who prefer the rule of Israel rather than independence. Under Solomon, we have peace, protection, and are not poor."

"It is sad and difficult," Solomon said, "when brother contends with brother for a throne. As I had Adonijah, you have Hanan. How much support does he command?"

"Little among the people but much among the court nobles. Our small but dedicated army is his captive."

"Do you yet sit on the throne?"

"Yes, but uncomfortably. Threats of death to my daughter and myself reach me daily. We are told we will live only if I step aside."

"Permit me to dispatch five captains, each with a minimum of a thousand men, to Rabbath, and we shall hear no more of Hanan," suggested Benaiah.

Shobi agreed. "For this purpose have I come, to petition Solomon to send a force of men adequate to rid me of my brother."

"Such means bloodshed, and I cannot countenance it," Solomon replied.

"Then Israel will lose Ammon," Shobi said. "Israel will lose a strategic neighbor. My brother will not pay tribute or supply laborers to Solomon as I have. No caravan destined for Israel will be permitted safe passage through Ammon."

"I will arrange a meeting with Hanan and we will come to terms without the clash of arms. He will negotiate sensibly."

"My brother has already anticipated Solomon's preference for negotiation. He counts on Solomon's reputation as the sovereign of peace. He knows he cannot best Israel in battle, and so he will not declare war. But war may come when his plans to build the army to full strength are complete. For now, Hanan is certain that Solomon will not invade Ammon. He diminishes Solomon as a woman who brought Gezer to heel only through the might of the Egyptians. Hanan adjudges Solomon a coward."

Solomon bridled slightly. "Is it cowardice to seek peace instead of war?"

"In the eyes of my brother, yes! Therefore he makes his bold attempt to usurp my throne. Solomon *must* send soldiers!"

"Under no circumstances!" His answer was firm, unequivocal.

"There is then but one alternative."

The king knew before it was said what was about to be said.

"If Solomon will not march, he can keep Ammon safe for Israel only by marrying my daughter. If Solomon and I are in league through marriage, Hanan, who is ambitious but not unintelligent, will give up his pretentions to my crown, knowing that the king of Israel will have no choice but to protect the position of his wife and his wife's father."

Solomon was snared, suddenly compelled to decide between war and a marriage for which he had no longing. If he followed the advice of Benaiah and Shobi to send the army, he would quickly remove Hanan and his arrogant mischievousness. Yet the prospect of even a small war that he could win handily was horrifying. If he ordered an invasion, Hebrew lives would be lost and he would be contradicting the basic ideal of peace to which he had shackled himself. However, if he married Naamah, he would again face the same criticism and complications that his marriage to Nagsara had brought. And what of Yahweh? Would such a marriage displease Him? He wasn't certain. But he recalled that Yahweh had not expressed any displeasure with his Egyptian wife.

"If I agree to this marriage," Solomon inquired of the girl, "how will you worship?" Naamah, dancing several steps toward him, her uncommon beauty irresistible, said in a feather-light, iron-strong voice, "As I have been taught from infancy, I will continue to follow Moloch."

She was as forthright an idolatress as Nagsara. Solomon noted that despite the heavy heat not a shred of perspiration showed on her bare arms or finely wrought features. Nor was her trim yellow cloak stained. From the cascade of spun chestnut hair to the eddies of her black eyes, past the waves of her breasts and down to the swell of her thighs she appeared as cool as the Great Sea.

Solomon asked: "It is the custom, is it not, for those who worship Moloch to cast their firstborn into his metal, fire-filled bowels?"

"Yes!" she replied unhesitatingly. "It is more than custom. It is a duty demanded of Moloch's true believers."

"Would Naamah so act if we had a child?"

Her dark eyes flared. "How better to show love for my god than by giving to him that which is loved and is most precious to me?"

"Such love is peculiar and irrational."

"I am pledged to Moloch, and I would incur his wrath by sparing him his rightful sacrifice."

"I would forbid it! Forbid it not alone because it would be my child, but because it needlessly and fiendishly butchers the innocent and defenseless." Solomon tried, not with complete success, to control his vehemence. "The custom is barbaric, obsolete. Casting children to Moloch has denied Ammon of who knows how many teachers, architects, statesmen, singers of songs. Moloch is a god of hate who consumes voraciously and indiscriminately. Moloch is a vulture of evil."

Shobi waded in, his reverence for his throne obviously outstripping his fidelity to Moloch. "The child can be taken from Naamah the moment it is born, and so it will live."

Solomon could not help but admire Shobi's deft compromise. "Would Naamah agree?" he asked, somewhat mollified.

"On the birthstool I would be powerless to resist." She seemed now a helpless child attempting to accomodate a stern parent.

Solomon dared to hope that Naamah might transfer her allegiance from Moloch to Yahweh. She was, after all, very young. And the young were most susceptible to change. Her intense feelings for Moloch were perhaps not as hardened or ingrained as she had indicated.

* * *

The marriage was performed the following day in the palace before a mere handful of onlookers. Zadok gave them one to another with the same resignation as when he had joined Solomon to Nagsara. Bathsheba was a reluctant, angry witness. Benaiah's expression was neutral. Only the face of Shobi glistened approval. The solitary advantage of Nathan's illness was that he could not attend the wedding. Solomon had not discussed this new marriage with the prophet, knowing he would object and that the inevitable argument would do nothing to restore his health.

After a small wedding feast, remarkable for its lack of conviviality, Solomon, lured by Naamah's overpowering beauty, took her with curiosity and high anticipation to his couch. He found Naamah a disappointing partner, wooden and impassive. She made no apology for her failure to return his ardor, accepting him with barely disguised contempt and passionless obligation. She made clear her distress and unhappiness that she, an Ammonite princess, had been forced into a hasty and unwanted marriage.

Since he had been in a similar position, Solomon sympathized with Naamah. He remained patient and considerate, trying to win her to Yahweh, to Israel, and to himself. His efforts were unavailing. By the third month of their marriage, he no longer invited Naamah to his chamber, and he gave up his attempt to convert her. He had totally misjudged her capacity for change and growth. She remained as frigid to Yahweh as to himself.

In his discussions with her, he found Naamah intellectually shallow. Poorly educated, her mind rigid and unimaginative, she was incapable of abstract conversation on any subject. Her personality was overwhelmingly tactile—what she could not touch or see was beyond her comprehension. Her only affection toward him was expressed when he gave her gifts of jewelry and perfume, and indulged her love for pets, presenting her with cats, lap dogs, and parrots imported from Egypt and Phoenicia.

Naamah spent long hours in front of her mirror, endlessly combing her reddish-brown hair and applying so many ointments to her skin that she secreted an obnoxious odor. Instead of tempting him, it caused near-nausea. Her capacity for food was prodigious. How she managed to retain the suppleness of her figure mystified Solomon. Naamah's capacity for gossip was also prodigious. Hour after hour she laughed, whispered, and screeched (not unlike her parrots) with other foreign women in the harem.

Solomon came to understand the seductive power of gods such as Moloch who were represented in imposing images, usually larger than life and with carved faces that were stern and fear-inspiring. Moloch was a grotesque conjuring of deity, his most blatant feature being an open-flame stomach, the cavity into which firstborn children were hurled. The sheer sight of the idol was awesome . . . yet reassuring! How much less demanding to bow before a lifeless idol than to please the invisible God who scudded the clouds with matchless majesty and power. Moloch was a deity for the primitive and superstitious who mistook representation for reality. Moloch was a god to whom much was given and little returned. He was, in tragic reality, a suitable god for Naamah.

Only one positive result emanated from the marriage. Shobi once more was in complete control of the Ammonite throne. As he predicted, the opposition of Hanan and his supporters melted away. Hanan could no longer risk offending or challenging Solomon, realizing the emperor's marriage to Naamah was a pointed warning to him. He had been outflanked by the Hebrew king. It would now be a matter of uncompromising honor for Solomon to dispatch his soldiers to protect the throne of his father-in-law. Hanan knew that Solomon could not do otherwise, should it become necessary. Bitter but helpless, his intrigues at an end, he withdrew into exile outside Rabbath.

In the Jerusalem palace, the exile of Naamah from Solomon was as complete as Hanan's from the Ammonite capital. Naamah's unyielding fanaticism for Moloch, her self-indulgence, her lack of depth for things of the mind, and her predilection for trivia nullified her physical beauty in Solomon's eyes. Her lone gift was the preservation of peace.

Having served that noble purpose, Naamah would have escaped completely from Solomon's mind. But one nagging thought persisted. At their first meeting, they had discussed the possibility of siring a child. Now he did not wish a royal heir from his deficient Ammonite wife. He feared that Naamah's blood would produce an inferior offspring.

The prospect of a child, however, was improbable, for they had known each other as man and wife only once. Besides, he concluded, Yahweh would not deal so unkindly with His people. Yahweh would not permit the birth of a son who unquestionably would be an unbridled disaster for Israel, threatening the continuity of his work and the future of Zion.

Hopefully, Naamah would prove as barren as Nagsara.

Chapter Seventeen

Informed by his court physician that Naamah was with child, Solomon was appalled and frightened. Yahweh *had* dealt unkindly with him and Israel.

Turned moody and ill-tempered, Solomon's only solace became his brief visits to the burgeoning temple. For a time, he tried to forget about the child by ignoring Naamah and immersing himself in the tasks of empire and spending long hours at his writing table. But the sublimations proved ineffective. He cursed Hanan, Shobi, and Naamah, anxiously reliving the sequence of events that had compelled his marriage and imminent fatherhood.

Would it have been preferable and wiser, he wondered now, if he had permitted Benaiah to send soldiers to dispose of Hanan?

It was too late for regret, and in calmer, more reflective moments he realized, had he to make the choice again, he would have chosen as he did—*peace.*

Also in those reflective moments he began to consider his fatherhood in terms of its real significance. According to Hebrew belief, Yahweh had not been unkind, but was providing him with a blessing, a challenge. A child was not merely the impulse and result of a natural act, but part of a father's sacred relationship with God. For Hebrew king or commoner, a child was a gift and a special source of wealth from the Lord. In the highest sense, the fruit of his loins would belong not to him, Naamah, or the nation, but to Yahweh.

Gradually, he accomodated himself to the impending birth. His child was springing to life as was the temple—two gifts from God and two for Him.

Suddenly the birth was very important to him.

He dispensed with his estrangement from Naamah and frequently looked in on her during her pregnancy. The visits were never pleasurable. Naamah complained bitterly that not only was Moloch to be denied her firstborn, but the growing infant jarred the symmetry of her figure. Motherhood, Solomon thought, had accomplished what gluttony could not. But the more Naamah bewailed her fertility, the more Solomon was filled with anticipation.

From the moment his son issued from Naamah, the infant was surrounded with the greatest care. The midwife adroitly severed the funicle of the umbilical from the placenta and half-a-dozen equally skillful and reliable women servants saw to all the needs of his newborn manchild. He was bathed at once and before being wrapped in swaddling clothes he was rubbed with salt, the traditional cleansing to strengthen him against demonic power.

After recovering from the rigors of childbirth, Naamah astonished her women attendants by smashing a water pitcher against the wall when she was told she had a son. "He should be dead!" she screamed. "Each day he lives is an insult to Moloch!"

The artful solution concocted by Shobi and tacitly consented to by Naamah was carried out. The healthy, squalling baby, which carried Solomon's blue eyes and his mother's dark coloring was whisked from her and given to a wet nurse.

Solomon was now made aware of the majority opinion in Israel regarding Naamah and his son. From those closest to him he learned that the consensus believed the nuptial had been a profound error. His marriage to Nagsara neutralized a powerful neighbor and bred a prosperous alliance. Ammon was another matter. It was a conquered, subdued nation. The advantage gained by circumventing a relatively minor insurrection, was more than cancelled by the possibility of a half-Ammonite king some day ruling the empire.

But for his part Solomon viewed his son as half-Hebrew, not half-Ammonite. And through Solomon's personal instruction, he would become completely Hebrew. He would also be schooled in the ways of God by the most learned of the Levite priests. Thus, in every way, Solomon came to regard his son as a child pledged to Yahweh.

The first, perhaps most vital consideration, was a name, which Israeli parents believed must be selected with exactness since it would influence the child's personality and govern its future. Solomon was dubious that a name alone could determine the path his son would take. But what of his own name? Meaning peace, was it the force that had sent him lusting after the one golden, glittering goal which was the hallmark of his life?

As his firstborn son, the child had a prior, though not absolute, claim to the throne. Short of an Absalom-type rebellion, an Adonijah-like duplicity, mental incapacity, an early death, or the birth of a more talented, more suitable heir, preferably mothered by a Hebrew, Solomon had to assume that this son would succeed him. Therefore he selected the name of his son with great care, and in doing so he honored Hebrew custom.

He called him Rehoboam—*"may the people expand."*

That was Solomon's most fervent wish, that after his death his son would magnify, enlarge, amplify, broaden, and augment the peaceful expansion of Yahweh's people.

Solomon decided it was an exceedingly suitable name, and he was well satisfied with the choice as he repeated over and over, "My son, Rehoboam, Rehoboam my son . . . may the people expand."

When he was eight days old, the child was circumcized. And in a ceremony over which Zadok presided, Solomon paid five shekels to redeem Rehoboam from Yahweh, since another Hebrew custom held that the eldest son of a family belonged to God not in an abstract sense, but directly and personally.

Solomon went even further to counter and ward off resentful and negative feelings toward his innocent son bred by an idolatrous wife. He publicly consecrated Rehoboam to God at the tabernacle with sacrifices, and in his son's honor ordered a daylong feast of herb-sprinkled lambs.

Solomon then publicly proclaimed throughout Israel that Rehoboam would be educated as a Yahwehite, and he himself would prepare his son for the delicate art of kingship. Solomon also declared Rehoboam would remain uncontaminated by the heathen god of his mother. To achieve this last objective, Solomon banished Naamah to a house on the outskirts of Jerusalem. He also forbade her from ever seeing Rehoboam.

She had concurred with obvious enthusiasm, telling Solomon as she left the palace, "I have no son." Naamah hoped that by disowning Rehoboam she would placate Moloch because the furance of his craw had been denied.

The day following Naamah's departure, Solomon went to the quarters of the wet nurse and peered down at his son lying in his crib. Only Rehoboam's brightshining head showed above the purple coverlet.

"The blessing of the Lord be upon you," Solomon whispered aloud. Then lines of a psalm he would later commit to papyrus rolled through his mind:

> *"Lo, children are an heritage of the Lord:*
> *And the fruit of the womb is His reward.*
> *As arrows are in the hand of a mighty man,*
> *So are children of the youth.*
> *Happy is the man that has his quiver full of them:*
> *They shall not be ashamed,*
> *But they shall speak with the enemies in the gate."*

Solomon bent low and kissed Rehoboam with the same affection Abraham had kissed Isaac. And Solomon visualized for him the same dream as Abraham had for his son.

No longer thinking of him as a disaster or a threat to Israel's posterity, he said reverently, prayerfully, and optimistically, "Rehoboam, my son, you are the hope and future of Israel. Go forth, my son, expand the people."

Chapter Eighteen

"The temple is all that keeps me alive." Nathan coughed out the words and expectorated a wad of agate bile into his beard as Solomon sat shaken at his side.

The condition of the prophet was rapidly deteriorating. Since the day that he had fallen ill, Solomon had not been able to bring himself to add to Nathan's burdens by conferring with him about anything except the progress of the temple. Solomon knew the events occurring in the palace were carried to Nathan by his other visitors and the physicians and servants attending him. Rehoboam had been brought into Nathan's chamber once and the prophet had prayed for him, but he made no comment to Solomon regarding the momemtous implications of his marriage to Naamah and the birth of his son.

"My day has passed," the prophet told his king. "Events have swiftly outpaced me, and my lord's actions while I have lain helpless are for the judgment of Yahweh. As to my judgment before the Most High, I have done what was possible though perhaps I have not done all that was truly possible. Of the things which I have done, three give me the most contentment: leading David to repentance, aiding Solomon to the throne, and uttering the words of the Lord which gave Solomon divine affirmation to proceed with the temple."

With difficulty Nathan managed to bring his face closer to Solomon, his voice washing away to an almost inaudible murmur: "My final request is that I be granted time enough to address Yahweh in his new dwelling place. When will the house of the Most High be completed?"

"Shortly," Solomon answered. "Already we plan the dedication. The ceremony will stir Nathan and all Israel."

Since Nathan had been too weak to make a single trip to Moriah, during each visit Solomon brought Moriah to the prophet. Nathan now insisted Solomon speak again of the temple. As the prophet listened wide-eyed, his only interruptions were harsh, spasmodic coughs from the depths of his lungs.

"I have made silver and gold as plenteous in the temple as dew and sunshine," Solomon said of his mountain poem. "Cedar trees as abundant as sycamores.

"The porch at the front of the nave of the house is overlaid on the inside with pure gold.

"The house is adorned all about with precious stones, and the doors are of gold and olive wood.

"South and north the pillars are reared up before the temple, higher than seven-hundred feet, and carved at the top of each are chains of a hundred pomegranates.

"On the walls are gold cherubim, those angelic creatures which are the symbol of the presence of God, each with a wing-span of eighteen feet.

"Of gold, too, are the carved flowers, the lamps and tongs and spoons, the dishes for incense, and the firepans.

"The most holy place—where the Ark will rest—is overlaid with gold, and the veil at the entrance of the holy of holies is of fine linen, blue, purple, and crimson.

"The altar is of perfect bronze—and the weight of all the yellow brass in the temple cannot be found out.

"The molten sea, for the washing of the hands of the priests, is from brim to brim two hundred and ten feet.

"It is a structure," he told Nathan, "more rare and beautiful than the three days of snow which fall each year in Israel. It appears higher than ice-capped Mount Hermon."

Solomon had not yet completed his recitation of the temple's magnificence when Nathan's eyes closed. The prophet was asleep, smiling.

A few months later, Solomon could tell Nathan, "It is finished, the end of seven years of labor and prayer. The abode of the Lord is reality."

Weak though he was, Nathan's face was filled with an ethereal, other-worldly expression. He was so overcome with gratitude and thanksgiving that he found the strength to rise on his couch, extend the limbs of his arms and embrace Solomon.

Then, all at once, Solomon's second deathwatch ended. The

king heard a gasp from deep inside Nathan, his frail body sputtering, and Solomon knew that Nathan had gone to be with David. There was a final spasm, a rattling, as Nathan gave up his spirit.

With him, something left Israel that could never be replaced. Nathan had been more than prophet to his father and himself; he had been the conscience of Israel and Yahweh's heroic spokesman.

Solomon gently disengaged himself from the prophet's embrace, sliding his hands across Nathan's eyes to shut them in sleep.

Nathan's life had ended poignantly, his final request refused. But Solomon took solace from the realization that he had brought to Nathan's bed of sickness the grandeur of the temple. As best he could, he had moved into Nathan's chamber, stone by polished precious stone, layer after layer of pure gold, the mountain poem that belonged to the God he had served so tenaciously all his life.

Nathan had been denied the opportunity of apostrophizing Yahweh at the altar of the temple. He had died, like David, full of days, riches, and honor. Unlike David, Nathan *had* lived to see the temple.

* * *

Warmed by sun and God, Solomon was in the middle of the courtyard of the Lord's house, kneeling on the brazen scaffold—the five-foot-high platform that had been especially erected for the dedication ceremony.

As when Joshua had commanded the sun to stand still, this day was also to be like no other.

The Ark was already in the Most Holy Place, transported earlier in solemn pilgrimage from the tabernacle by the Levite priests wearing their most splendid white linen robes. It rested now, that which had been cherished, guarded, and passed carefully and lovingly down the centuries from Moses, under the sheltering wings of the cherubim.

From all Israel, an overflow congregation had journeyed to Moriah for the consecration of the house of the Lord to hear Solomon speak of this, His dwelling place.

Solomon's view encompassed a congress of the nation's mighty men from all the provinces, of priests and elders, an eye-filling flock which pressed against the brazen scaffold and were dazzled by what had been wrought on Moriah. The king could glimpse, too, all the officials of his court. Benaiah, Zadok, and Bathsheba holding the infant Rehoboam in her arms. His heart ached because he could not see Nathan, who had been buried near David's sepulchre, but even Nathan's absence, ordained by Yahweh, could not dim the luster of this day.

A blanket of stillness covered the throng as Solomon lifted his face to the heavens and declared:

"The Lord has said that He would dwell in the thick darkness. But I have built an house of habitation for You and a place for Your dwelling for ever."

For Solomon and Israel, the moment was burnished. A new covenant was being forged.

"The Lord, therefore, has performed His word that He has spoken; for I am risen up in the room of David my father, and am set on the throne of Israel, as the Lord promised, and have built the house for the name of the Lord God of Israel. In it have I put the Ark, wherein is the covenant of the Lord, that He made with the children of Israel."

The brazen scaffold had been transformed into an altar, Solomon proclaiming his benediction in the graceful, unmatched language reserved for speaking to Yahweh:

"O Lord God of Israel, there is no God like You in the heaven, nor in the earth, which keeps covenant and shows mercy to Your servants that walk before You with all their hearts. You who have kept with Your servant David, my father, that which You have promised and spoke with Your mouth, have fulfilled it with Your hand as it is this day.

"Now therefore, O Lord God of Israel, keep with Your servant David, my father, that which You have promised him, saying, 'There shall not fail a man in My sight to sit upon the throne of Israel, if only your children take heed to their way to walk in My law, as you have walked before me.' "

He paused, and though he was looking directly into the sun, felt no discomfort.

"Now then, O Lord God of Israel, let Your word be verified, which You have spoken to your servant David."

Silently he added: "Verify Your word, O Lord; give Israel, give this congregation, give me another sign of Your acceptance of this house."

Reverently he continued: "But will God dwell indeed with man on the earth? Behold, heaven and the highest heaven cannot contain you; how much less this house which I have built!"

In a final plea that was a psalm tethered to a prayer, Solomon, protector of the Promised Land, said:

"And now arise, O Lord God,

and go to your resting place,

you and the Ark of your might.

Let your priests, O Lord God,

be clothed with salvation.

and let your saints

rejoice in your goodness.

O Lord God, turn not away

the face of your anointed:

Remember the mercies of David your servant."

As Solomon concluded, the new sign broke upon the assemblage.

Fire fell from heaven and consumed the burnt offerings which had been prepared for the sacrifices. The clouds, billowing in from the sea to the west, reverberated in a mighty thunderous crash.

Then all were witnesses to the miracle of the Lord who filled His house with glory. The effulgence so filled the temple that neither Solomon nor the priests could enter.

When all the children of Israel saw how the fire came down, that the glory of the Lord was upon the house, they bowed themselves with their faces to the pavement stones, worshipping and praising the Lord, saying as one:

"He is good: for His mercy endures for ever!"

The king and the people presented new sacrifices before the Lord, and the priests sounded their trumpets and psalteries and cymbals.

Solomon's offering was twenty-two thousand oxen and one hundred and twenty thousand sheep.

The feast of rejoicing, now that the Lord's home had been lashed to the mountain and elegantly, eloquently dedicated by Solomon, lasted seven days.

On the evening of the eighth day following the presentation of the temple to the Most High, Solomon was both satisfied and discontented. How could he be certain that the Lord had accepted His house? He felt a magnetic pull, something driving him again to Moriah. He made the journey alone in his chariot under a night necklace of silver stars and a golden half moon.

Mounting the brazen scaffold he once more considered the dwelling place of the Lord. With expectation and assurance, he waited. And he was not disappointed.

"I have heard your prayer," said God, appearing before Solomon a second time, "and have chosen this place to Myself for a house of sacrifice."

Transfixed, Solomon listened.

"If I shut up heaven, that there be no rain, or if I command the locusts to devour the land, or if I send pestilence among My people, if My people, which are called by My name, shall humble themselves, and pray, and seek My face, and turn from their wicked ways, then will I hear from heaven, and will forgive their sin, and will heal their land."

God had heard his supplication and was granting deliverance in exchange for obedience.

"Now My eyes shall be open," the Lord said further, "and My ears attentive to the prayer that is made in this place. For now have I chosen and sanctified this house, that My name may be there for ever. And My eyes and My heart shall be there perpetually. As for you . . ."

Solomon dared hardly breathe.

". . . if you will walk before me, as David your father walked, and do according to all that I have commanded you, and observe My statutes and My judgments, then will I establish the throne of your kingdom, according as I have covenanted with David your father, saying, 'There shall not fail a man to be ruler in Israel.'

"But if you turn away," warned the Lord of lords, "and forsake My statutes and My commandments which I have set before you, and shall go and serve other gods and worship them: then will I pluck them up by the roots out of My land which I have given them. And this house, which I have sanctified for My name, will I cast out of My sight. And will make it to be a proverb and a byword among all nations.

"And this house, which is high," the voice of God continued, "shall be an astonishment to everyone that passes by it; so that he shall say, 'Why has the Lord done this to this land, and to this house?'

"And it shall be answered, 'Because they forsook the Lord God of their fathers, which brought them forth out of the land of Egypt, and laid hold on other gods, and worshipped them and served them; therefore, He brought all this evil upon them.' "

Thus did the Lord speak to Solomon that enraptured night on Moriah.

The wonder of it made Solomon's heart race. So exalted did he feel that he lifted his hands to the heavens, and it seemed he was the only man whose fingers could clasp the moon and touch the stars. So strong were his intimations of invincibility that he felt nothing would be beyond his grasp for the rest of his life.

PART III

"And who knoweth whether he shall be a wise man or a fool? yet shall he have rule over all my labour wherein I have laboured, and wherein I have shewed myself wise under the sun. This is also vanity."

—Ecclesiastes 2:19

Chapter Nineteen

Now the song of Israel was the music of the hammer, a joyful, ringing, resonant exclamation for the Lord, homeland, and empire a-thrum and a-clatter.

The song of Israel was the prodigious echo of Solomon's obsession to build. Israel's song was the melodious, clanging, colliding slam of iron transforming the face of the Promised Land.

The tumultuous song of construction—the peaceful hammer blows more exciting to Solomon than the ruthless riff of war trumpets—had been sounded and set loose on the brazen scaffold by the resplendent reception of fire, glory, and approbation from the Most High.

Solomon viewed the second visit from the Lord as more important and significant than the first. At Gibeon God gave him wisdom. On Moriah God supplemented his sagacity and suffused him with boundless stamina, fresh inspiration, and dreams for Israel that curved beyond the horizon. Yahweh had removed from him any lingering splinters of self-doubt or hesitation to act out his convictions. Terminated was any consideration other than a lust to achieve success for Israel. With God driving him onward, flagging approval, watching and motivating him, failure would be as alien as Baal. Solomon now possessed the inner fortitude to put his wisdom to practical use. He now wanted to transfer ideas into action and ripples into reality of all the plans he had harbored since coming to the throne.

Although his natural bent veered to reflection and analysis, he concluded that wisdom was wasted unless it was the midwife to achievement. Wisdom by itself never tilled a single acre of land.

The noble protagonists of Israel had all been engines of action as well as sages of life.

Abraham, the founder.

Moses, the lawgiver.

David, the warrior.

And now: Solomon, the builder and peacekeeper.

That, he thought with enormous satisfaction, would more than suffice for his epitaph. That, he thought without immodesty, would lock him into the footsteps of his gigantic forebears. To bring a time of peaceful nation-building would force Israel's growth and challenge it to function at full potential.

But such objectives were only the water's edge. There were yet boundless seas and oceans to conquer. Solomon determined to make Israel the foremost power of the world in all things, thereby spreading Yahweh's bottomless bounty to the heathen and His miracles among all people. Consecrating himself to a purpose less noble or ideal than casting a leviathan shadow for Yahweh and Israel—while mastering the earth with the armor of peace—would be shallow service to Him. For one whose fingers could caress the firmament, Solomon's ambitions should match the span of his reach.

Already the future boded well. The struggles and strife from Mamre to Machpelah to Mahanaim had led to the triumph on Moriah. As Solomon had foreseen, the temple, more than the throne, was serving to amalgamate his countrymen. For the past two years, pilgrimages to the Lord's house from throughout Israel had been ceaseless. Where once all roads for all devout of Yahweh had led to the modest tabernacle and the lofty places, now all led to Moriah.

Solomon set an example of adoration to God by visiting the temple frequently and sacrificing generously at least three times a year at the altar. This occurred during the Feast of Unleavened Bread, which marked the barley harvest; at the Feast of Weeks, celebrating the bringing in of the yellow-stalked wheat; and at the Feast of Ingathering, during which he prayed and gave thanks for the expected largess of wine grapes and autumn fruits from the vast orchards and gardens he had planted in a broad valley between Bethlehem and Hebron.

In no other nation was there a single house of God around which an entire people could rally for worship. Neither was there a temple so grandiloquently conceived, appointed, and executed where an entire people could find exhilaration and meet God in the dwelling place in which He had chosen to enthrone Himself.

The temple was more than a victory of craftsmanship. It was a vindication of Hebrew persistence and spirit. It was a denunciation, by its very existence, of all other gods. By its existence the temple and Solomon displayed to mankind the majesty of Israel's God. So long as Israel stayed in the bosom of God, there was no question of its merely surviving. The only question was how formidable the rugged flower of the desert would become among the nations of the earth.

For Solomon, the temple was a beginning and an ending. Gladly, fervently, he had brought the Lord's house to fruition. But all Israel knew the colossal structure for Yahweh had been a Hebrew imperative since Abraham built the first stone altar to Yahweh and Moses pitched a tent-tabernacle for God during the travail in the wilderness.

In constructing the temple, Solomon acted as his father's surrogate. He had been deputized to carry forth David's dream, and had done so with loving, passionate dedication, giving the testament of his father the precedence it deserved. Fulfilling his father's dream, however, was not the same, not at all the same, as dreaming his own dreams and extending his own vision. In the strictest sense, the temple was *David's* offering to God. David had been the creative force and true architect of the Lord's home.

Now Solomon wished to be the architect of his own monuments.

He became a zealot without equal for Zion from Dan to Beer-sheba, following the announcement of his empire-wide network of building projects. He carefully supervised each undertaking, issuing stern, detailed orders as work progressed and until every project was completed to his satisfaction.

In everything to which he gave his attention—his architectural enterprises, relations with foreign rulers, mediating flare-ups among leaders of the tribal provinces, his palace audiences, the amassing of more wives and concubines—Solomon displayed ferocious, tireless labor and efficiency.

On one occasion when Benaiah feared for his king's health and urged him to slacken his pace, Solomon replied, "Whatsoever your hand finds to do, do it with all your might." Pleased with the observation and strengthened by its lean, uplifting truth, he quickly committed the thought to papyrus. *Whatsoever your hand finds to do, do it with all your might* became his lodestar.

Though he was in the prime of his years, Solomon was acutely conscious of his mortality and the swiftness of the engulfing night when all labor for God would be snuffed out. Youth fled from a man before he realized he had lost the honey-sweet, virgin beginning; the middle years disappeared like a man overtaken by an avalanche; and old age was filled with afflictions of body and mind. Solomon resolved that when he reached the winter of his days, he would have little, if any, cause for regret. He wanted to look back on a life of ambitions realized, and before his death, he desired to pass the crown to a successor—a king greater than he. Then he would spend his old age placidly, writing poetry and philosophy, and taking pleasure in sauntering through his orchards and gardens.

That season of his life assuredly would come. In the interim perhaps he might find the love and companionship of one devoted wife and a quiver of children. But for now he must continue to dedicate himself to his obligation of changing the visage of the land. By so doing, Solomon was convinced, he was mobilizing his kingdom for peace.

He had already made good his promise on the night that he, Nagsara, and Benaiah witnessed the decimation of Gezer. Solomon sent his Egyptian wife labor crews and materials to restore and extend the ruined walls and dwellings of his dowry city.

Nagsara had insisted, Solomon concurring, that the initial rebuilding project be the water channel running from a low hill outside the gates. Ever after it was called the Aqueduct of the Pagan Daughter.

Gezer was now a polygot and a much larger city after Solomon persuaded several thousand Hebrews to settle among the Philistine survivors. The Hebrews who went voluntarily to Gezer found new opportunities and helped make the outpost mightier and more prosperous than before. Under Nagsara, Gezer was unswerving in its loyalty to Israel, and, most importantly, it was pacified. His inauspicious marriage to the daughter of the Nile had, after all, been successful. As he had anticipated, Nagsara was ruling Gezer wisely, vigorously, with charity and understanding. Among the people she was a popular monarch, and no further disturbance emanated from what had been an enemy stronghold prior to his wedding in Thebes.

His next building projects were for trade and defense.

Strung out like a series of oases, Solomon laced his dominions with a chain of fortified, self-contained store-cities. The principal edifices were long, narrow, cool, thick-walled warehouses where the monthly supplies for his household were cached before transshipment to the palace. They also held weapons, barracks and food for his garrisons.

He built one of the most vital store-cities at Lachish, strategically located a scant twenty-five miles southwest of Jerusalem. Solomon's domination of Lachish served to protect Israel militarily and safeguarded the richly rewarding commercial caravans that traveled the coastal highway to Egypt.

Ten miles north of the Sea of Galilee were the ruins of Canaanite Hazor, once ruled by King Jabin, who had made the mistake of going to war against Israel. Soundly defeated by Joshua, a military genius more talented than Joab, the city was sacked. A century later, Hazor once more took up arms against Israel and was again defeated, pummeled to oblivion at the Battle of Taanach by an army under the leadership of Deborah and Barak. To protect the important Plain of Huleh, Solomon rebuilt and fortified Hazor.

In the hills of Judah at Beth-horan, Solomon made the area secure by raising a fort at Aijalon. The valley was another of the few remaining approaches that left Israel vulnerable to surprise invasion.

Built and fortified, too, were Tadmor and Hamath, north of Damascus and not far distant from the Euphrates. Both were caravan junctions on the long, hot trek to Jerusalem.

Solomon took full advantage of the latest knowledge in constructing each stronghold—insisting that his Phoenician and Egyptian architects (their services one more reward for his alliances with Hiram and Simeon) utilize another recent military innovation, *two* series of walls. Even if an enemy should breast the heavily guarded outer bulwark, he would find himself trapped between the two walls and helpless to make any maneuver save surrender or suicidal battle.

Built by foreign laborers toiling alongside Hebrew men—Solomon wanted the sons of Israel to become adroit at all things—the empire now had massive fortress protection, as impregnable as human design could achieve. Yet Solomon was not satisfied that Israel and its territories were safe from attack, that his military deterrents were the last word in discouraging would-be foes from aggression.

And so he added to his defensive system by building a string of eight chariot cities, the most impressive at Megiddo. The thirteen-acre position crested a mount on the Great Road through the Plain of Esdraleon. The summit of Megiddo—the name meant place of troops—had a commanding view to the hills of Galilee in the north, Mount Carmel to the west, and eastward toward Mount Gilboa where the plain dropped away to the Jordan Valley.

The chariot cities bordered the length and breadth of the empire. Together they contained a military force of twelve thousand charioteers and four thousand horses. They were a new thing under the sun, built with heretofore unknown care and mathematical precision. Each had a barracks, a communal kitchen, plus all other necessary supporting equipment for troops. The stables provided exactly ten feet of space per horse, an individual stone trough for every animal, and cedar-roofed sheds for shodding. Solomon commanded Benaiah to issue standing orders for battle exercises to be held twice weekly so that men and animals would remain in fighting trim. With three warriors to a chariot, the peal of horses' hooves sent up volleys of thunder which were heard in the capitals of potential aggressors against Israel.

Next Solomon turned his attention to no less a project than building a new city, that would rise full-blown from all but naked earth.

Ezion-geber, "the giant's back bone," ran in an almost sentry-straight line down the Plains of Moab to the Red Sea. The site had been ignored even prior to the exodus. When Moses crossed it on the flight from Egypt, a woebegone village near the water was a miserable collection of mud huts under the neglected stewardship of the Edomites. Indifferent to progress, the Edomites made no attempt to develop or take advantage of its most alluring attribute—cheek-by-jowl proximity to the Red Sea. David, after conquering the entire region of Edom—Ezion-geber thrown in as a doubtful, unnoticed bonus—had also made no attempt to augment what Solomon considered another imperative for Israel—its own huge port that would outstrip Joppa.

Although desperately required by Israel, the raising of Ezion-geber from ground up, in some ways his most ambitious and daring project, presented one crushing, perhaps insuperable problem. As a result of his building activity, Solomon's funds were temporarily depleted. Rather than increase taxes to construct Ezion-geber, he elected another method to finance the vast enterprise. The plan was complex, fraught with danger, and it hinged on the cooperation of Hiram—an extremely bold and unconventional approach that carried the risk of alienating his staunchest foreign ally as well as his own countrymen if anything went amiss.

Solomon dispatched Benaiah to Hiram with a plea to borrow a huge amount of gold. In exchange, Solomon offered the Tyrean king twenty Israelite villages near the Phoenician border. Hiram accepted the bargain—but when news of the arrangement became public knowledge in Israel, criticism was hurled at Solomon by the mighty men of the empire down to the humblest miller. Even the prostitutes in Jerusalem, who ordinarily evinced no discernible allegiance to the nation, felt that something hallowed had been lost, and felt with all Israelites that madness had overtaken Solomon.

The question on everyone's lips was how Solomon, the guardian of Israel's sacred soil, could forsake his holy responsibility to keep every inch of Zion inviolate.

The crisis deepened when Hiram inspected the Galilee villages that Solomon had given him and found them sparsely populated, drab, without any apparent riches. To his Hebrew friend, the king of Tyre sent a terse, sarcastic, and angry message.

"What cities are these which you have given me, my brother?" Hiram asked.

Solomon was prepared for the complaint and he responded by explaining to Hiram that ceding him the Galilee strip was only a temporary arrangement, advantageous to Tyre since it would provide interest on the loan, not in gold, but in foodstuffs worth as much as gold. He advised Hiram to have his people work the land, plant, and take for himself all the valuable crops it produced—the wheat, fruits, and vegetables that were always in short supply in rocky, wind-swept Phoenicia.

Disgruntled, but recognizing the wisdom of Solomon's suggestion, Hiram assented. Meantime Solomon stormed Ezion-geber into being on a crash basis. Hundreds of Israeli laborers and thousands of Edomite slaves under the supervision of the ubiquitious Phoenician and Egyptian architects labored in shifts from sunrise to sunset, encasing more than two miles of the city behind a twenty-six-foot-high wall, which in some places was thirteen feet wide. The main gate and entry way faced the sea.

Ezion-geber also became Solomon's headquarters for the smelting of copper, the final processing point where ingots which had been worked up in crude form at the nearby mines of Arabah were refined.

More significantly, Ezion-geber made of Israel what it had never been before—a sea-going people.

Solomon built hundreds of sturdy, sail-propelled cargo carriers, and the Phoenicians taught the Israelites to man them. Soon Hebrew crews were making long journeys aboard the ships of Tarshish, particularly to far-off Ophir. Solomon no longer had to depend on Hiram to obtain the treasures of the near-legendary land that was reached in a three-year round trip. To Ophir the huge Israeli merchant fleet carried produce, copper, chariots, and horses, returning with gold, silver, apes, peacocks, and almug wood. The hard, close-grained almug trees were second only to the cedars of Lebanon in value and versatility. The wood had been used in the temple and was preferred for the fashioning of lyres and harps.

When two immensely profitable voyages to Ophir had been completed, Solomon's profit allowed him to repay the loan from Hiram and reclaim the Galilee strip. The Tyreans withdrew, and the Promised Land was kept free of foreign incursion. As with Gezer, Solomon called for voluntary repopulation of the twenty villages, and the new Hebrew settlers shortly made themselves self-supporting through farming and the raising of livestock.

When the wheel of Solomon's plan had come full circle, the criticism turned to approval among Israel's leaders and people. Everyone had benefited. The economic viability of Israel was restored, it had a bustling port and copper center, and Solomon, in effect, had expanded the Promised Land, broadening its arable territory through the resettlement and productivity of the Galilee villages. Such, he thought, were the rewards of creative peacemaking.

Hiram, too, was well-satisfied. His gold had been returned. He had received several years of free, much-needed crops. His subjects withdrawn from the Galilee area had brought home with them the new skill of farming. Historically a nation of sailors, builders, and merchants, Phoenicia began to develop a small but important agricultural industry, despite its hardscrabble soil. In addition, the richer Israel became, the richer Phoenicia became. Profitable trade between the two nations was growing daily. More than ever, Hiram became Solomon's admirer. So much so that he proposed to Solomon by correspondence that their friendship be further consolidated through a political marriage to one of his daughters.

Solomon swiftly agreed and Hiram sent the Princess Apphia to Jerusalem. She was young, dark-eyed, neither ugly nor beautiful. Fortunately, Solomon found her undemanding, uncomplicated, unambitious. They were quickly and quietly joined in wedlock. Apphia, in name at least, became one of Solomon's chief wives, but immediately after the marriage ceremony she agreeably melted into the anonymity of the harem.

Bound by a tested friendship and now by marriage, Solomon felt free to seek further aid from Hiram. The king of the Hebrews' far-flung building program was not complete. He wished another structure, as necessary to Israel as the temple, the fortresses, and the chariot cities.

The arrangements were easily made with Hiram, the agreement identical to the conditions that had made possible Solomon's other works. He would supply Hiram with gold and foodstuffs in exchange for his architects and craftsmen. The Tyreans were soon at work again on Moriah . . . at work on a new palace for Solomon.

The structure, which would almost complete his master plan of construction, was not an idle whim. All the monarchs of which Solomon was aware, himself excluded, ruled from splendid edifices built for personal indulgence in luxury, as an extension of ego, for pomp, and to overwhelm their peoples. Prepossessing palaces of polished stones, fine wood, brick, and gold suggested solidity and unassailable power—even for thrones that often were rooted in sand.

For Israel, however, there were unique reasons for the new palace—practical, symbolic, holy.

David's palace was hopelessly obsolete in functional terms alone. It was surprisingly small, drafty, and overcrowded. Courtiers, women, and servants contended for space like a swarm of bees. His household, personal and official, had simply outgrown David's residence.

But that was a comparatively minor reason for erecting the palace that was bounding to life south of the temple.

In Solomon's mind, and he was certain the nation agreed, it was appropriate, desirable, and necessary that God and king be linked together by dwelling abreast of each other. When it was finished, the palace would jut and shine from Moriah side by side with the house of God, the two structures connected by a gilded passageway, thus combining the house of the Lord and the house of His anointed, earthly sovereign.

Nor did it escape Solomon's notice that Hebrew and heathen alike would be doubly overwhelmed by the splendor of the two buildings. The palace would be a minor pearl in comparison to the temple, but a pearl nevertheless. Both would attest to Israel's greatness.

And this was as it should be, Solomon thought, even though he hadn't found anyone, not even Benaiah, who remotely shared or understood the titanic scope that God had given him concerning the greatness of Israel. More and more, Israel was becoming a power, a force, a thrust, an idea, a body of unparalleled laws and morals and ethics handed down from Sinai. With each passing day Israel and her values loomed larger in the world, and would loom large through all the generations of man, no matter how many enemies might assail, vilify, and smite her.

Israel was God's child of light in a universe of darkness.

The position of Israel, therefore, cried out for the palace. The Lord had not given him instructions to build it—and he had asked for none. But he reckoned that God would not object to this celebration of Israel since it would convey an exalted message from God to the world: See what the people who have served God nobly and humbly have achieved; see how Israel has been blessed; see what the only God has done for His children.

As the temple served for a central rallying point for the Lord, reasoned Solomon, the palace would function as the epicenter for the crown. The spreading influence of Yahweh and the secular affairs of Israel would flow efficiently from impressive, commodious quarters. Also, visiting potentates could be entertained on a grand scale. And from the incomparable throne room which would be the heart of his new residence he could, hopefully, inject into the bloodstream of Israel a contagion of culture. Solomon's hope was an intellectual ferment of literature, art, and science that would throttle the notion that Hebrews were an upstart nation of coarse farmers, sheepherders, warriors, and greedy merchants.

The palace was to be the home of the king, but it, too, as the temple, would belong to Yahweh and all Israel. Therefore he had issued instructions to the Phoenicians that the palace must eclipse the regal houses of Pharaoh, of Hiram, of those incredibly rich monarchs in the kingdoms of the other side of the Great Sea. As the temple was second to none, the palace must be second to none. He again became a constant visitor to Moriah, taking vast enjoyment and satisfaction from the slow but steady growth of the gold, cedar, ivory, and hewn-stone edifice.

Where the temple had been gingerly crafted to the accompaniment of muted noise, Solomon reveled in the raising of the palace to the loud, crackling melody, the unabashed cadence of the tools of building. The temple had been an act of near-silent reverence; the palace a work of booming, zestful celebration.

Happily, gratefully, he noted that the music of the hammer remained the song of Israel. The music of the hammer had so changed homeland and empire that if David were to come back to life, Solomon knew his father would scarcely recognize the kingdom of the lands he had conquered. The temple alone would have dazzled him and brought tears of joy to his eyes.

Solomon was cognizant that not everyone in Israel shared his enthusiasm for building. Among his critics were some leaders of the tribal provinces, a smattering of priests, merchants, and average citizens who felt that his construction program would inevitably bankrupt the nation. They thought he was misinterpreting God's will that change was proceeding too fast, and the old ways were preferable. He considered such complaints false, petty, and short-sighted, and did not take them seriously since he was certain the overwhelming majority of his countrymen approved of his past achievements and assented to all he was presently accomplishing. Not even the king could travel to Dan if the people wished to journey to Beersheba. He buffered himself against his opponents by recalling that Nathan had said that he who builds for the Lord builds not in vain.

It suddenly occurred to him that a prophet to replace Nathan had not appeared . . . and he wondered why . . . wondered if this was an unfavorable sign from Yahweh.

After much reflection he concluded that holy men of the stature of Nathan were almost as rare as wings on a cat, that Israel could count itself extremely fortunate if a servant of Yahweh such as Nathan rose up once in a generation. He wondered, too, if God, by denying him a prophet, was trusting Solomon to ascertain His will. Was he now being showered with the twin responsibilities of kingship and acting as his own prophet? It was not an unprecedented occurrence. Moses had been both leader and prophet to Israel. Solomon did not wish to carry both responsibilities, but he finally and reluctantly decided that until the coming of a new Nathan, he must play the dual roles.

Besides Moriah and his favored mulberry grove, Solomon found another retreat, a place for him to meditate, relax, and revive his spirits. As often as he could manage a brief hiatus from Jerusalem and the palace, he went to his orchards and gardens.

Today was ripe with summer sunshine as he drove his chariot to the valley between Bethlehem and Hebron. He roamed without pattern among his spreading stands of grapevines that led to his groves of olive, nut, and pomegranate trees. All were irrigated by three pools, walled cisterns of stone and masonry that he had built specifically for the watering of his brimming fields. The reservoirs, which made possible his longheld craving to grow his own wine grapes and fruits, were constantly replenished from an ever-flowing underground spring that also ignited gorgeous patches of white, fragrant lilies. Sown for sheer beauty, the bell-shaped flowers were scattered like grounded clouds under the shade of the trees. Free-running wildflowers, violets, hyacinth, and climbing greenbriar added to the riot of color and radiance that abounded in the once dry, dead soil. These were tended now with care and skill by a year-round crew of hundreds of harvesters and landscape artisans.

As he walked, enjoying the profit of the earth, so, too, was he still basking in the yield of his personal transfiguration after learning from the Lord seven years before that he had built God a worthy house. Since then, much had been realized. His architectual glories had brought a period of almost total harmony to Israel and his navy had unfurled the pennants of Yahweh and Solomon throughout the world.

He had been secretly delighted but somewhat puzzled when his ambassadors and ship captains reported that the enormity and versatility of his works had resulted in his name becoming a legend beyond the far reaches of Israel. He was told that in distant lands it was believed the clever, resourceful God of the

Hebrews had made at least twelve men kings of Israel and called them all Solomon. How else could all that emanated from the throne of Jerusalem be explained?

Surely no one man could be king and emperor, builder and architect, wizard of diplomacy, merchant unrivaled, prolific poet, philosopher and psalmist, composer of songs, speaker of thousands of wise proverbs, master strategist of an indomitable army who would not readily fight a war, but against whom a war could not be won. Solomon was also held in awe because it was reputed that his harem was so large he took a virgin to bed with him each night. It was also believed he possessed the gift of speaking with the birds, beasts, and fish.

But within Israel his reputation was more realistic. Benaiah and others confided that he was considered a tirelessly inventive ruler who kept the nation and conquered peoples wheezing to keep pace with him, the best of men always several steps behind, the worst of his contemporaries hopeless stragglers.

The description he treasured most—and this was said of him both abroad and at home—was that he was a king who would give his life for peace.

The only discordant note at this juncture of his life, one which gave him profound concern, was the behavior of his son. The first years of Rehoboam's life had been unpromising.

Naamah had not seen Rehoboam since his birth, yet there appeared to be in the young prince of Israel more of Moloch than Yahweh.

For all Solomon's wisdom, his son presented an enigma for which he had no solution. Was it possible, Solomon asked himself, that he achieved success in everything to which he turned his industrious hand—except in his son?

Thus far, as he stooped and picked a bouquet of lilies for Bathsheba, Solomon had to admit candidly that the answer was yes.

Chapter Twenty

The sun had not yet bulled its way across the horizon as Solomon and Benaiah reached the courtyard of the palace. The king's chariot had been prepared for an early dawn ride to Moriah so Solomon could indulge his major pleasure and obsession, observing the progress of the new royal house that the artisan-wizards of Tyre were crafting so brilliantly. There hadn't been an opportunity for more than a week to visit the mountain and Solomon was eagerly anticipating this morning's trip.

His hope of leaving with Benaiah while everyone else was asleep was shattered when he heard a distant shout and saw a running, arm-waving figure racing toward him.

The running figure, flitting from nowhere, quickly materialized into Rehoboam. In lagging pursuit was Bathsheba, puffing far behind with slow, cumbrous strides. Solomon's annoyance changed to delight and anticipation when he recognized his eight-year-old son. When Rehoboam was only a few feet away, he leaped into the air, fully confident he would be caught on the fly. Solomon opened his arms like a spring blossom, but Rehoboam landed in the brawny grasp of Benaiah, who swung him to a straddling position on his shoulders.

Snubbed, Solomon attempted to submerge his disappointment and humiliation. Under the circumstances, the snub was understandable. Benaiah and Rehoboam were close, his general often mesmerizing the boy with his feats of war while in the service of David. Solomon could not match Benaiah's lurid stories with his own tales of striving for peace, which would strike his son as pallid and boring by comparison. The abrasive truth was that Rehoboam apparently felt more kinship with Benaiah than himself. He had been so engrossed in serving as father to all Israel

that he had not met his obligations to Rehoboam. But his neglect, however real, was unintentional. He had consigned Rehoboam to the background because as king his attention always
seemed to be needed elsewhere. He had broken promise after
promise to visit Rehoboam's chamber, and Benaiah, acting from
the best of motives, had filled his son's need for diverting, adventurous, adult male conpanionship.

"Forward, Benaiah!" Rehoboam urged as if the general were
a horse.

Laughing, Benaiah swiftly and dexterously transferred the boy
onto one of the chariot stallions.

Rehoboam grabbed the reins, and like a young warrior he
commanded the animal to charge full-speed into an imaginary
fray.

Bathsheba came up, breathing hard.

"When Rehoboam saw the king from his window," she said,
"he insisted on running to his father despite my forbidding him
to approach Solomon until later in the day."

"It is of no consequence," Solomon replied, grateful that his
mother tactfully ignored Rehoboam's affinity for Benaiah.

Protectively, Bathsheba went to Rehoboam to hold him
steady on the horse. The boy was furious that his mount had
remained stationary. He kicked its flanks as viciously as his small
legs could manage and turned the reins on Bathsheba, one leather strap catching her face with a thrashing blow.

Although he was outraged at Rehoboam's pugnacious, inexcusable behavior, Solomon hadn't the will or capacity to punish
his son. The slap of the rein must have stung Bathsheba painfully
—but she would not say or admit anything. She also made no
move to discipline Rehoboam.

Young as he was, Solomon thought, Rehoboam by now should
have developed two of the cardinal attributes that any father in
Israel expected from a child—unquestioning obedience and respect for his elders.

He regretted giving Bathsheba the prime responsibility for the
care of Rehoboam and the task of supervising his education.
After almost three years of breast feeding by a wet nurse, it had
seemed logical to entrust his son to his mother. And Bathsheba
had been pleased and anxious to attend Rehoboam. It appeased
her hatred for both Nagsara and Naamah, particularly the latter.
Bathsheba would never forget that Uriah, the husband of her

youth, had been slain by Naamah's Ammonite compatriots. To her credit, Bathsheba had not transferred her animosity for Naamah to Rehoboam. She, too, thought of him as Hebrew rather than Ammonite. But Bathsheba erred in going too far in the opposite direction. She had become a doting, indulgent grandmother, far too anxious to apologize and justify any breach in Rehoboam's conduct. She was more to blame for the failings of Solomon's son than he was. At least he had the excuse of preoccupation with an empire; Bathsheba was with Rehoboam constantly.

"Where is the ambitious fire for my son that you stoked into me when I was a child?" Solomon demanded. "Why have you dismissed every one of his teachers?"

"They are too harsh," Bathsheba replied. "They demand too much too early of the boy."

"Much will be demanded of him if he becomes king," Solomon argued. "The child is obstreperous and spoiled."

Bathsheba challenged: "Then let the king of Israel attend his own son and guide him in the way he should go."

"It was my mother who urged me to have a son, and circumstances compelled me to place him in your charge. But you have failed to care for him properly."

"You judge the day by only the first clouds of morning," Bathsheba said. "It is too soon to discern if Rehoboam's life will be filled with storm or sunshine."

It was a gleaming remark which obscured the truth. If Rehoboam's development continued as heretofore, there would predictably be more storm than sunshine in his future. Yet Solomon could not entirely blame his mother for his disappointment with Rehoboam. The child had inherited Naamah's passion for the sensuous and her aversion to concepts. Rehoboam could not read or write well for his age. As did his mother, he adored pets and was especially fond of horses. His chamber was strewn with toys, most of which he had broken in fitful and baffling bursts of temper.

"It has always been in my heart," said Solomon, "to be as much a father to my son as Abraham was to Isaac. But events have conspired against such a blessing."

Bathsheba's face softened. Kindly she said to Solomon, "Rehoboam needs little more than your time and attention. Is anything more important than intimacy between father and son?"

"Yes, there is, and no, there is not. I fear it is impractical to be both a proper king and a proper father."

Bathsheba shrugged helplessly. For a moment, Solomon considered whether Moloch was somehow wreaking vengeance because he had been denied Rehoboam. Was the Ammonite god that powerful? He banished such thoughts as nonsensical. Yet . . .

"My son knows little of Yahweh, for my mother has also dismissed his priestly teachers."

"They have been weak, ignorant, and unsuitable. Send me another Nathan so Rehoboam may be taught as you were taught."

"I will assign new tutors and priests for my son's instruction," he said firmly. "My mother is not to discharge them without my approval."

His glance caught Rehoboam, who hadn't budged from the horse. Solomon still yearned for intimacy with his son. What kept them apart was not only his lack of time and the lack of shared experience between them. Those were merely superficial reasons. The underlying cause, he decided, was that he seemed bereft of the instinct or knowledge to reach out and show Rehoboam love, anger, any emotion whatever. But the problem defined was not the problem solved. His vaunted wisdom had not provided a solution to why he was incapable of expressing his feelings to Rehoboam.

"Come, Benaiah," Solomon said gruffly. "The temple awaits our inspection."

Rehoboam dismounted and sprinted to the general. "Will Benaiah come to my chamber this evening and tell me again how he slew the lion in the pit and the warriors of Moab and the Egyptian giant?"

Benaiah had no wish to displace his king in the affection of his son. He had begun his tie to Rehoboam innocently, in an avuncular spirit. Now he felt embarrassed and uneasy that the child apparently relied on him above his father. Benaiah looked at Solomon for approval or disapproval.

Solomon's agenda for the remainder of the day was full. And he was leaving tonight on a routine but necessary inspection trip to Ezion-geber. Prior to his departure he was scheduled to deal with the irksome, unavoidable task of meeting Elihu, the out-spoken leader of Judah, who would be bristling with complaints about taxes and labor conscription.

With relief, a strange feeling that a burden had been removed from him, Solomon told Rehoboam, "As usual, Benaiah will visit your chamber."

* * *

By the time the horses tugging the chariot broke stride and came to a halt in the forecourt of the partially built royal resi-dence, the unpleasant incident with his son had been temporarily forgotten.

Solomon's expression, as his eyes avidly girdled the rising structure and the temple, verged on the gluttonous. "Once they are wedded," he said to Benaiah, "the palace and tabernacle will both give sublime service to God. But I would have built them for their beauty alone!"

Startled, the lines across the general's face straggled like rout-ed infantry. "I am a Yahwehite and a soldier. How would the cause of all we hold most sacred be advanced by buildings that exist solely for beauty?"

"So they could be enjoyed for their own sake, to celebrate pure, individual craftsmanship and talent. So the artist need not be chained to any purpose other than the creation of the exqui-site."

"Perhaps that is a goal best left to the future," said Benaiah, still resisting the notion. "Perhaps it is an indulgence that Israel may never be able to afford."

"Beauty in and of itself has value as truth and goodness by themselves have value. Does Benaiah realize that everything in Israel is built for utility, and when beauty occurs it is acciden-tal?"

"We are a nation of only one million who remain preeminent over scores of millions because God has given us inspiration, courage, and wit, which we have been compelled to reinforce with weapons." Benaiah countered. "Many in Israel are un-satisfied and restive. The empire is not free of treason. The king's life is perpetually in danger from malcontents. A strong minority remains unreconciled to the leadership of my lord. Yes, we have built for utility, and wisely so. We have not built for beauty, and that too has been wise. We have built for survival, for defense. That is the wisest course of all."

"Benaiah is correct, although I wish it were otherwise. I cannot help but wonder why a building cannot be as beautiful as a lily of the field. The lily is the handiwork of God, and we delight in it for its form since it has no function save as a feast to the sight. Unfortunately, the time is distant when we can build only or primarily for beauty. It is also unfortunate that Yahweh forbids us to create beauty in sculpture and painting, for such, we are told, is a temptation to idolatry. Yet why should it be so? Why not sculpt the likeness of David and those of our other esteemed ancestors? Would we come to worship their statues, forsaking Yahweh? I think not. Why shouldn't Israel produce artists free to use their imaginations to paint the crossing of the Red Sea and the full galaxy of surpassingly important events in our history? Would such paintings not bring us closer in allegiance to the Most High and remind us of what we owe Him?" Solomon discharged a deep sigh and shook his head in bewilderment before continuing. "However, we have made a beginning. In our temple and palace utility at least has become a partial partner of beauty. The form very nearly equals the function. The structures please the eye as well as the soul."

They traversed the polished hewn stones of the forecourt, moving in a slight upward climb. Solomon abandoned further thought of art unattached to function, thinking that such a concept now was undoubtedly a vagrant dream, an aesthetic impossibility.

Bidding Benaiah to halt, Solomon looked down at the high gloss of the mirror-bright stones. He took a near sensual pleasure in describing the details of the handiwork.

"The stones are fifteen and eighteen feet," the king said. "They have been perfectly matched and graded, an arduous and difficult accomplishment since they are laid on uneven ground. Yet each feels solid and firm underfoot."

When completed, the palace would constitute a compound of several vast buildings, far more than only the personal quarters of Solomon. Moving through the high retaining wall that surrounded the entire complex of temple and palace they passed under a graceful colonnaded porch, quadrangle in shape, and entered the Hall of Pillars.

"Eighty feet on each side," Solomon said appreciatively,

"adorned with gold and all manner of valuable gems. Here the king's visitors may wait amid splendor and comfort. Benaiah, if it is your inclination, station guards in this place to search those desiring an audience, thus attempting to protect me against the assassins you so greatly fear."

"My lord appears to treat his life lightly, as if his safety were a matter of little consequence."

"For all the strategy and plans Benaiah concocts, though you provide a host of ten thousand to watch over me, if it be God's decision, I will be killed. I do not, in truth, fear that much for my life. There are occasions when I wish my death would come to pass. Is life really so precious that a man should dread the return to dust? Does life hold so many pleasures that a man should cling tenaciously to it?"

"Yes!" declared Benaiah without equivocation. "After Yahweh, what does a man have but life?"

"The peace of the grave."

"The king's mind is troubled. If my lord persists in such ruminations, he will suffer the same despair that afflicted Saul."

Solomon's thoughts had wandered back to Rehoboam's unmeaning cruelty. He could not cleave the incident from his consciousness. Was he cursed by an incapacity to love enduringly, meaningfully, or was the nature of his curse his own inability to engender love from anyone toward himself? He was failing as a father as he had failed to find a Sarah, a Ruth, a Bathsheba, whom he could love totally and intimately. What could be said of a sovereign who wished to give love, his most personal and valuable gift, and yet could not bestow it on his own son? What could be said of a king who had the world's largest number of wives and concubines, yet could not find one woman to love? What could be said of Solomon whose emotions could quickly mount from the rock of pessimism to the diamond of optimism? Wedlock only to the throne was still cold, punishing, and lonely for the most part, isolating him from the normal family relationship he craved.

The crown rested heavily on him at this moment and perchance Benaiah was right. Did he in some measure suffer from depression similar to Saul's? Perhaps his tragedy was deeper. He doubted if he would end his own life like Saul, but must he live only for what scant happiness could be squeezed from being the architect and peacekeeper of Israel? Life was a contradiction. As

Solomon the king and emperor, he had a sense of fulfillment; but as Solomon the man, his life was empty. Was it preferable for his life to end as did Saul's or for him to suffer year after year the ravages of an existence without the realization of his private longings for love given and love received?

He led Benaiah into the next building and his spirit was cheered somewhat as the gorgeous scent of the cedars overcame him in the House of the Forest of Lebanon.

"No woman was ever so fragrantly perfumed," Solomon said. "The Phoenicians have performed a wonder, transplanting living timber from wild mountain slopes, incredibly reconstituting it so that the wood still seems alive and growing, threatening momentarily to pierce the cedar roof."

He reflected that all the effort and expense for the palace were worthwhile. Running his hand across the bark of one of the cedars, he again allowed himself the luxury of intimate description. "This House of the Forest of Lebanon is one hundred eighty feet long, ninety feet wide, fifty-four feet high, but appears much larger. This House is a queen dressed in her finest cloak and jewels. Note, Benaiah, that there are sixty trunks of cedar in four rows, irregular in height, some twenty-six feet in length, some twenty-nine feet. They stand in clusters of two, and so ingeniously are they forked at the top with arched ribs that they give the impression of intertwined branches." He could not resist adding: "Here is form as well as function. Beautiful as they are, the cedars are not merely ornamental. They are the pillars on which this House rests."

The illusion of a living forest was so strong that Solomon would not have exhibited the slightest amazement had a leopard, its combustible yellow eyes blazing, suddenly sprung from behind one of the trunks.

As lambent rays of sunlight waffled in through the small square windows of the ceiling, Solomon pointed to the naves above the cedars and the two uncompleted upper stories, where he would store his chests of treasure, shields of beaten gold, and weapons.

There was nothing else to examine for the time being, and on the ride back Solomon felt regenerated. He no longer harbored thoughts of death or self-pity. The exhilaration he had experienced on the brazen scaffold returned. God had defined his mission precisely, and it was unchanged. He was to remain the builder, the king of peace, the keeper of His laws. Everything paled in relevance.

Chapter Twenty-one

"The all-wise king of Israel has forgotten that my brother, the lord David, never exacted a single shekel of tax from the nation," declared Elihu in a harsh medley of biting sarcasm and outrage. "What manner of ruler have we now who steals bread by taxing it from the mouths of his countrymen?"

The rasping words stung Solomon, but he made allowances for his formidable uncle. As a founding father of the empire, he had inherited tribal leadership of Judah, Israel's poorest province. One of Israel's noblest princes, Elihu commanded respect. He was one of the few still alive who had been an eyewitness to David's slaying of Goliath. In contending with him, Solomon vowed to keep his temper in check. Although he suspected that whatever he said, short of complete agreement, would not pacify the still spry and vigorous eighty-seven-year-old elder.

Tall and straight-backed, Elihu's long, trim beard was as white as his simple, immaculate cloak. He was not only formidable, he appeared overwhelmingly prepossessing. One of the few remaining links to the time of Samuel, Elihu had nearly become Israel's king. Samuel, wishing to depose Saul, had found much to admire in Elihu, particularly his intelligence and dedication to God. But the prophet had also found in him jealousy, pettiness, and a volcanic temper. And Yahweh directed Samuel to David instead of Elihu for anointing. Elihu had served Israel well, fighting bravely against the Philistines and laboring untiringly for his beloved Judean countrymen.

As much as he wanted to please Elihu, Solomon would not do so at the price of the entire program he had set in motion for Israel. Responding to Elihu's charge, he said, "While it is true that my father did not tax our fellow Hebrews and was undeniably popular because of it, he had a rich source of income that is unavailable to me."

"Did King David conjure this manna from the fruitful winds? Or was he more clever, enlightened, and generous to his people than his son?"

"He supported the nation from the booty of war, gold and silver taken from the lands he vanquished, lands which now have little more treasure to give. I have vanquished no new lands and thus have no choice but to keep us prosperous through commerce and levying taxes on our people so that I may provide them safety and bread for their spirit, in addition to the staff of life for their stomachs."

"A man's stomach must be fed as well as his spirit. Judah cannot eat the gold of the temple and the palace or the sun-dried bricks of the king's fortresses and store-cities. Solomon has a dubious distinction of being the first sovereign of Israel to raise a tax from the common purse, a tax which is too much and which the men of Judah consider too onerous."

"Would the good and gentle Judahites prefer to face my tax collectors or armed foes? I have built expensively and greatly, from Ezion-geber to Tadmor, but I have built for peace. A price must be paid for peace. However, it is a lesser price than war."

"What do we gain by peace if the price for it is our impoverishment?"

"Judah is poverty stricken, yet it is richer by far than if it had to pay in blood instead of shekels for its freedom. The tithe is modest. The tithe is necessary. The tithe will remain unchanged!"

"I cannot guarantee," Elihu bristled, "that the tithe will continue to be paid. The feeling in Judah against it runs high."

"Did not Abraham tithe to Melchizedek, the priest-king of Salem? Did not Jacob tithe to the Lord, saying, 'And of all that You shall give me I will surely give the tenth to You'? The finger of God, who wrote the laws for Moses on Sinai, did not abolish the tithe. In demanding payment from our people for the works of God, I break no virgin ground. I follow one of our oldest traditions."

"In one of David's psalms it is written, 'The meek shall inherit the earth; and shall delight themselves in the abundance of peace.' But peace among the meek of Judah has brought neither delight nor abundance."

"There is more to my father's psalm, which Elihu and his brethren choose to ignore or forget, though it gives even the poorest man sweet consolation. David also wrote: 'A little that a righteous man has is better than the riches of many wicked. For the arms of the wicked shall be broken; but the Lord upholds the righteous. The Lord knoweth the days of the upright: and their inheritance shall be for ever.'"

"Judah cannot afford the tax," Elihu persisted. "We are not as rich as the northern provinces who have lush soil yielding bountiful harvests."

"Judah suffers not because of the paucity of its soil but because it has been reluctant to adapt to the new way of things. It is commerce based on husbandry which gives the northern provinces their riches. A new wealthy class has arisen among them and the north profits handsomely from trade. They exchange their crops for horses, chariots, ivory, linen, gold, jewels, and spices from Egypt and Phoenicia, even while they tithe. Judah can do the same, if it is willing to change."

"We are not merchants, but shepherds and farmers. We have no wish to change."

"Judah is my own tribe, and I hold a special affection for it. But without change Judah will remain poor."

"Even if we are reduced to beggars, Solomon and his heir to the throne will come to realize we are intrepid people, capable of survival no matter what the hardships. One day we shall offer the throne a commodity more precious than gold and silver."

"And what may that be?" the king asked with genuine curiosity.

"Loyalty to Solomon and his progeny," Elihu answered with dignity.

As Solomon pondered the implications of his uncle's statement, Elihu filled the silence: "But loyalty does not mean unquestioning submission. So that my people may have the threat of hunger and thirst removed from them, I implore the king to exempt us from the levy or reduce it drastically."

"I have need for the loyalty of Judah, but I also have need for the loyalty of every province. Am I not king of all Israel? I cannot make an exception for the Judahites. If I do, the eleven other provinces will rightfully demand the same, and such would breed chaos."

"Solomon accords little honor to his native tribe in maintaining the loathsome tax. In the end, it will cause him great difficulty."

"The levy of a tenth is Judah's fair share, less than the twentieth demanded by the pharaoh from his people. Siamon explained his system of taxation to me, and it has much to recommend it."

"Solomon's Egyptian ally, in taking a twentieth of the people's possessions, is no more than a thief," Elihu said scornfully.

"Consider his system," Solomon replied. "In years of plenty, the pharaoh keeps twenty per cent of the produce of the land. It is laid aside and stored. When the inevitable years of famine arrive, there is no hunger because the pharaoh provides food for the people from the tax in grain and other crops which he has saved for such an emergency. Siamon, who is an eccentric but not an evil man, told me his tax collectors were met with anger and hatred during the years of plenty, but were greeted as heroes and saviors in the years of famine."

Unimpressed, Elihu said, "I seek a reduction in the tithe from a tenth and the king attempts to convince me of the advantages of taking from us twice as much. Is this Solomon's wisdom?"

"In all candor, I admit that I briefly considered the introduction of Siamon's method of taxation in Israel. But it would not be effective. I am not as absolute a monarch as the pharaoh, who personally owns all the land in Egypt, his people working the soil by royal sufferance. Siamon does not have to contend, as I do, with countless thousands of independent farmers whose land is theirs and inviolate."

"May it ever be so," Elihu said in a low, firm, almost prayerful tone.

"Yes. Our way suits our people and would be preferable under any circumstances. Siamon's procedure would clash with the Hebrew temperament. The custom of an Israelite's own vine and fig tree has come to mean much to him and is an incentive to achievement. And what he achieves brings us the tax which Elihu finds so distasteful. Yet the tax brings us an ordered government, peace beyond our borders, and much prosperity within our own frontiers."

"It also brings Solomon an extravagant palace and an extravagant number of wives and concubines."

"The palace is God's and the nation's; it is symbolic of Israel's strength and importance in the world. As for the women, they, instead of Judah's sons, fight our wars."

"What of the levy in labor? Solomon makes slaves of foreigners and Hebrews alike, thereby giving the servants of Yahweh unwanted equality with those who bow to idols."

"I see no evil," Solomon said, measuring his words carefully, "in the bondservice of foreigner or Hebrew."

"Though Solomon fails to acknowledge the evil, it is evil nonetheless."

"It was David who revived the ancient custom of indenturing enemy warriors and using the men from the captured populations for beneficial labor. He spared them primarily for that reason. By so doing, he showed them mercy and most were grateful. It is the rarest of men who prefers death to work. I had no choice but to continue my father's course. Without the compulsory service from foreigners, the temple and the palace could not have been built. Who would have felled the cedars of Lebanon? Who would be our stone-cutters and burden bearers? Who would have built our fortifications? Without the idolatrous workmen, all past and future construction would be impossible. There are also further advantages to such a system."

"I find it repugnant and see no advantage for any man to be denied his freedom."

"The foreigners are denied only freedom from death. Between one hundred fifty and two hundred thousand who are not of Yahweh toil for Israel. Most of them are from five of the seven tribes of heathen Canaan—the tall as giant Ammorites, the nomadic Perizzites, the cave-dwelling Hivites, the vanquished Hittites who once held Hebron and Beersheba in sway, and the Jebusites, who fought so fiercely until David took Jerusalem from them. They are fed, housed, clothed, and kept from mischief and conspiracy, from uniting against us by the long hours they toil. It is not a perfect system. I see the injustice of it and were our enemies not so numerous and dangerous I could afford Elihu's lofty and idealistic conception of freedom for all men. But the king of Israel must be practical and realistic. By so using our foreign captives Israel remains at peace and the work of Yahweh proceeds."

"But why then do you make slaves of brother Israelites?"

"Less than thirty thousand Hebrews are compelled to tithe their labor, most of them uncommitted to other worthwhile tasks. They serve no more than six years with respites to visit their families, after which their service is ended. Such is not slavery, but an opportunity for them to help Yahweh and the nation, which left to their own volition they would not voluntarily do."

"This is a new Israel," the octogenarian said. "I am glad I will not live to behold the outcome of what I still consider excessive taxation and unjustified slavery."

"If I did not utilize taxes and compel labor to foster the great nation sworn to us on the Plains of Mamre," Solomon said passionately, "this Promised Land, this throbbing work of God, this desert miracle, this Israel, this Zion, would be stripped clean of life by the heathen surrounding us."

Solomon went to Elihu and placed his arms on his shoulders.

"Peace, my uncle, does not automatically accrue to the righteous. Peace is the most arduous, rigidly demanding type of warfare. I know that rulers outside Israel praise me aloud for wisdom but privately hold me in contempt as a coward. Had they the resources of Israel they would go forth as kings go forth—to conquer, pillage, and rape. In their eyes I am a fool, a weakling, a woman, the runt seed of my father's loins. But what use have we for more conquest or territory? Of what use would it be to attempt to subjugate the world through war instead of with reason and God's truth?"

"Solomon speaks artfully as a statesman concerned with war and peace, as a king who has never known hunger and thirst. But I speak humbly, asking nothing more than bread, goat's milk, and wine for my people."

"Then let me help Judah," Solomon pleaded.

Elihu's eyes burned into Solomon, searching his face, trying to discern if David's son was offering deceit or sincerity.

"I beseech your permission and cooperation," Solomon added, "to lavish on Judah the same prosperity and bounty from Yahweh enjoyed by the provinces in the north."

There was a long pause during which Elihu's gaze did not stray from Solomon, during which the elder carefully weigned the words of this new king of a new Israel.

"Very well," Elihu said finally, a touch of skepticism in his reply. He could only hope that Solomon was acting from an open, generous heart, that the king was being truthful, that he cared for the best interests of Judah.

Solomon was gratified that he had kept his vow to hold his temper in check, knowing Judah, sensitive and proud, had always been Israel's most difficult and needy tribe. Moses considered Judah so impoverished that he asked Yahweh to grant the tribe a special blessing.

Solomon now repeated the ancient invocation of the witness to the burning bush:

"Hear, O Lord, the voice of Judah,

And bring him to his people;

With your hands contend for him,

And be a help against his adversaries."

Upon his return to Judah, Elihu told his brethren of Solomon's promises. Judah waited, doubtful that Solomon could or would change their way of life.

But soon its rocky soil was transformed, issuing bountiful crops because of the widespread network of irrigation canals that Solomon had immediately ordered into being. Pasturage turned green with new grass and the herds of sheep and cattle increased so there was a surplus. This enabled the province to initiate a lively commerce with its neighbors. The people of Judah readily became skilled in trade, and among them also grew a prospering merchant class. Solomon had brought not only irrigation and seed, but he built new houses, store-cities, and fortresses throughout Judah.

Three years after his memorable audience with Solomon, Elihu died. He had lived long enough to see—and approve—of the resurgence of the land he so deeply cherished. He passed into sleep astonished that change had come as a friend, not an enemy. Pleased, with a smile on his face, Elihu's final words were: "Solomon is wise."

For the following three years, Judah enjoyed a tranquil period during which she and the rest of Israel continued to flourish. This was a period when virtually everyone from Dan to Beersheba gave unquestioned devotion to Solomon. It was also the period when the Phoenician craftsmen suddenly departed from Jerusalem. The task for which they had come was completed.

Chapter Twenty-two

This was to be Solomon's last night in David's palace. Nearly asleep in his chamber, he planned to rise early, eagerly looking forward to taking up residence the next day in his newly wrought home.

He had left orders not be disturbed short of a crisis. Now he heard a tattoo of pounding at his door.

"Enter," he called, fearing the worst.

Bathsheba, plump, hair deeply ribboned with gray, swept in, driving Rehoboam before her. There was no mistaking his mother's choleric mood, and before Solomon could utter a word she proceeded to vent her anger.

"A palace guard," Bathsheba fumed, "has confided to me that Rehoboam, not yet fifteen years of age, spent last evening at the most notorious, shameless establishment in Jerusalem, a place of horrors where sodomites as well as prostitutes cater to all manner of appetites. Solomon the king has spawned a son who commits fornication and disgraces Yahweh and our house."

Solomon came fully alert and examined Rehoboam with curiosity. Tall for his age, he had dark hair and jutting eyes that protruded so precipitiously from their sockets they threatened to fall out. His ungainly body displayed more fat than muscle. Apparently he did not have the capacity of his discarded mother, Naamah, to eat heavily without showing weight.

"Is the charge true?" Solomon demanded of his son.

Rehoboam answered forthrightly, almost with hauteur. "With the young men who are my friends I went to the establishment described by my grandmother. I knew my first woman, an experienced girl, whose father, so she said, is a decent and respectable merchant in Dan."

"The child is disgusting," Bathsheba said, her fury unabated. "Far from contrite, he arrogantly boasts of his sin."

"The son of the king of Israel should not besport himself like a drunken soldier." Solomon somehow felt more uncomfortable than outraged. "Your conduct brings grief to my heart and embarrassment to the throne."

"My father has many women—"

"My women," Solomon interrupted, "their number and use, are as yet no concern of my son."

"It was time to prove my manhood," Rehoboam said without hint of apology.

"Is my son to become another Adonijah?" Solomon asked. "Why did you not pray to our Lord for the restraint suitable to a prince of Israel? Why did you not come to me and speak of your passion?"

"Because my father is as alien to me as is God."

"The boy is not only unashamed of his fornication, but denies God," Bathsheba declared incredulously. "May God protect us if this creature of sin is to be the future king of Israel."

Solomon asked calmly, "Does my son indeed deny God?"

"I do not deny Him and I do not accept Him. My Levite teachers and my grandmother have shown Yahweh to me as a stern God, empty of joy. I am more comfortable with the belief of my companions, who wonder, as I do, why God should deny pleasure to young men."

"Such a belief *is* very comfortable. Has it occurred to my son that by not accepting Yahweh, he is in fact denying Him. If one day Rehoboam should rule Israel, he would assume the throne of the Lord while denying the Lord. That is untenable, and God will have vengeance on a king who does not hail and affirm Him."

Rehoboam shrugged.

"Have not the priests told my son that Yahweh tests men but does not expect His people to succumb to enticement?"

Uncowed, filled with swagger, Rehoboam unexpecetly challenged: "Unless I am allowed to see my mother, I will visit the establishment at every opportunity. The experienced Danite extended me an invitation to return."

Solomon had given no more than a few random thoughts to Naamah since she had agreed to exile in Rabbath. Nor had he seen or communicated with her after their rancorous parting.

"Why does my son suddenly express interest in the woman who would have sacrificed him to a horrific god, the woman who gave him life but not love?"

"As my father also gave me life but not love," retorted the son.

Startled by Rehoboam's candor, Solomon searched helplessly for a reply. His love for his son was still profound but he was yet incapable of expressing it. And his long dereliction of fatherly duty to Rehoboam would make any assertion of love sound hollow.

Rehoboam let his eyes roam from Solomon to Bathsheba. "On the infrequent occasions when my grandmother has spoken of my mother, she has been set before me as a woman of complete evil, lacking all merit. I wish to meet her and judge for myself."

"In all probability," Solomon said, "Naamah has no wish to see her son. Even if she did, the meeting would end in disenchantment for Rehoboam."

"Your mother," Bathsheba added, "is yet capable of scheming for your death, contriving to force you into the bowels of Moloch so as to placate him at last."

Rehoboam emitted a laugh. "I do not believe it, and I am willing to take the risk."

"She will be no better as a mother to you than she was wife to me," Solomon said. "As king and your father I must forbid the meeting."

Rehoboam's arrogance suddenly crumpled. His body went limp and he seemed a small, frightened child.

"I have nothing," he cried. "All is foreign to me. God has not appeared to me as He did to my father at Gibeon and the temple. God, my father, and my mother avoid me. Who then shall embrace me? Who then shall I embrace?"

Thanks to Nathan, Solomon thought, belief in the Lord God of Israel had come to him early in life. He had not experienced the doubts or indifference plaguing his son. Solomon recalled that David, sparse as his affection had been during Solomon's childhood, had given more love to him than he had given to Rehoboam. It was true his son had neither father nor mother. Worse, Rehoboam did not have the comfort and strength of Yahweh.

For these reasons and in hope that Rehoboam would reject his mother and her god and then turn to Yahweh, Solomon said, "So that my son's wish may be fulfilled, I will send for Naamah."

He could not recall the last occasion when Rehoboam hurried to his side unbeckoned, kissing and cleaving to him with spontaneous affection. Solomon cried within as he felt Rehoboam's tears of pleasure and pain touch his cheek.

* * *

The two citadels hung in a corona of splendid magnificence on Moriah.

The shimmering palace beside the temple was finished at last, everything in place, the hewn stones, the redolent trunks of cedar, and more gold than had ever been used in one structure.

Solomon's chariot horses had come to an instinctive halt in the palace forecourt. The king of Israel had made the journey to his regal mountain alone—he wanted to slip into his new abode unobtrusively, with no ostentation whatever.

He had rejected all plans for a public celebration in connection with his transfer to the new palace, feeling it was not an event deserving of pageantry, because it would invite comparison to the holy jubilee that had marked the completion of the temple. It would be presumptuous, a vainglorious display of disrespect to Yahweh. So he had commanded that not even a private banquet be arranged. Solomon also decisively refused Benaiah's well-meaning but immoderate suggestion that he arrive amid an escort of warriors adorned in golden shields, his way bombarded by trumpets and a cheering multitude. He was still not averse to pomp—and neither were his countrymen, who would welcome an unexpected feast and holiday. But this was not the appropriate occasion. That occasion would soon present itself with the arrival of the Queen of Sheba. Solomon planned to spread the city at her feet.

As his gaze cruised the palace and adjacent buildings, Solomon gave praise and thanks to the Lord for the twofold, overwhelming marvel he had dreamed, worked, planned, and willed into being.

The temple and palace were solid reality, vision mated to achievement, the coming together of his master plan, twenty years in execution.

Now, finally, temple and palace were food and wine for all who belonged to Yahweh. Altar and throne were one, Yahweh and the king of Israel dwelling and laboring beside each other, each in his own house. The junction, in Solomon's mind, was as natural, necessary, and inevitable as the rhythm of planting and harvesting, as harmonious as two perfect notes fondling each other on the lyre. Altar and throne must stand or fall together, each sustaining and supporting the other.

Every section of the new royal complex had been occupied as soon as it was completed. Already ensconced were Benaiah, the most important court officials, and many of Solomon's wives and concubines. Bathsheba and Rehoboam would move into their quarters shortly.

Solomon had shown what many said was undue favoritism, ungodliness, and needless extravagance by building a special, opulent house for Nagsara at the northwest corner immediately behind the palace. But for Solomon the house of Nagsara was no more than a necessary gesture of ongoing friendship to Siamon, whose favor he still valued. Nagsara seldom visited Jerusalem. Virtually all her days were spent in Gezer, where she continued to rule with flair and proficiency. She had proven an indifferent wife but a trustworthy vassal queen, and no one, in fairness, could fault her except on grounds that she did not publicly acclaim and worship God though she labored more strenuously for Him than many people of high and low station who gave but routine if not hypocritical homage to the Lord.

Except for the throne room, which he had not seen, wishing to savor it as a surprise, and Nagsara's dwelling, in which he did not plan to set foot, Solomon minutely inspected every other inch of the complex. Besides the Hall of Pillars and the House of the Forest of Lebanon, he visited his own richly appointed chamber, hung with gold and purple tapestries, the quarters for his women, the rooms in which his officials were already at work, and the commodious barracks which housed the royal body-guard.

Benaiah and Zadok were waiting in the throne room as Solomon entered. Seeing it for the first time took his breath away. He had expected much, but not the art and consummate craftsmanship which drowned him in an ocean of hard, brilliant gold and the lavish wood of Lebanon. So overpowering was his first impression that he briefly felt intimidated by the incredible room with its high, vaulted ceiling, walls and floor laid with the incomparable cedar, and countless sumptuously decorated golden chairs strewn about in clusters of twos and threes.

"No throne like this was ever made in any other kingdom," Benaiah said.

To Solomon, the comment was an understatement.

Fine gold adorned the throne itself as did inlays of marble, beryls and every conceivable gem. The stairway to the summit of the new royal chair was extraordinarily wide. At the edge of the twelve steps, one representing each tribe of Israel, reposed two golden lions and two golden eagles, the beasts and birds eye-to-eye with open jaws and poised talons.

He slowly climbed to the royal seat, distinctively round rather than square, and eased himself against a mound of lush pillows which formed his backrest. Above the throne was a curved, golden awning. On it rested a dove riding a hawk, signifying Solomon's yearning to deliver the world for Yahweh by means of peace through strength.

The adroit Phoenicians had also managed to intermix light, long-lingering scents of perfume around the entire area of the throne, which perfectly complemented the odor of the cedars.

Solomon, comfortably stationed in his chair, stared down at his general and high priest.

"No throne like this was ever made in any other kingdom," Benaiah repeated with undisguised approval and admiration.

"The work is well done," Solomon said, further words of praise failing him.

"Perhaps too well done," Zadok responded from a troubled countenance.

Benaiah's eyes came together like clashing swords. "Cannot Zadok fathom that in this place like no other there is glory for God, king, and Isreal?"

"The house of the king," replied Zadok, "the richness of it, will be misunderstood by many of the most devout and zealous children of Yahweh."

"In what way?" Benaiah demanded.

"In as many ways as there are foolish and myopic men ready to disapprove of what they do not understand," Solomon said with resignation, having anticipated and girded himself for the criticism. "The truth that eludes them is that the palace, despite its apparent opulence, is but a fragment of the temple."

"With all deference to my lord," the high priest continued, "it is said aloud among some of the priests and the people that by devoting more time to the building of the palace than to the construction of the temple, the king has shown disparagement of Yahweh."

"Explain then to those who trifle with fact," Solomon answered, "that the opposite is true. I had the temple rushed to completion as quickly as the sacred work could be accomplished. Fastening the palace to this mountain was done with comparative leisure. It required seven years to erect the temple, thirteen for the palace. The abode of the Lord, moreover, was built with quietness, but in raising the palace the ring of every tool of iron was heard louder than a harvest of thunderstorms. I did not build this residence in haste or stealth. I do not apologize for the palace since it is of God. My first and last allegiance remains with God. I would do nothing to displease Him."

"Yet the king's critics maintain that his allegiance now is to his own comfort."

"Explain then, furthermore, since it has obviously occurred to no one, that I could have ignored my father's wishes and built the palace *before* the temple, or *not* built the temple at all."

Zadok's face was a speechless pageant of horror. Even ever-loyal Benaiah was perplexed at what seemed to him Solomon's sacrilege.

The king allowed himself a brief smile.

"I have shocked my friends," Solomon said. Then, completely serious: "Building the Lord's abode was a command from David, yet I could have shirked, delayed, or forgotten it. But it was also a command from God and my conscience, and therefore impossible to disregard. Still, I could have been clever and cynical and not built the temple by postponing it indefinitely, as men are wont to postpone matters of conscience. I would have built the palace first if, as those who confide in Zadok maintain, my foremost motive had been my own comfort and indulgence."

Zadok sank weakly into one of the golden chairs while Benaiah decided to suspend judgment until the king completed his explanation.

"What profit, it may well be asked," Solomon said, "accrues to me from the temple if building it was the act of a selfish ruler interested only in comfort and wealth? The profit from the house of the Lord is spiritual and sacred, but such cannot be stored in my treasury. In contrast, the profit from the palace will be enormous, paying for itself many times over since it provides the setting to efficaciously govern the nation and the conquered lands and to conduct our commerce."

"But why the enormous size of the palace?" Zadok wondered. "Why is it so much larger than the temple?"

"Because of the sheer, practical needs of my personal and official households. But what does size have to do with the purpose of a building? The temple and palace cannot be compared on that basis anymore than the mountains of limestone in all the quarries of Jerusalem can be measured in value against a small hill of pebble sized diamonds." Solomon warmed to his peroration. "Those with eyes that do not see will note only the palpable, that the palace appears the richer and more imposing of the two structures. But is it? The temple holds the real, bottomless wealth of Israel—the tablets of Moses, the laws that have guided us in the past and guide Solomon now. These are the laws that perpetuate God instead of idolatry, commandments that constitute the code without which civilization would slip back into the hands of barbarians. One day, I dare to hope, the laws given to Moses will truly guide mankind, sowing friendship among all nations. Against this, the palace is but an afterthought."

Considerably mollified, Zadok had yet to clear his mind of another extremely irksome sore spot, one he was certain the king could not justify without admitting to at least a modicum of selfishness.

The high priest declared, "The king has made silver and gold to be in Jerusalem as stones, and cedars made he to be as the sycamore trees that are in the lowland for abundance. Gold is so plentiful in Israel that Solomon has applied not one, but two coats to overlay much of the palace. Why has the king used it with such profligacy? Why do the treasurehouses of the king burst with it?"

"As a priest, Zadok perhaps is not conversant with the logical use of gold," Solomon replied. "In this he is as ignorant as virtually everyone else in the world. I have discovered it is absolutely necessary for me to propitiously hoard gold, for there is great danger in flooding the nation with the metal. Too much gold in the land would drive its value down and make it worthless, leading us to grave economic peril. Too little in circulation would paralyze and stagnate commerce. Gold must be fed to the people as milk to an infant, in proper and prudent quantities. By feeding not too much and not too little, our finances are kept in balance."

"Yet the gold is not shared by all Israelites, many of whom are poor."

"Wealth is relative, dear Zadok. Its distribution is not equal. There are those among us with more riches than others. But it has always been so. Was not Abraham richer than his herdsmen? Unequal division of wealth is a reality that likely will be the condition of man forever since each individual is generally rewarded with gold in proportion to his effort, talent, wit, and circumstance. All wealth stems from the Lord, but the Most High takes a hand in dividing it unequally, why, I am not certain. Perhaps because the less a man sins the more proficient he grows. Yet sometimes evil men enjoy great wealth as did Shimei, the traitorous Benjaminite. Zadok laments for the poor in our midst. I readily admit there are many in Israel who will never taste luxury. But no Hebrew need starve, if he is sound in body and mind and willing to labor. If he is disabled and his days of toil behind him, the tradition is longstanding among us that he be fed by family, friends, or neighbors. Even the non-Israelite slaves eat well and their basic needs are provided."

"Still it is grossly unfair for some men to have so much more gold than others," Zadok said. "It brings discontent and spiritual corruption."

"Our merchants, farmers, and tradesmen, as they become more prosperous, develop expectations of even greater wealth. There is good and evil in such ambition, but more good than evil, for the honest pursuit of gold is blessed by Yahweh since it drives men to create further wealth which in turn is shared to a larger extent by more and more of our people. Can a man without hope of filling his stomach bring his full attention and adoration to the Lord? Can he remain steadfast in his faith? Already the average Hebrew has more riches than his counterpart in any other nation. In addition, Israel offers each Hebrew the opportunity of growing rich in the wealth of this world if he is willing to work longer and more diligently than his neighbor."

Solomon's answers seemed to sway Zadok, and Benaiah's faith in the wisdom of Solomon bordered on the worshipful.

"Now," the king said, "let us speak of another matter. I have received a message that within the year Balkis of Sheba will visit Jerusalem."

Impressed, Benaiah observed, "Some say she is more beautiful than rich, others that she is more rich than beautiful."

Solomon's eyes brightened with interest and anticipation.

* * *

After dismissing his two confidantes Solomon reviewed his discussion of gold with his high priest. As he did so, the vaccuum in his private life returned to haunt him. What he had failed to mention to Zadok was that all his yellow treasure had not yet purchased for him personal contentment, much less happiness or love. His women had swollen to a thousand, yet not one among them could he love intellectually as well as physically.

He reflected briefly on Balkis, scowling as he did so. He knew next to nothing of her but guessed she was hardbitten and possessed the masculine qualities of ruthlessness and brutality that allowed her to rule one of the most strategic and richest nations on earth. Otherwise she could not contend with the men surrounding her who would be probing for her weaknesses, searching out ways to usurp her power. A truly feminine woman could not long endure as a monarch.

From his royal chair he looked down and saw the first of an unending stream of petitioners who would be brought before him so that he could dispense justice. As he began listening to the conflicting versions of two farmers embroiled in a land and water dispute, all thought of the Queen of Sheba was swept from his mind.

Chapter Twenty-three

Five hundred of the finest, strongest, and most handsome of Solomon's Cherethites and Pelethites, their beards freshly cut and scented with oil, joined the long caravan of the Queen of Sheba as an escort of honor when her train entered the gates of Jerusalem.

The imperial troops were bedecked in the oblong golden shields of Solomon, which they wore lightly as summer cloaks although two hundred of the shields weighed twenty-two pounds and the heft of the three hundred small bucklers was about one-third that of the larger ones. Solomon had ordered a minute part of his surplus of gold beaten into the shields. Never before had they been seen publicly, and they were exhibited now as dazzling proof to Balkis of the wealth of Israel.

Strong rays of sunlight glinted against the precious ceremonial armor, and thousands in the elated crowd that cheered the way of the Sabean queen had to raise their hands above their eyes for protection against the reflection of gold colliding with gold.

Balkis was lovely, looking appropriately regal and tantalizingly fresh, as if she had just emerged from her bath. Wearing a white sapphire tunic, an exciting contrast to her dark skin, she ravenously gathered the sights surrounding her from quick, alert olive eyes. The alabaster city was impressive, but not as impressive as the warm outpouring of the people, an exceedingly friendly reception, far more enthusiastic than she had anticipated.

As the Queen of Sheba waved a slim, supple arm at the throng, she was fully cognizant that she was an idolatress in their midst —her god bearing no resemblance to the God of the Hebrews.

227

The generosity and sincerity of her welcome, therefore, was all the more remarkable.

The bargain of love between the multitude and Balkis was sealed when an eight-year-old girl, carried on her father's shoulders, pressed a glitter of bunched yellow wildflowers into the queen's hands. Balkis touched the child's cheek with a kiss and the roar of approval was deafening.

The queen's journey had been arduous and long. She had traveled fifteen hundred miles over mountains, sand dunes, and vast stretches of waterless, lifeless wasteland from her high country capital of Mariaba in southwestern Arabia where gold mines, beryls, and emeralds abounded. But the journey had already been worthwhile. Love from Solomon's people was also an emerald.

Not since the victorious entry of David after the battle of Jerusalem had a monarch arrived in the city amid such approving frenzy. Among the people lining the queen's path it was said that David had captured the city while Balkis was captivating it. And from mouth to mouth, the question rolled with the speed of a bird on the wing: Would king Solomon take this unimaginably rich, young, and beautiful ruler of the lush land beyond Canaan as a bride?

The Queen of Sheba sat atop a portable gold, gem-encrusted throne on the only white camel among more than a thousand in her wake. Clinging to the other beasts was Balkis' retinue of hundreds. The camels were also laden with heavy boxes, which the people assumed contained gifts for Solomon.

After winding its slow, triumphant way through the city, the procession made the gradual climb up Moriah and in the courtyard of the palace her appearance was punctuated by more exclamations of joyous welcome from Solomon's officials and servants.

Two huge Sabean attendants helped their queen dismount. Benaiah, appreciatively noting her exquisite comeliness, accompanied Balkis across a sheepskin carpet which did not end until they reached the throne room, where Solomon was waiting. His purple, tapered robe outlined his still trim figure. The only sign of his middle years were tines of gray that attractively speckled his raven beard and hair. His face was yet unwrinkled.

The Queen of Sheba bowed as the king of Israel rose from his chair and descended the dais. He came to within a few feet of her, finding it difficult to believe the gorgeous young woman before him was not an apparition.

"Blessed be the Lord your God," Balkis said respectfully and formally, "which delighted in you, to set you on the throne of Israel; because the Lord loved Israel for ever, therefore He made you king, to do judgment and justice."

Solomon felt sudden cold fire within him. Courtesy obliged him to respond to Balkis with equal respect and formality. But a ritualistic compliment would be inadequate—he must say to the Queen of Sheba words that were enchanting—words that were more than words. He became oblivious to everyone in the great chamber, the overflowing audience including Bathsheba, Zadok, Rehoboam, and the mightiest leaders of Israel.

Unaccountably, Solomon thought himself no longer in the throne room. He was alone with Balkis under an orange moon in the mulberry grove near the Gihon spring. Without shame or hesitation, he recited aloud the love lyrics from one of Israel's ancient wedding songs:

> *"How beautiful are thy feet with shoes,*
> *O prince's daughter!*
> *the joints of thy thighs are like jewels,*
> *the work of the hands of a cunning workman.*
> *Thy navel is like a round goblet,*
> *which wanteth not liquor:*
> *thy belly is like an heap of wheat*
> *set about with lilies."*

Solomon's voice was timbrel, shophar, psaltery, trumpet . . . and the strum of David's lyre . . .

> *"Your head upon you is like Carmel,*
> *and the hair of your head like purple;*
> *the king is held in the galleries.*
> *How fair and how pleasant you are,*
> *O love, for delights!"*

There was a bout of embarrassed coughing and a low, gruff, shocked murmur among many of the onlookers.

"The beard of Yahweh blushes crimson," Zadok whispered fiercely to Bathsheba, and Bathsheba replied testily, as she always did when assessing any foreign woman who enthralled her son, "This one is not *that* beautiful. If she is half the queen a queen should be, she will express her insult to my mad son whose language is as insolent as it is tasteless."

But there was cold fire in Balkis, too. In her mind she and this handsome, romantic king—already her suitor?—were afloat by themselves on a lake the color of wine. Or perhaps they were marooned in a bower garlanded by blossoms that no god had yet created, blossoms that stabbed the air with perfumes which none but she and Solomon had ever savored. And she lilted a Hebrew wedding chant that seemed most natural:

> "I am black, but comely,
>   O ye daughters of Jerusalem,
>   as the tents of Kedar, as the curtains of night.
> I am the rose of Sharon,
>   and the lily of the valleys."

Solomon responded:

> "I have compared you, O my love,
>   to a company of horses in Pharaoh's chariots."

And she chorused:

> "Behold, you are fair, my love;
>   behold, you are fair."

She stepped within an arm's length of Solomon and in silver, senuous, soliloquy sang:

> "My beloved is white and ruddy,
>   the chiefest among ten thousand.
> His head is as the most fine gold,
>   his locks are bushy, and black as a raven.
> His eyes are as the eyes of doves
>   by the rivers of waters,
>   washed with milk, and fitly set.
> His cheeks are as a bed of spices, as sweet flowers;
>   his lips like lilies, dropping sweet smelling myrrh."

Transfixed, their voices lifted together in harmony:

> "His (her) mouth is most sweet:
>   yea, he (she) is altogether lovely.
> This is my beloved,
>   and this is my friend,
>   O daughters of Jerusalem."

The eyes of Solomon and Balkis mated, and their child was instant, tender, mutual, certain love.

The moments of sharing a strange and other-worldly bliss, an intensely private communion in the midst of witnesses, the giving of themselves openly one to another in a manner which no one present could understand or condone, were shattered by a blast of Solomon's trumpeters announcing a parade of Balkis' attendants, who entered two by two carrying strongboxes fashioned of rare, exotic, and unfamiliar woods.

Balkis dipped her head—the movement similar to a rose bending before the wind. Her servants overturned the boxes, spilling gold, diamonds, and spices to the floor.

When the wave of gasps by those in attendance subsided, Balkis told Solomon, "My gifts are unworthy treasure for the king of the Hebrews."

"The gold and diamonds of Balkis," Solomon said, "do not shine as her skin. Her spices are rare, but more rare is the woman who is Sheba the Queen."

Saying nothing more, for to say more might lessen the perfection that had passed between them, Balkis turned and departed.

Watching her willowy body retreat was akin to chasing a shard of rainbow. For the first time in his life, Solomon understood the power of passion.

Chapter Twenty-four

The story of their efflorescent meeting in the golden palace on Moriah flew through Israel with the speed of a stone pitched from David's sling. Unlike the reaction of chagrin and distaste of many onlookers in the throne room, the coming together of Solomon and Balkis struck a romantic chord in the average Hebrew citizen, particularly the young. They and the bulk of their elders considered the episode an inspired interlude, approving of their king and the daybreak-lovely queen falling instantly in love as might any Hebrew man and woman.

The sensitive confrontation between Solomon and Sheba's queen became a pattern to epic romance. Scribes and singers of songs would recount and embellish it orally and on papyrus for many years. Later, lovers in other times and places would repeat the rhapsodic words exchanged by the two sovereigns. Each new generation would draw inspiration from their beautiful encounter.

The soaring incident, as far as most ordinary Israelites were concerned, far overshadowed the expected generosity of Balkis' gifts. The proffering of gold and diamonds for a ruler of her stature was but a token. Unexpected and much admired was her intimate acquaintance with the earthy, resonant chants of Hebrew tradition, and that she had given herself so warmly to Solomon. Among the populace there was certitude that Solomon and Balkis would be married, the setting of the far desert's rarest jewel into the crown of their king.

Solomon shared the common feeling. For him, the meeting with Balkis was life-changing. Suddenly he had found the woman for whom he had been searching so long. For Solomon, they were already one bone and one flesh. Except for Zadok joining

them formally, their dreamlike, provocative introduction in the
throne room had been a nuptial. Quickly they had vaulted the
steps toward wedlock: the initial physical attraction, the court-
ship of seductive lovers' words and vows, the joining of their
minds and thoughts as a single entity,

Yet within Solomon, there was an edge of doubt. Would Balkis
consider him a worthy husband? Was he beguiling himself, smitten as a young, love-sick shepherd? He could not expect their
first interaction—precisely because it had been so unusual and
rare—to continue at the same feverishly amorous pace.

Solomon decided to explore the relationship to its core. He
totally abandoned all other affairs to spend every possible moment at Balkis' side. He personally conducted her tour of Jerusalem and its outskirts, pointing out the site at Gihon where he had
been crowned and great Gibeon where God had come to him in
a vision. He walked with her in the mulberry grove and his
orchards and gardens, inspecting David's old palace, now con-
verted to quarters for many of his less prestigious wives and
concubines.

On a scarlet sunrise morning, he ran his chariot up the Mount
of Olives and showed Balkis the path leading over the crest
where David had been forced to flee when he could not initially
stem the revolt of Absalom. At the summit, they examined the
high place of worship used in Samuel's time which was abandoned after the construction of the temple. He explained that
here the rite of purification by the priests had been performed—
the burning of a red heifer to ashes as the first step in the preparation of the lustral water.

Nightfall brought the rising of a new moon, and he had Balkis
light the torches which traditionally signaled its coming. The
flames, Solomon said, could be seen twenty-seven miles to the
northeast.

He spent a day showing her the rooms of his palace. The next
day he ordered his Cherethites and Pelethites to again wear his
golden shields when Balkis attended with him a sacrificial
ceremony at the temple. Solomon gave the customary burnt
offerings to Yahweh. And though Balkis did not join in the
adoration she displayed surpassing respect and reverence.

The feast Solomon commanded in tribute to Balkis a week
after her arrival was held in the sumptuous banquet hall of the
palace. The guests were the pride of Israel: its noblest, mightiest,

and most important personages. Throughout the meal the chiefs of Israel came to the royal table and exchanged polite gusts of conversation with Balkis. Each departed reluctantly. To a man they were charmed by the aristocratic queen, fully appreciating Solomon's enchantment with her. Balkis was witty, intelligent, candid, curious, and civilized. Her manner conveyed to each man his eminence while at the same time inoffensively hinting that she was in fact superior. It was a quality the leaders of Israel found irresistible, and it did not seem to matter to them that she was not of Yahweh. If they could be said to have one common reaction, it was envy of Solomon.

Balkis even managed to please Bathsheba, who for once had lost her petulance and distrust of a foreign woman. She was enjoying herself, filling Balkis' ears at every opportunity with gossip from the harem. Rehoboam's eyes did not stray for a moment from the queen. But though she could not be much older than himself, Solomon's son did not know what to say to this sophisticated yet uncomplicated regal beauty. He counted himself fortunate merely to be at the table with the Queen of Sheba.

Zadok, embroiling himself happily in the gaiety of the occasion, allowed himself an unaccustomed luxury—a second goblet of wine, which he consumed too quickly. As the liquid fell like a spring rushet down his throat, he concluded optimistically that if he had to perform the wedding of Solomon and Balkis, the queen would be the foreign wife most easily won to Yahweh. Except for Solomon and Balkis, both relaxed and in highly convivial spirits, Benaiah was enjoying the feast more than anyone. He savored the delicious deer meat and regaled the queen with accounts of his battlefield exploits. And with amazement he learned that Sheba's standing army was no more than a few hundred men, and those were used more for ceremony than defense.

"The desert is our general, the sand dunes our warriors, the mountains our fortifications," said the queen of the isolated kingdom. "We are at peace with all nations, wanting nothing from them but commerce and friendship."

Benaiah's response was drowned out by a bellow from the assemblage. The entertainment was beginning and the guests immediately became engrossed with the clever pranks of trained baboons from Ophir and the deftness of a conjurer who appeared to draw a scorpion from the bodice of Balkis' carmine cloak. Solomon and the queen laughed uproariously. After the dancing, musicians and singers rendered innumerable Hebrew and Sabean ballads.

Balkis had noted the excellence of the meal, the attentive efficiency of the serving men and cupbearers, the elegance of Solomon's table with its eating utensils and drinking vessels of pure gold. She had been impressed, delighted, and overwhelmed by the rugged charisma of Benaiah and the other chiefs of the Hebrew empire, by the splendor of the temple and the palace, the white glory of Jerusalem, and all the works of these vigorous people. But she was yet to be persuaded of Solomon's wisdom. Despite his display of poetic skill, his attentiveness to her, his attraction as man and king, she hadn't discerned the brilliance of his mind. The infrequent travelers to her realm had relayed endless stories of his acumen. However, she had not herself beheld evidence that Solomon was as wise as his reputation.

When the music ended, Balkis said to Solomon, "Happy are your men, happy are these your servants which stand continually before you, and hear your wisdom."

Fending for a reply which would not betray conceit or immodesty, his glance caught Rehoboam slouching in his chair with his protruding eyes fixing Balkis with indecent hunger. His son was a living testament to his lack of wisdom. Recent reports concerning Rehoboam were negative and disappointing; his tastes still ran more to fornication and a penchant for idolatry than to scholarship and fealty toward Yahweh.

For the first time during the long night of celebration, Solomon spoke seriously to Balkis.

"Whatever the Queen of Sheba has heard concerning my sagacity is grossly exaggerated. I have not, nor, I fear, will I ever make total use of the wisdom given to me by our Lord."

Misreading the intensity of his mood, unaware of its source, Balkis asked, a thin cut of sharpness in her voice, "Is the discernment of the king truly undeserved?"

"My lord's fame for wisdom is justly earned!" Benaiah snapped with reflexive loyalty.

"The main reason for my journey to Israel was to prove the king with hard questions," Balkis said, her eyes riveted on Solomon. "Surely he will not refuse to answer them." Mischievously she added, "If indeed Solomon *can* answer them."

Solomon grimaced. Balkis's "hard questions" would be no more than a game of riddles, a game in which correct answers were mistakenly equated with wisdom by all desert peoples, Israel being no exception. Actually, riddles were a bore, a children's pastime. He remembered those David had dangled before him as a child. He had learned the answers by rote and they had ceased to be amusing. True wisdom, Solomon knew, lay elsewhere than the serpentine cleverness of language. He understood he was being challenged and tested, but had no inclination at this time to indulge in verbal swordplay. Besides, he had consumed too much wine and did not think he would acquit himself well. He was about to divert the attention of those at his table by removing from the inside of his robe a giant pearl, a gift for Balkis. But all at once Bathsheba was on her feet, calling out loudly, "The king will answer the queen's hard questions."

As ever, his mother's fascination for games could not be quenched.

The guests swiftly gathered in a large, closely pressed circle around the royal table.

"Ask on," Solomon said with forbearance. "Prove me, if you must."

Balkis' purpose was not to embarrass Solomon, only to satisfy her curiosity by testing the king and, she was sure, confounding him. In any case, the game would be harmless sport.

Balkis smiled confidently and began: "What is the clothing that a woman wears, which her husband never sees?"

"The garments of mourning," replied Solomon instantly.

"What is the plant that even the blind can recognize?"

"The thorn bush."

"What is as broad as the earth and can yet pass through the eye of a needle?"

"The wind."

The smile of Balkis was gone, her annoyance evident as she continued:

"What runs without having feet, and roars without having a mouth?"

"The sea."

"What is it that a god never sees, a king seldom sees, and most people see every day?"

"An equal."

"What was yesterday and will be tomorrow?"

"Today."

The guests applauded Solomon spontaneously and loudly. In spite of his earlier reservations, Solomon was deriving pleasure from the competition. His only uneasiness was for Balkis. Nostrils flaring, she seemed irritated that he had matched a perfect answer to each of her riddles.

Stubbornly Balkis demanded, "Is the king prepared for further questions, the most difficult that the learned men of Sheba have been able to originate and gather?"

There was no artful way of bringing the game to an end, but perhaps it would be hospitable if he intentionally gave incorrect answers, permitting Balkis a victory as he had sometimes deliberately permitted Bathsheba to defeat him at hounds and jackals. He was still toying with the notion of allowing Balkis to save face when she posed the next riddle:

"There are three things that are never satisfied, like a leech forever craving more."

"The grave, the barren womb, and earth that is not filled with water," Solomon answered correctly. He would have given Balkis her triumph except that she attempted to deceive him by ommitting the last of the riddle. "Forever unsatisfied, too," he added, "is the fire which never says, 'Enough.'"

Her confidence not completely shattered, Balkis doggedly went on: "What three things are too wonderful to understand?"

"The way of an eagle in the air. The way of a serpent upon a rock. The way of a ship in the midst of the sea." Again she had tried deception. "And the fourth," he said pointedly, "is the growth of love between a man and a woman."

Vexed, Balkis realized it was she who was suffering embarrassment. She had not only failed to confound the king but had twice been caught attempting to mislead him.

"There are three things," she persisted, "that make the earth tremble." Then she caught herself quickly, refusing further deviousness. "No, there are four things that trouble the earth."

"A slave who becomes a king," Solomon responded easily. "A fool who is filled with meat. An odious woman when she finally marries. And a servant girl who becomes more precious to a husband than his wife."

"I have two more hard questions, by far the most perplexing," Balkis said, her humiliation transposing itself to growing admiration of Solomon.

"Very well," the king retorted quietly, with no suggestion of superiority.

"What are the four things which are little upon the earth, but they are exceedingly wise?"

"The ants are a people not powerful, yet they store up food for the winter. Cliff badgers are a feeble folk, delicate little animals who protect themselves by living among the rocks. The locusts have no king, yet they go forth, all of them together in swarms so that they are united and strong. And the spiders are not difficult to catch and kill, yet are found even in the palaces of kings."

"Tell me then, finally, the names of the four stately monarchs of the earth?"

"The lion, which is strongest among beasts, and turns not away from any. The peacock. The he-goat. And a king, against whom there is no rising up."

Balkis stood and bowed to Solomon.

"My beloved," she said, "it was a true report that I heard in my own land of your acts and of your wisdom. Howbeit I believed not the words until I came and my eyes had seen it. And, behold, the half was not told me; your wisdom and prosperity exceeds the fame which I heard."

There was a long hush in the great room.

How, Solomon wondered, could he respond to such an expression of praise, which he considered more florid than accurate. Since any retort would make him sound arrogant or pompous, he decided to say nothing. Instead he rose and extended his arm to Balkis. Together they walked from the banquet hall as the musicians resumed playing and the guests dispersed to their places. They agreed that the riddle contest had been the highlight of the evening's entertainment.

As Solomon escorted Balkis to her quarters, the queen, still astonished by the depth of the king's mind, thought Solomon was a ruler unparalleled in the world.

For Solomon, Balkis' concession of defeat had been gracious and her estimate of his wit too generous. But now he interpreted her laudable estimate of him as the signal for which he had been waiting.

At the doorway to her chamber, Solomon retrieved the pearl from his robe. He reached for Balkis' hand and placed the huge white precious stone, imbedded in a gold ring, on her finger.

"Will Balkis be my wife?" Solomon asked.

"It is a privilege for me to love Solomon and greater privilege to have his love returned."

The flow of her smile was a current of promising assent.

But the Queen of Sheba, to Solomon's consternation, closed her door without replying one way or another to his marriage proposal.

* * *

The visit had lasted more than a month, and the tiers of ministers rendering assistance to Solomon and Balkis had readily come to written arrangements for trade and reciprocal respect for the inviolability of each other's territory. Hebrew grain, fruits, and horses would be exchanged for Sabean gold and minerals. The two rulers had signed their names to the treaties of commerce and friendship.

Solomon and Balkis were sitting now on a blanket of earth in the tranquil mulberry grove. They were dressed carelessly, and their attendants remained a discreet distance away out of hearing.

They talked for an hour of small things, then wolfed a meal of figs and melons, quaffing a good portion of a skin of wine in sheepherder fashion. Holding the skin aloft they pressed it, letting the liquid spurt in a curve into the back of their mouths. Neither was expert at the maneuver, and when they missed they stained their faces and clothing, then chortled like misbehaving children.

"Dearest one," said Solomon, and it was not the wine but his heart giving tongue to his feelings, "she who was meant for a thousand delights, rise up, my love, my fair one, and come away with me."

Hers was the laughter of pleasant things under the heavens.

They had not again discussed marriage. Solomon had been dumbstruck when Balkis had enigmatically refused to accept or reject him. But since she had not refused, he assumed she was exercising a woman's prerogative to be coy. He was confident their marriage was a certainty. How could it be otherwise? The visit had proceeded flawlessly, their closeness increasing each day.

Now he believed the mood and moment were propitious for him to repeat his proposal.

"The king of Israel wishes the Queen of Sheba for his wife."

"And the Queen of Sheba wishes the king of Israel for her husband," she answered.

Solomon's face was alight with pleasure and satisfaction.

"The time of the singing of birds is come," he said joyously, "and the voice of the turtle is heard in our land. Our wedding will be magnificent and our marriage glorious."

"Dearly beloved," she said gently, "there will be no marriage between Solomon and Balkis and yet the king of Israel and the Queen of Sheba shall be married."

"For such a riddle, I have no answer or understanding. Does Balkis refuse and mock me at the same time?"

"I refuse marriage, but I do not refuse the king of Israel."

"Balkis persists in her riddle," he said, his joy turning dark. "Two empires joined by marriage as the result of a king and a queen who love each other. Where is the harm in it? How better may we serve our nations and ourselves?"

"As man and woman, everything brings us together. If there is perfection for mortals, we are ideally suited. But as king and queen we are irreconcilably set apart, and thus there can be no ordinary marriage between us."

"If it is my other wives and concubines that trouble Balkis, I shall rid myself of them and place you at my side as my equal after you have accepted Yahweh."

"Such gesture from Solomon would be noble, but foolish. Solomon cannot shed himself of his women and keep peace for Israel. The king himself has explained to me the wisdom of collecting females as an instrument of statecraft. Without his wives and harem, Solomon forsakes his throne and Hebrew freedom. The people of Israel would surely be conquered and enslaved, if not exterminated. The great nation of Yahweh would be no more."

"Balkis understands well the peculiar circumstances of my throne. However, if my women are not a deterrent, I will keep but ignore my wives and concubines, which is already the situation."

"It is not the dismissal or retention of the women that separates us. What keeps us apart is that I do not, cannot, and will not accept Yahweh."

"But why? Yahweh would look with favor on our marriage. We are already linked closely in the matter of God. Sheba and

Israel have a common father. It is written in our scrolls that
Keturah, the second wife of Abraham, whom he married because
he was lonely after Sarah's death, was the mother of six sons.
Sheba was one of the lands founded by a son of Abraham and
Keturah."

"Keturah was a lesser wife than Sarah, little more than a
concubine. And though it is true that we share common ancestry
it is also true that we do not in any way share the same god. I
worship Attar, who is the sun."

"It is but a step from worshipping the sun to worship of Yahweh, who made the sun."

"It is not a small step. And if it were, I could not take it. I can
no more abandon Attar than Solomon could desert Yahweh.
Attar is female, which is why women are held in high esteem in
Sheba. To her I owe all my power and allegiance, as Solomon's
loyalty is to the God who inhabits the temple on Moriah."

"What then shall become of the love I bear for Balkis? It
cannot easily be set aside. Many waters cannot quench love,
neither can floods drown it."

"Between love and god, the preference must be god."

"Yes, but I question if it is truly the will of Yahweh that we
not be joined in marriage. I have married many foreign women
with strange gods, yet my Lord has not condemned me."

"There is more to consider than our diverse gods," Balkis said.
"My people would not support their queen even as the equal of
Solomon, for they regard her who rules Sheba as superior to all
the monarchs of the earth. And in the eyes of Israel, I am an
idolatress and thus unacceptable as queen. Our thrones cannot
be linked through marriage. One of us would have to abdicate.
Solomon cannot give up his throne. Nor can I. Formal marriage
between us would be disastrous. Solomon cannot rule Sheba and
I cannot rule Israel."

She moved closer to him, moving her hands to his cheeks. "As
queen, I am allowed as many husbands as the king of Israel is
allowed wives, but they must be servants of Attar. I will in all
likelihood marry many men, but I will love none of my husbands
as I love Solomon. Yet, as I told the king, I wish to be married
to him, but in a manner that I pray both our deities will understand, if not condone."

Solomon stared at her blankly.

"For this special marriage of ours," Balkis whispered, "I wish a special gift from Solomon."

"I have offered my empire, my throne, and my love. Barring my devotion to Yahweh, which is sacred and sure and cannot be changed, what else can I give the Queen of Sheba?"

"So deeply do I love King Solomon that he can give me a gift to treasure all my life—a son."

"You would have my son and not his father!" Solomon said in amazement.

"Upon reflection, Solomon may agree the circumstances are not unusual. The king has Rehoboam, but does not have his mother."

"Such was not my intent. Though the marriage turned lame, we were wed by Zadok with Yahweh as a witness. Balkis asks the impossible, to father a child conceived in fornication."

"Conceived in love," she amended. "Yes, I wish Solomon's son, a son that he will never see as we will never see one another again. For if I were to share once more the sweet and honeyed companionship of Solomon, my resolve would weaken and I would destroy the trust reposed in me by Attar and my people, who need me as I need them, who need me as Israel requires the indispensible Solomon."

Now she quickly ran from him and directed one of her attendants to carry her back to the palace astride his horse. Solomon watched in dismay as she disappeared swiftly in a swirl of dust.

That evening they were again alone in Solomon's apartment. Again he implored her to marry him. Again she refused, saying, "Let us speak together as we spoke when first we met, in the poetry of your chants." And she sang:

> *"Let him kiss me with the kisses of his mouth, for your love is better than wine."*

And Solomon chanted:

> *"Your teeth are like a flock of sheep that are even shorn, which came up from the washing; whereof every one bears twins, and none is barren among them."*
> *"Because of the savor of your good ointments your name is as ointment poured forth, therefore do the virgins love you."*
> *"Your lips are like a thread of scarlet, and your speech is*

comely: your temples are like a piece of pomegranate within your locks."

"The king has brought me into his chambers: I will be glad and rejoice in you; I will remember your love more than wine; the upright love thee."

"Your two breasts are like two young roes that are twins, which feed among the lilies."

"You are all fair, my love,
There is no spot in you."

Then Solomon gave the Queen of Sheba what she had requested.

* * *

Less than a year later a letter arrived from Balkis.

"Dearly beloved," she wrote; "I have given birth to our son, whose name is Menelek. He is as playful as a young lion. I believe Attar is well pleased, and all Sheba celebrates, for I have not kept it secret that Israel and Sheba are thus united."

Unable to read further, Solomon crushed the damning papyrus in his hands. He thought of the son he would never see and of the dark and lovely Balkis who he would also never see again. *"Until I have no more breath, I shall love you, fair one,"* he breathed. And he thought once more of the uselessness and bitterness of gold and power, and that the sum of all he had and was could not bring him the Queen of Sheba.

The time since her departure had been a morass of corrosive pain and long-suffering, of anxious meditation, of attending to the tasks of the throne out of instinct rather than intelligence.

He knew that in losing Balkis he had become a different man. In ways not yet fully charted, something of inestimable worth was gone from him.

Chapter Twenty-five

The world that Solomon had known as a younger king was crumbling. As the siege machine and chariot had brought a revolution in warfare, the four winds of change howled pell-mell toward his throne with billows of insurrection against peace.

A fresh realignment of power within and without the perimeters of the Hebrew empire had unleashed dangers so menacing that chaos beckoned if the shifts in strength were allowed to proceed unchecked.

The continued possession of the conquered lands was already in dire jeopardy. The very survival of Israel as an independent nation was threatened. Most depressing and discouraging of all, Solomon faced a plethora of newly risen, belligerent adversaries who could not be reasoned with, who seemed to be bent on destroying the peace he had so assiduously fashioned. He had apparently sacrificed his private life for a goal that now appeared doomed to failure.

The latest blow was the fall of Damascus, the first parcel of his dominions to be wrenched from his grasp since he became king. More frightening, according to the fragmentary information Benaiah had received from a courier, was that Rehoboam had almost been killed in the battle for the distant oasis. In the company of other survivors, Rehoboam was now returning to Jerusalem. Solomon had ordered Benaiah to meet his son and bring him immediately to the throne room for his eyewitness report.

As he waited, wondering if Rehoboam had been wounded, Solomon considered the collection of problems besetting him.

Unceasing demands still flowed in for lower taxes and the abolition of compulsory labor—these volatile issues would not die and his explanations were not understood nor accepted by an increasing number of Hebrews. He realized that these two policies which continued to vex the nation, particularly the ten northern provinces, might fan open rebellion if a new, dynamic leader emerged to exploit the discontent. Solomon had a gnawing presentiment that such a champion would spring from the people to cause him blistering grief.

He brushed the unpleasant foreboding aside, attempting to gird himself with the armor of confidence. He was still king and could yet conquer any internal or external antagonist. Had he not, in more than thirty swiftly gone years of overseeing Israel and the vassal states, coped with and defeated all his enemies?

But his confidence did not flower as he thought of the recent developments in Egypt, which were far more ominous than his domestic difficulties and the loss of Damascus.

Siamon had been murdered in his palace by Shishak's Libyan barbarians. The new pharaoh held undisputed sway over the land of the Upper and Lower Delta, and had displayed blind, uncompromising enmity to Israel.

Shishak had permitted Hadad, prince of the defeated house of Edom, to sneak back to his homeland and begin guerrilla warfare. Hadad had spent long years in exile in Thebes, where he had been sent as a child when Joab began his six-month bloodbath of retribution, killing every male in the conquered kingdom. During Solomon's visit to Egypt he had tactfully avoided mentioning the asylum Siamon was affording Hadad. Since the prince of Edom no longer seemed a threat, Solomon had been content to let him remain undisturbed in exile. Solomon's father-in-law would have delivered Hadad at Solomon's request though the Edomite had married Tahpenes, an Egyptian princess. The Egyptian-Hebrew alliance was more important to both kings than the life of Hadad.

Now Hadad's opportunity for vengeance had come. Sacrificing the comforts of Thebes, he lived as a marauder with a band of several hundred followers, most of whom he recruited in Egypt. Ensconced in the hills and scrub-bordered trails, the band ambushed small caravans and two- and three-man Israeli army patrols.

Despite Benaiah's strenuous objections, Solomon would not send his army to ferret Hadad and his men from the hills.

"A leopard does not contend with a locust," the king told his commander-in-chief. "To do so invites derision. I will dispatch the army only if Shishak provides Hadad with considerably more aid in men and weapons, only if the locust becomes a leopard. For now, you are to station as many men as necessary along our southern frontier. Their mission will be to intercept Hadad's supplies from Shishak. Also, you are to provide strong contingents to guard every caravan. Hadad will soon be paralyzed and his raids against us will cease. When those who follow the Edomite prince become aware their leader is helpless, they will abandon him and Hadad will return to his Eyptian wife."

The strategy did not prove completely successful. The hit-and-run raids of the Edomite chieftain diminished but did not stop. Whatever slim hope Hadad nourished to free Edom from Israel was no doubt being kept alive by the unpredicatable Shishak, with whom Solomon had made every effort to seek an accomodation . . . to no avail.

Solomon composed letters to the pharaoh suggesting that they meet to discuss the renewal of their treaty guaranteeing peace, friendship, and commerce. The correspondence had been insultingly returned to him—unopened! Then his ambassadorial staff in Thebes was expelled. Trade between the two nations had reached a standstill. Shishak could not be bargained with. He was irrational, and as Siamon had called him, "a savage."

Solomon thought, morosely, that Siamon's overthrow by the intractable Libyan had canceled out all the positive diplomatic and political effects of his daring first marriage to Nagsara. It had canceled out his hard-won peace with an ancient enemy, bringing Israel and Egypt to the brink of war.

Solomon did not expect that during his lifetime, Shishak would attempt an armed invasion of the Promised Land. Israel was yet too strong and essentially united. Hebrews might disagree among themselves, often abrasively. However, they would rise as one to defend their sacred soil against an Egyptian attack. But he realistically feared the sweep of events after his death. If the ten provinces of the north, talking more and more boldly of breaking away from Judah and Benjamin, made good their threat, Israel would be so eviscerated that the disunited nation would invite attack and defeat. The northern provinces would not dare the step of declaring themselves independent of the south while he was alive. He would, he had let it be known, chastize them with whips if that became his only recourse to keep Israel intact. But if the fissure occurred after his death, his legacy would be war and schism instead of peace, plummet, and line.

The ambitious Libyan would certainly move against a divided Israel. Again Sons of the Covenant would be broad-axed and Hebrew women violated. The temple would be desecrated if not destroyed, stripped of its gold, thus depriving Israel of its transcendent symbol of unity. The question, therefore, of his successor daily grew more important. His successor should be cast of iron. But since he had fathered no other acceptable sons, the heir to his throne would assuredly be Rehoboam, and he was made of clay.

He knew he had failed, miserably so, to groom Rehoboam as Israel's next king. But David had not been groomed, either. The youngest of Jesse's six sons, he was no more than a stripling shepherd when Samuel anointed him. And Solomon had been selected to rule at the age of twenty without preparation, then the Lord had given him wisdom and the capacity to successfully oversee and maintain the empire—thus far at least.

A potter could make of his manchild an able potter, and the progeny of a farmer could be molded into proficient farmers. It was perverse and puzzling that a king seldom, if ever, could pass on those qualities which make his heir an effective monarch.

If Rehoboam did ascend the throne, perhaps Yahweh in His perfect wisdom would thrust greatness and sagacity on his son.

Rehoboam's unachieved excellence, or even competence, was not entirely his fault. He was the product of a ragged, diffuse, confusing environment, weaned prematurely from the soaring inspiration of Yahweh and exposed via his mother while too young and impressionable to the dark, angry Moloch. Even as Solomon attempted to give Rehoboam every justification, a scorching thought followed: As matters stood at the moment, his son was a heart-flutter from power. Was there an idolater waiting in the shadows who, in the event of his sudden death, would inherit the crown? What then of Israel's future?

As he had promised Rehoboam, Solomon brought Naamah, still the graven-image worshipper, back to Jerusalem and built for her a capacious, costly house at the edge of the city. His hope that his son would reject Naamah was in vain. Rehoboam had instead gravitated to a mother who was a creature of leisure and mischief, having little to do but play the spoiler and wreak revenge on a husband she despised. Spending countless hours with her, Rehoboam had grown closer to Naamah and Moloch than to himself and Yahweh. As king, he had been so absorbed by his obligations and continuing inability to communicate his love to Rehoboam that he had lost his son by default. Solomon had won only one victory—absolutely refusing the frequent requests of both Naamah and Rehoboam to journey to Ammon. He was fearful that Naamah would somehow contrive to sacrifice his son to Moloch.

Solomon had finally concluded that it was useless to compete with Naamah for Rehoboam's affection and loyalty. He gave up castigating his son for drawing close to his mother and her god. Such arguments widened the gulf between them. Desperately he had confided his distress regarding Rehoboam's behavior to Benaiah, who immediately made a pragmatic suggestion: a warrior's tour of duty to a remote station. "Damascus," said Benaiah, "would have the twin advantages of separating the lord Rehoboam from his mother while forcing him to make good his obligation to serve the nation. It would give him a sense of responsibility and an opportunity to taste and observe a corner of the empire which he may someday rule."

Solomon had instinctively objected. "I have no desire for my son to be schooled as a warrior. The idea is repugnant. It contradicts my yearnings for Rehoboam as a potential king to be dedicated to peace."

"I do not urge that Rehoboam take up the sword," Benaiah argued, "only that he beholds from a soldier's viewpoint, without the presence of his father or mother, what the sword has won. Quiescent Damascus, where there is small chance of danger, would be ideal."

Realizing that his wish to be close to Rehoboam was as forlorn as it was unrealistic, Solomon relented. He ordered his son to the oasis, where no trouble had occurred since David had conquered the strategic outpost and made it a tributary of Israel.

The decision brought Bathsheba's vigorous disapproval. Although her now thirty-year-old grandson still wounded her with abuse, disrespect, and indifference, she remained loyal and loving. Still spry in body and mind, her face a mass of wrinkles, Bathsheba had declared: "It is criminal to risk the life of Rehoboam among a people who are unfriendly to us. Solomon sends his son into perilous exile."

"My son is an exile to me in Jerusalem. As for danger, Benaiah assures me it is minimal."

"If the heir of the house of David must serve in the field, why should it be with heathen? Why not send him to a friendly Hebrew province, where Yahweh is worshipped? Why Damascus?"

"Why not Damascus? Place has little to do with commitment to the one true God. Rehoboam has lived in Yahweh's land all his life, and is yet hostile to the Lord. I would rather see my son in Damascus than have him remain under the influence of his devious mother. Naamah is more perilous to Rehoboam than the Damascans."

Naamah, on the other hand, had been delighted with Rehoboam's assignment. She had appeared before Solomon for the first time in years, asserting brashly, "I pray each night to my god that Rehoboam is engaged in battle and dies a death of honor. Then Moloch will finally have his offering."

He dismissed her with disgust—"Naamah is more a curse than a mother."

Rehoboam himself had been all but flogged into the chariot waiting to transport him to Damascus. In the end, he had gone because there was only one disgraceful alternative, which carried the threat of severe punishment.

"If Rehoboam refuses the post of Damascus," Solomon said, "the court and people will consider him cowardly. Your choice is to serve or to be banished from the palace and your position as heir-apparent. You will be penalized as are others who evade the army, by seven years labor in the quarries. The patience I have shown my undeserving son is at an end."

"Does the wisdom of my father amount to no more than this transparent effort to force my service like the king's slaves who have no choice but to render obedience?"

Solomon replied: "In time I pray you will come to see that there is wisdom in commanding you to participate in the work of the empire instead of continuing your pointless and parasitic life, which is as much to be condemned as your fascination with idolatry. Your whoring and your admiration for Moloch are products of your idleness."

"I tire of these accusations of idolatry. I have still not given full allegiance to any god. If there is idolatry in me, it is my father who is to blame. He married my mother knowing she was pledged to Moloch. And it is my father who has married many other women not of Yahweh. Between us, who is the idolater?"

"My marriages of convenience to women with other gods have not brought condemnation from the Most High. And for good reason, a reason which accounts for the difference between us. I love and fear the Lord, and Rehoboam, alas, does not."

"Whatever the king wishes, he justifies by invoking the approval of Yahweh. Is this not taking the name of the Lord in vain? How can I love such a God and love a father who shows himself to be a hypocrite."

Before Solomon could answer, Rehoboam turned on his heel. He left Solomon wondering if the charge of hypocrisy was true. Would it have pleased Yahweh more if he had married only one or a few Hebrew women? But if he had done that he could not have cemented the nation and empire through alliances. The foreign marriages had been difficult and fraught with complications, but Israel had survived and flourished. And so the Most High must be pleased.

The unpleasant scene had occurred more than two years ago, and Solomon had decided to hold back any announcement of a successor to his throne. Yahweh might yet show him a replacement infinitely more suitable than his son.

Now he heard a scuffling of feet, a jangle of armor, and Solomon saw Rehoboam and Benaiah hastening toward the dais. With relief he noted that his son wasn't wounded, but he looked ragged and disconsolate, the hapless victim of a failed mission.

Without formalities Rehoboam related: "Our garrison at Damascus has been slaughtered, our warriors beheaded and disembowled. Of our force of more than two hundred, only nine survived the massacre."

Solomon accepted the baleful tidings without comment.

Benaiah, still doughty but shamefaced, added: "Three of my men under the protection of a moonless night managed to rescue the lord Rehoboam during a pause in the attack. Only the protective, merciful intervention of God saved the king's son from death, and the king's general, who severely misjudged the danger in Damascus, from the unbearable sorrow of knowing he had a part in sending a prince of Israel to a premature grave."

"I beseech Rehoboam and Benaiah," Solomon replied calmly, "not to overly concern yourselves with the loss of a waterhole."

Benaiah's eyes screamed surprise. "Surely my lord is aware that Damascus is far more than an oasis. Damascus guards our caravan and military routes north to the Euphrates, westward to Phoenicia, and southward to our own Jerusalem."

"My father has not heard the worst of it." Rehoboam said wretchedly. "Rezon, the accursed leader of the Damascans, is as dangerous as a hungry viper. He has not forgotten or forgiven the shame that befell his mentor, Hadadezer."

Solomon quickly reminded himself of the long-ended battles between David and King Hadadezer. David had soundly defeated the dogged Hadadezer three times.

"Rezon now considers himself so powerful," Rehoboam continued, "that he has declared his independence of Israel. He calls himself King of Damascus and refuses to pay further tribute to Israel."

For Benaiah, the solution was clear and obvious. At last his crack Israelite army would be sent into battle. "Shishak, Hadad, and Razon are all devoted to our destruction," said Benaiah. "Yet our army is strong and anxious to protect Israel and each foot of the empire. Damascus can be reclaimed in a day, and Hadad routed from his mountain hiding place in a week. If we act swiftly and demonstrate our strength and resolve, the Libyan pharaoh will be cowed and not dare to march against us."

"Despite the three prongs of opposition poised against Israel," Solomon responded, "I cannot countenance direct military action. Before engaging in war, we must explore all paths to peace and discover how to turn foe into friend. At the same time we must keep our territory and prestige unimpaired."

"Hadad, Shishak, and Rezon will never be friends of Israel. Let the army attack," Benaiah pleaded.

"I mourn the deaths of good Israelites at Damascus and Edom," Solomon countered. "But my soul would cry out in deeper anguish if additional Hebrews were to be sacrificed before the search for peace was exhausted."

Benaiah challenged: "Then my lord would permit the slayers of our brethren to go unpunished?"

"Rather than uselessly compound the letting of blood . . . yes! Benaiah is too quick to commit us to a course that could lead to a battle on three fronts simultaneously, and his expectations of lightning victories are perhaps too optimistic. If we now move in force against Hadad, Shishak may use our action as a pretext for sending his legions across our border. As for Rezon, he is merely another locust masquerading as a leopard."

"My father is a coward!" Rehoboam said hotly.

The charge of cowardice was an old one, but it had always to be answered.

"If love of peace is cowardice," replied Solomon patiently, "I am a coward. But the God of Abraham and Isaac, Jacob and Moses, of David and Solomon is not a coward. If war is demanded of us, Yahweh will show me the absolute necessity for it. I have not yet been given that command from the Most High."

"We must have vengeance!" cried Rehoboam, ignoring his father's rebuttal. "The murder of our men is a call to vengeance."

At least, thought Solomon, his son's service in Damascus, though it ended in horror, allowed him to observe firsthand the sordid underbelly and malignant motives of Israel's enemies. Rehoboam was no longer a troublesome palace adornment, born to privilege while eschewing responsibility. As he himself had changed, so, too, had Rehoboam become a different man. The Damascus experience propelled him into a confrontation with reality.

"Nathan taught me early in life that only Yahweh is permitted vengeance," Solomon said. "My son has been unduly influenced by Moloch who instructs his followers to seek revenge and human sacrifice. What difference would there be between the teachings of Yahweh and Moloch if I sent sons of Israel into battle needlessly? If Rehoboam knew more of the ways of Yahweh instead of Moloch, he would understand his father as well as our Lord."

"I have a deeper understanding of Yahweh than does my father, who has made the Lord of Israel a craven, fearful God, bereft of courage. David interpreted Yahweh correctly. My grandfather considered himself the instrument of Yahweh's vengeance. What if the shepherd of Judah had been as timid as my father? There would be no Israel, no empire. If David were now our king, he would follow Benaiah's advice—and that of Yahweh—by smiting our enemies."

"My son," Solomon answered with conviction, "there is a time for blood, and a time for the absence of blood."

"David," Rehoboam continued, again ignoring Solomon's response, "would send the host of Israel, swords in hand, to annihilate Rezon and Hadad. He would also march to the pharaoh's palace in Thebes and destroy him!"

This was too much even for Benaiah. "An invasion of Egypt is unthinkable," he said hurriedly. "But we must institute heavier reprisals against Rezon than we have with Hadad. Damascus must be retaken. Otherwise Rezon's defiance of my lord Solomon will spread to the other Aramean kings who are among us throughout the empire. For the moment they remain our vassals, but these petty rulers could incite their peoples to rebellion. And they are capable of forming a confederation against us. The Aramean leaders are restive and grasping. As the sun probes the dark places of the earth to shed light, the conquered Arameans search for our weaknesses and will unleash the blackness of total war with high loss of Hebrew lives and possible defeat of Israel unless we strike first. Only then will we have peace."

"Vengeance," Solomon declared, "is a stark, superficial act which breeds further vengeance and death. Vengeance is a primitive weapon to be used only under the most extreme circumstances, when all else has failed, when there is no choice but to fight for Yahweh. Only then does it become meritorious and honorable. Vengeance by itself ill befits a great nation ruled by a God unsurpassed. We must use the mind to conquer the mace. Again we must choose the far more difficult paths of compassion, forgiveness, subtlety, and reason to find peace. We must use these unviolent substitutions instead of revenge, for that is the essence of Yahweh. The effort must be made to defeat Rezon, Shishak, and Hadad without battle."

With a wave of his hand, Solomon indicated to his son and general that their audience was at an end.

Departing, Benaiah trembled inwardly for the future of Israel, and Rehoboam raged at the enigma separating a wise man and a fool. Both were convinced that Solomon could find no solution that would keep Israel free of war.

Chapter Twenty-six

Solomon *did* keep Israel from going to war, which proved to be the least of his concerns in the closing days of his life and reign. Before final sleep, he would have to contend with two overwhelming crises, which both dwarfed his Damascan difficulty. Solomon's premonition that an appealing, rebellious leader would rise from the people was to come true. And far more significant, God would visit him a third time—but on this occasion with a stinging rebuke, disapproval, and condemnation for setting in motion a chain of disasters for Israel that would endure thousands of years.

Unmindful of the climactic sweep of events facing him, Solomon tended to his immediate task. He planned to utilize strategy, diplomacy, the prestige of his position reinforced by gold, and, inevitably, marriage.

The more he considered a military reprisal against Damascus the more he came to abhor the idea. His stewardship of Israel had been marked most strikingly by the absence of Hebrew participation in any hand-to-hand conflict. A battle now would revive Israel as an imperial, warlike nation, severing Zion from the umbilical cord of peace. Rezon's taking of Damascus did not pose a direct threat to the homeland. And Benaiah's assessment that Damascus could be retaken in a day was wishful thinking. A battle to take Damascus would be grueling and strewn with useless loss of Hebrew life, even useless loss of Damascan life.

Rezon refused a meeting to settle their differences. But Solomon perceived a way of regaining the advantages afforded by the Damascus terminus without physically attempting to reoccupy it.

Such a victory would be sufficient.

Damascus was strategically located, but it was not strategically indispensable. What Rezon had in fact conquered was an oasis, a small population of poor, backward subjects living harshly in an undeveloped land. Rezon was the self-declared king of a stab of geography which was important though not vital to the interests of Israel.

The key to preventing war lay with the clutch of Aramean kingdoms and their rulers. By themselves, as Benaiah had made clear, none of the small city-states was strong enough to fight Israel, but if amalgamated they could present devastating opposition. However, Solomon felt that Benaiah erred in assuming the Arameans would act as one. Solomon sensed that these vassal kings would each be more concerned with his individual welfare than with Rezon and his ambitions for further conquest.

Solomon thus convened a conclave of the Aramean kings and they came to Jerusalem, half in fear, half in perplexity. What could the Hebrew emporer be seeking from them? Among themselves they considered Solomon more devious than wise—he was well known to have as many bends to his mind as a crooked stick. Moreover, they never before had been accorded such importance.

Solomon found the ten Aramean kings distasteful, none completely barbaric, none completely civilized. He talked with them singly and together, finding them sensual, selfish, rude men who ignored the golden forks at his table to eat with their fingers. And as he suspected, they were totally immersed in themselves, caring little for their own people, much less Rezon. Solomon's feeling that they were essentially disunited proved correct. He listened closely and with interest to their petty tales of woe, bickering, and jealousy. All of them denounced their fellows. His impression was that any one of them would slit the throats of any of his peers for a few hundred shekels.

The Arameans spent a week as Solomon's guests in the palace. They were gall and wormwood, but they were also shrewd, and whenever Solomon turned the discussion to Damascus they turned the advantage to themselves.

This was Solomon's intent. Before presenting them with more formal proposals, he met alone with each of them, finding without exception that each was amenable to bribery. He negotiated, in exchange for their loyalty to him, a sum of gold for their own

treasury. Some haggled, some did not. In the end, all made a
settlement; all had a price.

Solomon thought he might one day tell Zadok of this further
use of gold, how a king could buy peace like a jug in the marketplace. He chastized himself for offering the bribes, but justified
it on obvious grounds. It was better to pay for peace in gold
rather than lives. But not for a moment did Solomon trust the
word of any of the Arameans. He cannily insisted, therefore, that
his payments to each king be parceled out over a period of ten
years.

When he gathered them for their final meeting, he set down
conditions carefully tailored to appeal to the self-interest of each
Aramean king. Their self-interest, fortunately, coincided with
his needs.

Solomon offered them additional gold for their armies, making
the terms especially attractive since he guaranteed he would
never use their troops as fighting mercenaries. He wished only
that they keep their armies neutral in his dispute with Rezon.
The Arameans agreed. His second proposal was the lessening of
tolls for their caravans into Israel. The kings stamped their feet,
signaling approval. Then Solomon suggested, and for this too
there was unanimous assent, that he take from each of their
families a wife or a concubine.

King Talmai, of Geshur, one of the more powerful of the
Aramean rulers, was swept away by Solomon's generosity. He
asked, "Will the king of the Hebrews accept for his son Rehoboam one of my daughters in marriage?"

Solomon acquiesced, remembering that David had married a
Geshurite named Maacah who became the mother of Absalom.

The Arameans left Jerusalem in high spirits, knowing they
were richer by far than when they had entered the gates. They
also felt they had bested the astute Solomon, given little, and
gained much. They left Jerusalem thinking it miraculous that
so great a fool as Solomon had somehow amassed so much
gold.

Solomon had purposely filled the Arameans with gold and
wine. He knowingly allowed them their smugness while disdain-
ing them as stupidly self-satisfied, short-sighted, and greedy as
Ephron had been when the Hittite had sold the Cave of Machpelah to Abraham. For Solomon, the conclave had been a huge
success. Again he had avoided war, and the confederation of

Arameans that Benaiah had so feared became a confederation allied not to Rezon, but to him.

Over the next few years, Solomon's policy of containment was extremely successful. Damascus and Rezon became no more than minor thorns in his side. It was true, as some said, that he had lost a piece of the empire, but in actuality he had, as in his maneuvers concerning the Galilee strip, increased the riches of Israel. Because of the lesser tolls, trade between Israel and the Arameans grew. The profit earned from this commerce far exceeded the amount of gold Solomon spent to buy the neutrality of the Arameans. He had thus maintained peace at a profit in lives as well as gold.

The caravans of the Arameans that would normally have stopped at Damascus simply avoided the way-station, bypassing it for alternate oases. Damascus was the only immediate area where Rezon held power. Rezon became only another locust masquerading as a leopard. By himself the king of Damascus could not prevent the flow of increased trade into Israel. In addition, the westward road to Phoenicia was closed to him. Hiram of Tyre found Solomon a far more agreeable and reliable ally than Rezon. The roads south into Israel were also closed to Rezon as were the northern routes to Zobah, Hamath, and Tadmor, near the Euphrates.

To tighten the circle, Solomon ordered five thousand men from the fortress and chariot cities to surround Damascus. Solomon permitted food to pass through, but weapons were confiscated.

As long as the Israeli-Aramean alliance held, Rezon was helpless to cause further trouble. The Damascan ruler became a prisoner within his own narrow kingdom.

Solomon's strategy also served to discourage further provocations from Hadad and Shishak. Hadad grumbled sullenly in his Edomite mountains, helpless as a deer before a lion. It was only a matter of time, Solomon calculated, before Hadad returned to his Egyptian wife. Meantime, Shishak was busily engaged in consolidating his power. Not all Egyptians had been pleased with his usurption of Siamon's crown. Many had preferred the murdered pharaoh, and there were pockets of resistance holding out against Shishak. As Solomon was dealing with internal enemies, so, too, was the Libyan. Shishak therefore made no move against Israel, perhaps biding his time. But his flow of weapons to Solomon's enemies within Israel subsided to an ineffectual trickle.

Content with the progress and success of his moves against Rezon, Hadad, and Shishak, Solomon turned his attention to further building, fortifying the Jerusalem wall in the northwestern portion of the city. Begun during David's reign, the Millo, as the wall was called, needed lengthening and widening so as to give the alabaster city absolute protection. Solomon set several thousand laborers to the job of repairing and extending the breach.

One hot and humid afternoon, Solomon, accompanied by Benaiah, rode down from Moriah to inspect the wall. As always, the king, impatient for the work to be done, wished to note and measure the daily progress. As they rode at a slow gallop, Solomon spied a tanned, long-haired, long-legged worker moving efficiently among the builders. Solomon had Benaiah halt the chariot, and for a long time he watched the handsome, sweating figure at work. Smoothly he directed the masons, burden bearers, and stonecutters through their tasks. Solomon noted the workers not only obeyed the man but grinned as they did so, and grinned harder, the more demanding his shouts for them to toil more quickly. He had a discernible knack for leadership; by acting as a gruff yet agreeable comrade to the laborers rather than a leathery, one-dimensional overseer, he seemed to get twice the amount of effort from the men. He cursed and cajoled, gave encouragement, and chatted. Most impressive was that his section of the Millo was rising faster than anywhere else along the line.

Solomon ordered Benaiah, to bring the man to his chariot.

Moments later he was bowing before the king, his smile as white as the wall he was erecting.

When Solomon asked his name, he replied, "Jeroboam, an Ephraimite from the village of Zeredah."

"The work proceeds well," Solomon said.

"I beg the king to consider that more than stones are needed for the Millo in order to protect Jerusalem."

"The stones are wide and high. Will they not suffice?"

"To make the holy city invulnerable, a moat is also required."

More impressed than before, Solomon declared with enthusiastic appreciation for Jeroboam's acumen, "Then build the moat."

Solomon soon put Jeroboam in charge of all construction on the Millo and came to greatly admire his industry and ability. From his governor in Ephraim Solomon learned by discreet inquiries that Nebat, the father of his new favorite, had been thrown from a horse years before and killed. His mother, Zeruah, was a leper. The family was of excellent repute and ardent in their worship of God.

Under Jeroboam's skillful and vigorous prodding, the entire wall and moat were finished before schedule, in less than a year.

To further test Jeroboam, Solomon made him overseer of all public works in Ephraim and Manasseh. The reports that first flowed back to Solomon were exciting. Jeroboam had made an auspicious beginning. Construction of the new city of Sarira on Mount Ephraim was proceeding smoothly. Like himself, Jeroboam was a dedicated, hard-working builder. He was committed to the nation and empire, and a true servant of the Lord. Jeroboam was everything that Rehoboam was not. He had strength and character and was seemingly devoid of weakness. He was everything Solomon yearned for in a son. So lofty was his opinion of him that Solomon began to consider elevating Jeroboam as his successor.

Then disturbing reports began to cast doubt on Jeroboam's loyalty. According to Solomon's governor, Jeroboam had become an opportunist. The king was shocked to learn that his protege had apparently made a league with the most conservative priests in Ephraim and Manasseh. He vowed to them that if the throne of Israel were his he would dispense with Solomon's tyrannical, spendthrift ways. It was also reported that Jeroboam upbraided Solomon as a perverter of the will of God. Too, it was declared that Jeroboam had rallied thousands of Israeli workers and had become their spokesman, promising that as king he would abolish the hated system of forced labor.

Hastily Solomon sent for Jeroboam, unable to believe he had been so severely mistaken regarding the young Ephraimite's motives, personality, and ambitions.

"Jeroboam arrives with three hundred chariots and perhaps a thousand men, crudely armed," said Benaiah. "But they will be no match for our troops. Yet Jerusalem crackles with tension and rebellion churns the air."

Jeroboam approached the throne, wearing hauteur and disdain like a sword. He was the first to speak. "The people hail me as the new king of Israel! To show my humanity—I will spare Solomon's life if he leaves the city by tomorrow after abdicating his throne and naming me his successor!"

Unintimidated, more disappointed than angry, Solomon answered, "Jeroboam is as Absalom. David, when the moment was ripe, would have gladly handed him his throne. But he too, was impatient. I had it in my mind and heart to name you king if you proved deserving. Now you have shown yourself a jackel in this wretched, clumsy attempt to unseat me. You act ignobly, disgracefully, and without honor for my equity as king, without regard for my age or what I have given to Israel." Solomon waited for a moment before continuing. "I am grieved beyond consolation over your actions, for I regarded you as my son."

Jeroboam laughed uneasily. "I would not have a father who so mistreats his people. If you refuse to step aside, I will be compelled to take the throne with force."

"Has God anointed you? By what authority do you dare claim the crown other than as the leader of a handful of deluded and ill-advised laborers and priests?"

"By the authority of Ahijah, the Shilonite prophet. I met the holy man in a field and he wore a new garment which he rent in twelve pieces, saying unto me: 'Take ten pieces;' for thus says the Lord, the God of Israel: 'Behold, I will rend the kingdom out of the hand of Solomon, and will give ten tribes to you.'"

"Your prophet is false. He is your co-conspirator and has led you astray."

"The prophecy is true. It will come to pass."

"I am a man of peace," Solomon said, standing to his feet and, angry now, shaking his fist at Jeroboam. "But I will fight to keep my throne. Only Yahweh can depose me, and til I hear from the Most High I will remain king."

"Let me scythe away his head," declared Benaiah.

"No," Solomon replied. "If Jeroboam renounces his treason and his appetite for my place, his life will be spared."

Jeroboam stalked from the throne room.

By the next day, Solomon had cause to regret his mercy. Jeroboam, had gathered several thousand men outside the gates of Jerusalem and they were preparing to attack the city.

"He has lifted up his hand against the king; his rebellion is serious and fraught with danger for Israel," Solomon said ruefully. Events had proceeded with such haste that a part of him still thought of Jeroboam as his son. Nevertheless, he gave the command he did not wish to give. "Very well, Benaiah, see to his execution."

Several hours later Benaiah informed Solomon: "My host easily managed the dispersal of Jeroboam's followers without inflicting any casualties. But Jeroboam escaped. Several of his men say he fled to Egypt."

Solomon was not entirely unhappy that the tall Ephraimite he had sighted at the Millo was still alive. Paradoxically, he still found qualities in Jeroboam he could admire. And in some measure he was able to think of Jeroboam as his son while he yet found little in Rehoboam to approve. Of late, Rehoboam was visiting and offering sacrifices to Yahweh at the temple, but Solomon was not convinced that Rehoboam's dedication to the Lord was genuine. He felt Rehoboam was playing a role and making a sham attempt to placate him. Solomon knew his son had evinced interest in succeeding him as king.

The fire of discontent in Solomon's soul was not cooled when Rehoboam came before him several weeks after Jeroboam's escape. Benaiah had confirmed through his spy network in Thebes that Jeroboam had reached Egypt safely and been welcomed warmly by Shishak. "It seems that I have no choice but to name you king," Solomon told his flesh and bone son. "How fares your relationship with Yahweh?"

"God draws closer to me."

Solomon said nothing more, but he had the inescapable feeling that Rehoboam's attachment to the Lord was not deep.

"I pray you," said Rehoboam in a conciliatory tone, "to see my mother. Naamah is old and she has a final request of my father."

Solomon agreed to give her an audience. Time had dimmed his rancor for his Ammonite wife.

Looking spent and ill, Naamah presented herself to Solomon, saying in a voice filled with dignity, "If it please the king, let me order servants to the Mount of Olives and there build an high place for Moloch. Solomon has kept me apart from my god since our marriage. Before I die, and the physicians inform me I will die soon, let me make peace with Moloch."

Despite his many disappointments, notably those regarding Balkis and Jeroboam, Solomon had lost none of his ferocious belief in the supremacy of Yahweh. The most significant change in his attitude toward the Lord of the Hebrews was a feeling of liberality and compromise, a feeling that Yahweh could co-exist in Israel beside other gods. The first commandment ordained, *"Thou shalt have no other gods before me."* Solomon had no other gods before Yahweh, but why could not Yahweh countenance the presence of high places, shrines, and altars to gods who were no competition for His might and truth. Where was the harm in granting the request of a now harmless wife who would build a lifeless idol?

"Go then and erect your high place for Moloch," Solomon said with virtual disinterest, feeling he had long ago made peace with Yahweh and could not offend Him. Besides, his mind was busy with plans for another imperative—writing a testament that would detail his life, a papyrus that perhaps would outlive his structures of gold and jewels.

But Solomon had understimated the significance of giving Naamah permission to build her high place. Now he was beset on all sides from his myriad wives and concubines that they also be allowed to construct places of worship to their gods. He had no choice but to honor all the requests. In fairness, he could not make Naamah an exception.

Soon on the Mount of Olives there was also a shrine to Chemosh, cousin to Moloch, which was erected by one of his Moabite wives. Then his Hittite, Edomite, and Zidonian wives and concubines pocked the landscape of Jerusalem with all manner of altars to their gods. At least, thought Solomon, the worship of these gods was now out in the open. They had been idolized secretly within Israel since the founding of the Promised Land.

Still, he was concerned that he had gone too far. If only he had Nathan to confer with, to buttress him. He now feared there was too much liberality and compromise, too gross a violation of the first of the commandments.

Less than a year following his acquiescence to Naamah to build her high place, God came to Solomon late one night in his chamber. In appearing before him now, Yahweh's voice was the voice of anger, his message brief but far-reaching:

"Wherefore, forasmuch as this is done by you, and you have not kept My covenant and My statutes which I have commanded you, I will surely rend the kingdom from you and will give it to your servant. Notwithstanding, in your days I will not do it, for David your father's sake; but I will rend it out of the hand of your son. Howbeit, I will not rend away all the kingdom; but will give one tribe to your son for David my servant's sake and for Jerusalem's sake which I have chosen."

And then Yahweh was gone.

"Lord God of Israel," cried Solomon, "do not condemn your servant, Solomon!"

Chapter Twenty-seven

Since catastrophe was to be his inheritance to Israel, Solomon's testament seemed more necessary than ever.

The desire to accomplish this task before he died burned in him like an unquenchable flame. When it was completed, the fragile papyrus would be given to his scribes for copying—and then his Book of Ecclesiastes would—he hoped—become an essential part of the wisdom literature of the ages.

But Solomon was not writing solely for the ages. Always he had felt more comfortable with the written word than the scepter, and his goal, as he shuffled his mound of papyrus into an orderly pile at the table in his chamber, was to assemble one life, the only life he knew. By holding a clear mirror to his three-score and ten years, he wondered, would he reflect the experience of one man ... or all mankind? His Book was to be an act of unsparing self-examination, a summation of an era, the record of a time that would not come again.

Most important of all, his Book was penitence for his transgressions and a search for repentance. David, earthy and viseral, had rent his clothes and begged publicly for forgiveness of his sins. But Solomon, king and emperor who had been excoriated by the Most High, was of a different cast, more cerebral and undemonstrative. He would seek redemption through meditation and declaration.

His reed writing instrument began to flash, and as he wrote, stopping after each passage to think through the significance of what he was composing, he felt like a climber on foot, without food or water, making his way step by tortured step to the summit of the world's highest mountain.

The climb would be long and danger-strewn, for there was

much to reflect upon, much to regret, and much to reclaim. And he knew not if he would reach the summit . . . nevertheless, the trek must be made.

"The words of the Preacher," he began, "the son of David, king in Jerusalem. 'Vanity of vanities,' says the Preacher, 'vanity of vanities; all is vanity.' "

He remembered one of the shorelines reached in the drifting sea of his days—that morning when Nathan had awakened him to say that his father had passed the crown to him. But the throne had been vanity—emptiness, a hollow triumph. No matter the accomplishments of his tenure. Even for a king life was fallow. Presumably the most blessed and fortunate of the earth, even a king could have little while having much.

And if a king found it so, how searingly sad must be the lives of the multitudes who never know much beyond raw contention for survival and simple satisfactions.

"What profit has a man of all his labor which he makes under the sun?"

If life was measured in terms of toil and struggle, there was no reason to attempt anything of value for nothing had lasting value.

Had he not worked almost non-stop for Israel and yet been rejected by the Lord? Was he not cruelly despised by many of his countrymen, defamed as nothing more than a tyrant, his alleged wisdom counting for nothing. Beyond Israel, in lands where he had sought only friendship, he had only enemies.

Was this his reward for four decades of heart-bursting effort? Who was there to comfort, thank, and extend even token appreciation of him?

All was emptiness, the sweetness of the honey of life extracted, leaving a vomitous stench in his mouth.

"One generation passes away, and another generation comes; but the earth abides for ever."

Where was man's place in such a disordered, capricious scheme of things?

David had been king and now was dust. He was king, and soon would be dust, the only use of his decayed flesh to perhaps rekindle a farmer's pasturage or to be swept by the wind to the Great Sea. Where was the purpose of life if the end was dust?

How was it that the earth endured forever and man for only an instant? Now his generation, alas, was passing to Rehoboam, and already his son's rule was blighted because his father had sinned grievously in the eyes of God.

Surely all was vanity and chaos.

"The sun also rises and the sun goes down, and hastens to his place where he rose. The wind goes toward the south and turns about to the north; it whirls about continually and the wind returns again according to his circuits."

In the earth there was order, purpose, and plan for the sun and wind. God had ordained this chain in nature ... favoring the earth, the sun, and the wind above man. And so man was not the equal of a harvest, a sunrise, a sunset, a zephyr ...

There was no logic to the thought that unthinking dirt and the elements were immortal while that a thinking man, who could fashion a wheel, concoct a poem, carve beauty into a mountain, master the earth, and utilize the sun for his comfort and sustenance was destined to vanish.

Why did God so waste a man made in His image and His most precious resource? Because man in Eden had eaten of the tree of knowledge and therefore was punished with afflictions of mind and body and shortness of days? Would God have preferred man to remain ignorant?

No, He would have preferred man to keep his innocence.

"All the rivers run into the sea, yet the sea is not full; to the place from whence the rivers come they return again."

The myriad and diverse thoughts of a man fill his mind with passing contentment, but his dowry is unhappiness, which will inevitably come back to batter his dreams and hopes, teaching him that existence is as vacant as it is brief.

"All things are full of labor; man cannot utter it. The eye is not satisfied with seeing nor the ear filled with hearing."

He had built the temple and palace, cities and great fortifications, yet found himself weary and bored with what he had raised. The music of the hammer, the song of Israel, had ended— and what was there to replace it? Only unfulfillment. All that was within sight and sound was monotony, emptiness, and bone-tiredness.

"The thing that has been, it is that which shall be; and that which is done is that which shall be done; and there is no new thing under the sun. Is there anything whereof it may be said, 'See, this is new'? It has been already of old time, which was before us."

Abraham's altar and the wilderness tabernacle of Moses had preceded his grandiose temple. But at root and essence they were the same, committed to the identical end of serving Yahweh.

God put a limit on thought and experience. Life was not alone empty, but repetitious; only conceit or stupidity made man believe otherwise.

The Lord gave him wisdom, but without realizing it until now, he had not been able to originate one new idea.

"O Yahweh, how puny You made Your servant, man!"

"There is no remembrance of former things; neither shall there be any remembrance of things that are to come by those that shall come after."

Remembrance of things past was an abomination to most men: memory caused guilt and fear. It was a reminder that the past was father to the future—and the future was death. The more a man looked backward the more aware he became of his own mortality.

Who recalled with honest sorrow the pangs of Abraham, the grief and glory of Moses? Who cried now because Moses only sighted the Promised Land from afar?

The travail and works of Solomon would also be forgotten— the agony of keeping peace, the energy devoted to over twenty years of building the temple and palace on Moriah. The structures would fall one day to the weather, to an invader, or be replaced by new kings with new monuments. Then they and their works would in turn be forgotten.

"I the Preacher was king over Israel in Jerusalem. And I gave my heart to seek and search out by wisdom concerning all things that are done under heaven; this sore travail has God given to the sons of man to be exercised therewith."

The more he had learned and the wiser he had become, the greater his disenchantment. His wisdom was proverbial and he had made his kingdom Israel the eye of the world . . . and yet he had no surcease of sorrow.

"I have seen all the works that are done under the sun; and, behold, all is vanity and vexation of spirit."

He had lived fully, deeply, had sought out all manner of pleasures, explored all the possibilities life offered a rich king. But even the possessor of limitless gold and a thousand wives and concubines had not found inner rest. King or commoner, all men shared the burden of disappointment. At the road's end lay woe in wait like an avenging angel.

"That which is crooked cannot be made straight ..."

Happiness was not only impossible, but life was a never-ending paradox. A problem solved was not a final solution. Like the wind, the grief returned. He had allied himself with Egypt only to see Egypt turn again against him in hostility. He had made straight a crooked, long-lasting enmity only to find it again turned crooked. The beginning of a thing was identical to the end of a thing.

"... and that which is wanting cannot be numbered."

Love unattained; rest for Israel; a good and righteous son. These were among his hundred thousand wants, some yet undreamed. But why dream when everything was to be denied him, including community with Yahweh, which was his greatest want?

Life was a masquerade, an anomaly beyong the power of man to understand.

"I communed with my own heart, saying, 'Lo, I am come to great estate, and have gotten more wisdom than all they have been before me in Jerusalem;' yea, my heart had great experience of wisdom and knowledge. And I gave my heart to know wisdom ...''

God had granted him much, including wisdom, but wisdom was not the same as capturing the total knowledge of the divine, knowing-feeling-understanding the ways of Him who was the wheel in the middle of a wheel.

"... and to know madness and folly: I perceived that this is also vexation of spirit."

There had been moments of pleasure, moments of release from the taut string of life, but sadness bounded back. He had inherited the wind. The north, west, south, and east corners of his mind and spirit whirled uncontrollably with a storm of strife —troubles without termination.

"For in much wisdom is much grief; and he that increases knowledge increases sorrow."

Paradox again. The humiliation of man was that the more he knew the less he knew.

His gift of wisdom from God had been incomplete.

A sage was no better than a stonecutter. Nay a stonecutter was better than a sage, for the laborer's lack of wisdom often shielded him from sadness.

"I said in my heart, 'Go to now, I will prove you with mirth, therefore enjoy pleasure;' and, behold, this also is vanity. I said of laughter, 'It is mad;' and of mirth, 'What is it?' I sought in my heart to give myself to wine, yet acquainting my heart with wisdom; and to lay hold on folly; till I might see what was that good for the sons of men, which they should do under the heavens all the days of their life."

He had eaten from heaping platters of pleasure and wisdom, but both had jaded him. If pleasure was unsatisfactory and wisdom unrewarding, what was left?

"I made great works; I builded houses; I planted vineyards;

I made gardens and orchards and I planted trees in them of all kind of fruits;

I made pools of water to water the wood that brings forth trees; I got servants and maidens and had servants born in my house; also I had great possessions of great and small cattle above all that were in Jerusalem before me."

He had been king of kings and yet no match for the Lord of Lords, who had said, "Because you have not kept My covenant and My statutes which I have commanded you, I will rend the kingdom from you."

Everything for which he had labored, save the combined tribes of Judah and Benjamin, was to be given to Rehoboam. All else was to be wrested from him.

"I was great, and increased more than all that were before me in Jerusalem; also my wisdom remained with me."

From where the world began to where it ended, there never was a sovereign such as he. His wisdom saved the life of a harlot's infant, and he had uttered three thousand proverbs which commended the pursuit of wisdom, piety, liberality, domestic faithfulness, and honesty in commercial relationships. His proverbs condemned the vices of intemperance in eating and drinking, licentiousness, falsehood, sloth, contentiousness, and the keeping of bad company. But all his wisdom came to naught —in his final failure to keep Israel from public idolatry.

Rehoboam also had the mark of failure upon his brow, though he knew it not. And so did Jeroboam, Shishak, Hadad, and Rezon. Great and lesser kings were doomed to flicker and then mix with the dust, forgotten.

Life was a candle lit so briefly. A tree would outlast a candle, a rock outlast a tree, and a mountain would live longer than a rock. Only God lived longer than all.

"Then I saw that wisdom excels folly as far as light excels darkness. The wise man's eyes are in his head; but the fool walks in darkness . . ."

Surely there was more reward in doing right instead of wrong, practicing good rather than evil; more satisfaction in knowledge than ignorance. Knowledge created. Ignorance accepted or tore asunder.

Without knowledge life would be unbearable. Never to know the loftiest thoughts thought by man, never to have the capacity to discern between true and vulgar wit, never to know the cadence and beat of poetry or the subtleties of music, never to know the difference between what was worthwhile and what should be valued at less than a sheckel—yea, there were good things under the sun. Still:

". . . I myself perceived also that one event happens to them all. Then I said in my heart, 'As it happens to the fool, so it happens even to me; and why was I then more wise?' Then I said in my heart that this also is vanity."

The wise man died, aware of regret. The fool died, sensing regret. But both wise and foolish descended to dust.

"For there is no remembrance of the wise more than of the fool for ever; seeing that which now is shall all be forgotten in the days to come. And how dies the wise man? as the fool."

The grave was the leveler. It made king and sheep herder equal. Worse, their deeds and their lives went unremembered. Life was here and now . . . for the living; mourning for the dead and the works of the past was pointless and brief.

How long had he mourned David? Too briefly. How long would Rehoboam mourn him? Even more briefly.

"Therefore I hated life; because the work that is wrought under the sun is grievous to me; for all is vanity and vexation of spirit. Yea, I hated all my labor which I had taken under the sun because I would leave it to the man that shall be after me."

The proud monuments he had achieved—the abode of the house of the Lord, the palace, the fortresses and chariot cities, Ezion-geber, his navy and all the host of his mighty army, the walls of Jerusalem—all of it would not even pass to Rehoboam, who was to be king over only one tribe. Who would rule the rest of the nation and empire?

Jeroboam?

Shishak?

A stranger?

"And who knows whether he shall be a wise man or a fool? Yet he shall have rule over all my labor where I have labored and wherein I have showed myself wise under the sun. This is also vanity."

He had prayed and hoped for a suitable successor, but had failed his son as he had failed God. He had neglected, deserted, and abandoned Rehoboam and God. Rehoboam had come of age and was to follow him on a diminished throne. As king, Rehoboam would be weak, wanting, and self-indulgent. He was not a scholar of peace. There was little likelihood that Yahweh would visit Rehoboam with even the limited gift of wisdom Solomon had received.

"I pray, Israel, for you. I pray, Zion, for you."

For this Promised Land now shorn of promise I pray righteously and fervently, though my prayers be heard by a God who has judged me severely. O Israel, Zion, the Promised Land ... I prophesy that soon your last free breath will be taken for generations unnumbered ...

The rule of David my father and his son Solomon spanned eighty years ... Israel's golden morning, noon, and night. David did much that was good. Therefore this Jerusalem will for ever be called by his name, the City of David. As for me? There have been worse guardians of Israel. I built a house in which the Lord chose to dwell. And that was wise. And I let places be built that were an abomination to the Lord. And that was not wise.

I have been a wise fool.

What poor implements are words, for how can a man be wise *and* a fool? Study this testament of Solomon and you will know.

"There is nothing better for a man, than that he should eat and drink, and that he should make his soul enjoy good in his labor. This also I saw, that it was from the hand of God."

To ease those fear-ridden hours when a heart takes not rest in the night, perhaps it is good that God granted man the capacity for pleasure. Assuredly, if happiness did not exist there would be no unhappiness, but why was there more unhappiness than happiness? God gives man the desire for enjoyment, yet he is in an ambush hiding grief.

"To every thing there is a season, and a time to every purpose under the heaven; a time to be born, and a time to die . . ."

Life began in pain on the birthstool, then was dotted with fleeting joys, eventually to lamentation. From the moment of the beginning of life the grave waited.

Felled now like two of the rarest cedars of Lebanon were Bathsheba and Benaiah, taken to the sleep with no awakening. Also dead were the accursed Naamah, who had led him to his idolatry, and Nagsara, though Gezer remained loyal under the rule of a trusted governor.

Gone, too, was Hiram of Tyre. Only Zadok remained, but he was in his senility and no aid to Solomon in this period of his deepest sorrow and longing. At sixty, Solomon had had his time to be born; soon it would be his time to die.

". . . a time to plant, and a time to pluck up that which is planted . . ."

He paused in his writing and went to his chamber window. It was the harvest season, and out beyond his view in the Hebron Valley were orchards and gardens, good things from the soil, being reaped. Now the harvest of his life was nearly over. He returned to his table and continued his testament, still climbing toward a summit that was perhaps out of reach.

"A time to kill . . ."

He had knowingly taken only three lives: Adonijah, Joab, and Shimei. Adonijah's slaying was Yahweh's judgment. The deaths of Joab and Shimei had been David's decisions, not his. He had the chance to kill Jeroboam for rebelling against him, but he had delayed the execution order, and he was not sorry that his would-be son still lived although Jeroboam hated his would-be father.

What of those whom he had not killed? Thousands upon thousands of sons of Israel were spared due to his persistent dedication to peace.

Sadly, there was a time to kill, but there was also:

". . . a time to heal."

He had been the great healer as Israel contended with foreign nations and its enemies within. He had kept peace for four decades when war would have been easier. Where before in history had there been a four-decade respite of peace?

"A time to break down, and a time to build up."

Gezer. The villages of the Galilee. Ezion-geber. The vastness of all his other works of line and plummet. He had built up more than he had broken down.

"A time to weep, and a time to laugh; a time to mourn, and a time to dance; a time to cast away stones, and a time to gather stones together; a time to embrace, and a time to refrain from embracing; a time to get, and a time to lose; a time to keep, and a time to cast away; a time to rend, and a time to sew; a time to keep silence, and a time to speak; a time to love. . . ."

Laughter and love also ended in their time. He remembered: dark and lovely Balkis, burning, burning in my lonely heart and soul. Hers was the laughter of good things under the heavens. His son by Balkis was of age, too . . . and he would not know him if he appeared this instant in his chamber. Was Menelek a son greater than Rehoboam? According to the infrequent dispatches he had received through the years from the Queen of Sheba, he knew Balkis and her throne yet thrived . . . save for building the temple, the possession of Balkis had been his dearest wish.

". . . and a time to hate; a time of war, and a time of peace."

He had despised wicked men and been disenchanted by his wives and concubines. He pitied them, but did not hate them. It was useless to hate because it troubled the soul of him who hated more profoundly than he who was the object of hatred.

"What profit has he that works in that wherein he labors? I have seen the travail which God has given to the sons of men to be exercised in it."

The Lord gave trouble to a man who labored, but what, after all, could be accomplished that was worth accomplishing without trouble? The mirth, satisfaction, and challenge was in fighting the difficulties head-on and conquering them. Had he crossed the first precipice on his climb to the summit?

"He has made every thing beautiful in his time . . ."

If one looked closely he would discover fitness and glow in life and death.

A maiden, tender of age, was expectedly beautiful in the blossom of her years. But the maiden grown old was also beautiful in her way, especially if she gained a sensitive spirit for pride, wit for arrogance, charm of manner for charm of flesh.

". . . also He has set the world in their heart, so that no man can find out the work that God makes from the beginning to the end."

Serving the God of Israel was filled with mysteries. For some men, it was enough to seek to obey the Commandments and question God no further. For other men there were always more questions.

Of all the intriguing mysteries of God, the most elusive was the difference between time and eternity. Yet not completely elusive. Time was the stuff of a man's life; eternity the possession of God. But did not man live by God?

"I know that there is no good in them but for a man to rejoice and to do good in his life. And also that every man should eat and drink, and enjoy the good of all his labor; it is the gift of God."

All things were God's, even the wine that gives mirth. Man should enjoy his work and his leisure, and when he does he is serving the best interests of both himself and God.

"I know that whatsoever God does, it shall be for ever; nothing can be put to it, nor any thing taken from it; and God does it that men should fear before Him."

Man should never be so brash as to compete with God, for such competition is impossible. God is perfect and majestic; man imperfect and constantly betrayed by sin. Therefore do men quake before Him.

"That which has been is now, and that which is to be has already been; and God requires that which is past."

Though life is a cycle within cycles, history is not dull repetition nor fruitless circuits, but rather the blood-racing, indispensable prologue to the future.

For without the humble altars of Abraham and Moses, Solomon could not have built that which was now enshrined on Moriah. In order for him to have lived and worked, it had been necessary for Abraham and Moses to have preceded him. Life was not only a running chain of events but a chain of generations.

"And moreover I saw under the sun in the place of justice that wickedness was there, and in the place of righteousness that iniquity was there. I said in my heart, 'God shall judge the righteous and the wicked, for there is a time there for every purpose and for every work.' "

Some men are more wicked than good, some more good than wicked; but man is a poor judge of his own acts, therefore it is right for God to judge as God had judged Solomon for permitting the burning of incense and sacrifices to evil gods.

"I said in my heart concerning the estate of the sons of men that God might manifest them, and that they might see that they themselves are beasts. For that which befalls the sons of men befalls beasts—even one thing befalls them: as the one dies, so dies the other; yea, they all have one breath, so that a man has no preeminence above a beast, for all is vanity. All go to one place; all are of the dust and all turn to dust again. Who knows the spirit of man that goes upward, and the spirit of the beast that goes downward to the earth?"

His moods veered wildly. On these strips of papyri he seemed to be fighting his first war, with the prize of his inestimable soul. Against the soul of a man, what was gold and silver?

The lowest beast putrefied as did a man. But the idea that a man was no better than a beast was found wanting. Letting his mind soar, he saw one day man being lifted to heaven, putting him, as was right and just, above the beast.

He remembered a long-ago conversation in Thebes with Nagsara when they talked of the coming of the Hebrew Messiah. Would this in fact come to pass, would that Savior be the Son of God in a special and unique way? Would man, in exchange for dedicating his life to the Lord, have *body and spirit* pass into heaven? It had not yet happened, but it had been forecast. Nathan had spoken of it to him often in the mulberry grove. Was there not the future possibility of resurrection and eternal life?

In God all things were possible.

Curling through him now was the same intimation of immortality, not for him, but for generations unborn when the Lord God decreed heaven and ordained for men the way, the resurrection and the life.

Until the Messiah was made manifest, a man should labor for good and do good in his life and works. He had traveled at least to this realization, that work was exalted, necessary, useful, worthy. What if king and commoner did both end in the grave! In the living of a life, in the kind of life possessed, there was a difference!

"So I returned and considered all the oppressions that are done under the sun, and beheld the tears of such as were oppressed, and they had no comforter; and on the side of their oppressor there was power, but they had no comforter."

He himself had been a slavemaster, but a gentle and merciful as circumstances allowed. When the Messiah came, would He comfort the powerless, offering heaven to the oppressed? Would He banish the abomination of slavery—yea, *that* would be a new thing under the sun!

He had reached the point where he saw the absolute necessity for the coming of the Messiah. Why had not the Savior come yet? How long must man suffer in his sins? Not until the Messiah flowed to man like cool water, washing him clean and new, would the end soar higher than the beginning . . .

"Better is an handful with quietness than both the hands full with travail and vexation of spirit. Then I returned, and I saw vanity under the sun."

He had been too fortunate and successful in the amassing of gold. A man with half a loaf of bread was often richer than one with two loaves. A smaller amount of gold was better than a larger amount. The man with half a loaf of bread and a slighter fortune had less to fear from his fellows, less to lose to a thief.

"Two are better than one, because they have a good reward for their labor. For if they fall, the one will lift up his fellow; but woe to him that is alone when he falls, for he has not another to help him up. Again, if two lie together then they have heat; but how can one be warm alone? And if one prevail against him, two shall withstand him; and a threefold cord is not quickly broken."

The Queen of Sheba, the king of Israel, and their son. How exquisitely, perfectly happy they might have been as man and wife worshipping the true God, their quiver filled with child and contentment to the time when they were ripe with days and a good old age.

"Better is a poor and a wise child than an old and foolish king who will no more be admonished. For out of prison he comes to reign; whereas also he that is born in his kingdom becomes poor."

Before his first growth of beard, David, who had been humble and the youngest of six brothers, was anointed to reign. Though he had been captive of the dung of his father's sheep, he had caught Samuel's eyes. The prophet knew in his heart that David without a shekel had more than the richest man in Israel, because he had zeal and spirit and longlastingness for the Lord. His father had shown more wisdom than he, having repented without hesitation before the Lord. The Lord accepted David's apologies like an offering, gladly and freely given. David thus had died blessed in the arms of the Lord.

He had been born in David's palace when his father was already king and had not suffered travails in becoming the first man among the Israelites. Therefore he had not appreciated the crown as had his father. Then he had committed the final foolishness, becoming in his dotage the poorest man in Israel by ignoring the two personal admonitions of the Lord to walk in His statutes and commandments. For his disobedience, he and Israel would pay a fearful price.

"I considered all the living which walk under the sun, with the second child that shall stand up in his stead. There is no end of all the people, even of all that have been before them; they also that come after shall not rejoice in him. Surely this also is vanity and vexation of spirit."

Rehoboam was forty-one years old and would rule one tribe following Solomon's death. Jeroboam was younger, and the Lord had strongly implied he would rule the rest. But in their time they also would be rejected as he had been—if not by the Lord then by the people, who were uneasy with the presence of a king who stayed too long on the throne.

At best, as the corridor of time lengthened, David, Solomon, Rehoboam, Jeroboam, and all the others who were once mighty on the earth would only be dimly remembered. The people alone would endure.

* * *

He continued writing his Book until it was completed, scarcely noting that the shaking of his fingers was gone. Once more he summed up and read aloud some of his themes of life and death, wisdom and folly, cynicism and hope, man and God. His eye caught and he read in a soft, contented voice:

"Be not rash with your mouth, and let not your heart be hasty to utter any thing before God; for God *is* in heaven, and you upon earth. . . . When you vow a vow to God, defer not to pay it for He has no pleasure in fools; pay that which you have vowed. . . . A good name is better than precious ointment. . . . For there is not a just man upon earth that does good and sins not. . . . I returned and saw under the sun that the race is not to the swift, nor the battle to the strong, neither yet bread to the wise, nor yet riches to men of understanding, nor yet favor to men of skill; but time and chance happens to them all. . . . Wisdom is better than weapons of war; but one sinner destroys much good. . . . Cast your bread upon the waters. For you shall find it after many days. . . . As you know not what *is* the way of the spirit, nor how the bones do grow in the womb of her that is with child, even so you know not all the works of God who makes all. . . . And moreover, because the preacher was wise, he still taught the people knowledge; yea, he gave good heed, and sought out, and set in order many proverbs . . . of making many books there is no end, and much study is a weariness of the flesh."

He fell asleep at his table, and when he awakened after a long, deep slumber, he took pen in hand again, feeling his Book somehow incomplete. Hour after hour he mediated and then added two final verses:

"Let us hear the conclusion of the whole matter: Fear God, and keep his commandments, for this is the whole duty of man. For God shall bring every work into judgment, with every secret thing, whether it be good, or whether it be evil."

His life testament was done . . . he had come to the summit . . . and he felt the exhilaration and exhaustion of a work accomplished. Short days later he went to his couch and did not rise again.

A time to be born, and a time to die.

His life, he thought in the last throbs of his heart, had been wise *and* foolish. He had lived heroically and tragically. But he was dying peacefully because he had journeyed back to God.

And it was good, he also thought as darkness began to blind his eyes, that he had written all the wisdom he knew. Like travail and vexation of spirit, there was no end of wisdom. The story of Yahweh would go on beyond the life of David's son, beyond the life of whatever glory Solomon had represented. And in God's continuing wisdom there was one certainty: the Messiah would come to further instruct man.

For he had not idly written:

"To every thing there is a season, and a time to every purpose under the heaven."